**Pension Strategies
in Europe and the
United States**

CESifo Seminar Series

Edited by Hans-Werner Sinn

Managing European Union Enlargement
Helge Berger and Thomas Moutos, editors

European Monetary Integration
Hans-Werner Sinn, Mika Widgrén, and Marko Köthenbürger, editors

Measuring the Tax Burden on Capital and Labor
Peter Birch Sørensen, editor

A Constitution for the European Union
Charles B. Blankart and Dennis C. Mueller, editors

Labor Market Institutions and Public Regulation
Jonas Agell, Michael Keen, and Alfons J. Weichenrieder, editors

Venture Capital, Entrepreneurship, and Public Policy
Vesa Kanniainen and Christian Keuschnigg, editors

Exchange Rate Economics: Where Do We Stand?
Paul De Grauwe, editor

Prospects for Monetary Unions after the Euro
Paul De Grauwe and Jacques Mélitz, editors

Structural Unemployment in Western Europe: Reasons and Remedies
Martin Werding, editor

Institutions, Development, and Economic Growth
Theo S. Eicher and Cecilia García-Peñalosa, editors

Competitive Failures in Insurance Markets: Theory and Policy Implications
Pierre-André Chiappori and Christian Gollier, editors

Japan's Great Stagnation: Financial and Monetary Policy Lessons for Advanced Economies
Michael M. Hutchison and Frank Westermann, editors

Tax Policy and Labor Market Performance
Jonas Agell and Peter Birch Sørensen, editors

Privatization Experiences in the European Union
Marko Köthenbürger, Hans-Werner Sinn, and John Whalley, editors

Recent Developments in Antitrust: Theory and Evidence
Jay Pil Choi, editor

Schools and the Equal Opportunity Problem
Ludger Woessmann and Paul E. Peterson, editors

Economics and Psychology: A Promising New Field
Bruno S. Frey and Alois Stutzer, editors

Institutions and Norms in Economic Development
Mark Gradstein and Kai A. Konrad, editors

Pension Strategies in Europe and the United States
Robert Fenge, Georges de Ménil, and Pierre Pestieau, editors

See ⟨http://mitpress.mit.edu⟩ for a complete list of titles in this series.

Pension Strategies in Europe and the United States

Edited by
Robert Fenge,
Georges de Ménil,
and Pierre Pestieau

CESifo Seminar Series

The MIT Press
Cambridge, Massachusetts
London, England

For information about special quantity discounts, please e-mail ⟨special_sales@mitpress.mit.edu⟩.

This book was set in Palatino on 3B2 by Asco Typesetters, Hong Kong.
Printed and bound in the United States of America.

Library of Congress Cataloging-in-Publication Data

Pension strategies in Europe and the United States / Robert Fenge, Georges de Ménil, and Pierre Pestieau, editors.
    p.   cm.—(CESifo seminar series)
Includes bibliographical references and index.
ISBN 978-0-262-06272-5 (hardcover : alk. paper)
1. Pensions—Europe. 2. Pensions—United States. 3. Pension trusts—Europe.
4. Pension trusts—United States. I. Fenge, Robert. II. De Ménil, Georges, 1940–
III. Pestieau, Pierre, 1943–
HD7105.45.E85P46   2008
331.25′22094—dc22

                                                                          2007020847

10   9   8   7   6   5   4   3   2   1

Contents

Series Foreword   vii

Introduction: Pension Systems in Europe and the United States: The Demographic Challenge   1
Robert Fenge, Georges de Ménil, and Pierre Pestieau

I Pay-as-You-Go Pension Systems

1 Optimum Delayed Retirement Credit   27
Eytan Sheshinski

2 How Elastic Is the Response of the Retirement-Age Labor Supply? Evidence from the 1993 French Pension Reform   37
Antoine Bozio

3 Optimal Response to a Transitory Demographic Shock   87
Juan C. Conesa and Carlos Garriga

II Democratic Sustainability

4 Demographics and the Political Sustainability of Pay-as-You-Go Social Security   117
Theodore C. Bergstrom and John L. Hartman

5 Free Choice of Unfunded Systems: A Preliminary Analysis of a European Union Challenge   141
Gabrielle Demange

III Funded Pension Systems

6   Public Policy and Retirement Saving Incentives in the United Kingdom   169

Woojen Chung, Richard Disney, Carl Emmerson, and Matthew Wakefield

7   Personal Security Accounts and Mandatory Annuitization in a Dynastic Framework   211

Luisa Fuster, Ayşe İmrohoroğlu, and Selahattin İmrohoroğlu

8   Aging, Funded Pensions, and the Dutch Economy   239

A. Lans Bovenberg and Thijs Knaap

9   Optimal Portfolio Management for Individual Pension Plans   273

Christian Gollier

List of Contributors   293
Index   295

Series Foreword

This book is part of the CESifo Seminar Series. The series aims to cover topical policy issues in economics from a largely European perspective. The books in this series are the products of the papers and intensive debates that took place during the seminars hosted by CESifo, an international research network of renowned economists organized jointly by the Center for Economic Studies at Ludwig-Maximilians-Universität, Munich, and the Ifo Institute for Economic Research. All publications in this series have been carefully selected and refereed by members of the CESifo research network.

Pension Strategies in Europe and the United States

Introduction: Pension Systems in Europe and the United States: The Demographic Challenge

Robert Fenge, Georges de Ménil, and Pierre Pestieau

Retirement systems throughout the developed world are facing major crises. These are particularly acute in the countries of Europe because of the speed at which their populations are aging, because of misguided earlier policy initiatives to encourage early retirement, and because of the extent of the development of the reliance on pay-as-you-go (PAYG) financing in a number of countries.

Pay-as-you-go pension systems were introduced in Europe in the late 1940s to provide benefits to a generation of retirees who had just gone through a long economic depression and a painful war. It is now widely accepted that, the good intentions of its founders not withstanding, this institutional innovation has had unfortunate consequences. There was, at the time, a possible alternative route—to issue public debt to finance the pensions of the retirees who had survived the war and to develop for their successors fully funded pension systems with the same redistributional characteristics as those of the PAYG systems actually adopted. Confronted with the magnitude of the explicit debt incurred by this pension scheme, governments probably would have been far less generous in expanding retirement benefits, and Europe today would not face a liability that is in many countries far higher than official public debt. There were, in principle, other virtues to the PAYG schemes: they allegedly permitted intergenerational transfers from well-to-do generations to generations suffering from unemployment and business-cycle troughs, and they had the capacity to compensate for missing or underdeveloped financial markets. Unfortunately, most work on generational accounts shows that such intergenerational redistribution has been of secondary importance, mainly indicating a one-direction redistribution—from future to current generations (see Kotlikoff, 1992). The verdict is still out on missing or underdeveloped markets.[1]

Indeed, countries with pay-as-you-go pension systems are prisoners of a liability they cannot dispose of quickly. It is now well accepted that shifting from a current PAYG system to private, funded accounts cannot be Pareto improving. Some believe that by removing the distortions prevailing in current PAYG systems there would be enough resources to finance the transition or to put it another way—to reimburse the famous "free lunch" awarded to those pensioners who received benefits without having contributed. There are in fact two types of distortions—those inherent to redistribution and those resulting from a less than optimal design of the tax-transfer systems. The first distortions cannot be disposed of; they would subsist in a fully funded system, achieving the same redistribution as the PAYG. The second distortions could be removed even within the PAYG pension system.

If one abandons the requirement of Pareto improvement, one can argue that a partial or total move toward funding can be socially optimal to the extent that it provides welfare increases to future generations at the expense of the current generation. In countries where voters weigh future welfare heavily, such reforms can also pass the political test of majority support.[2]

The Scale of the Crisis and the Diversity of Existing Systems

If public retirement systems in Europe and the United States were simply suboptimal, there would be time to debate the relative merits of the different systems. But the impending demographic crisis bears with it the clear implication that future budgetary burdens will be unsustainable in many countries. Table I.1 provides an overview of anticipated changes in the demographic structures of selected European countries as well as the United States. Dependency ratios are roughly expected to double between 2000 and 2050. Since these ratios assume that all workers retire at age sixty-five, whereas in most countries workers are effectively retiring increasingly earlier (see below), the nature of the problem is greater than the table suggests.

An essential feature of the pension crisis in Europe and the United States is the diversity of existing pension systems. The political geography of social arrangements for the provision of retirement income is strikingly different from country to country in Europe. Pay-as-you-go tax rates range from among the lowest (United Kingdom) to the

Table I.1
Dependency ratio: 65 and over divided by 15 to 64

	2000	2050
Belgium	25	43
Denmark	23	52
France	25	47
Italy	26	69
Netherlands	20	42
United Kingdom	24	39
United States	19	35
European Union 15	24	48
OECD	21	42

Source: European Commission (2003), OECD (2005).

Table I.2
Characteristics of pension systems (2000)

	First Pillar (percentage of GDP)	Second plus Third Pillars (assets as a percentage of GDP)	Redistributive Index
Belgium	10.0%	5.9%	64.8%
Denmark	11.8	16.3	22.9
France	12.8	6.6	46.4
Italy	13.8	2.6	4.0
Netherlands	7.9	111.1	5.7
United Kingdom	5.5	80.9	69.6
European Union 15	10.4	29.2	—

Source: European Commission (2003), OECD (2005).

highest (France) in the developed world. Table I.2 reports several measures of the differences across systems.

The pension system characteristics that differ the most across countries are the relative size and redistributive character of the PAYG first pillar and the relative size of fully funded second and third pillars. In the table, we measure the size of the first pillar by the ratio of its expenditures to gross domestic product and the size of the second and third pillars by the ratio of their total assets to GDP. Our measure of the redistributiveness of the first pillar is an index supplied by the Organization for Economic Development (OECD, 2005) that is based on a comparison of the Gini coefficient of annual earnings and the

Table I.3
Public pension expenditure before taxes as a percentage of GDP

	2000	2050	Change
Belgium	10.0%	13.3%	3.3%
Denmark	11.8	16.9	5.1
France	12.8	15.8	3.0
Italy	13.8	14.1	0.3
Netherlands	7.9	13.6	5.7
United Kingdom	5.5	4.4	−1.1
European Union 15	10.4	13.3	2.9

Source: European Commission (2003).

Gini coefficient of pension benefits, for the year in question. If the two Gini coefficients are the same, which they should be in a pure insurance scheme, the index is zero. If pension benefits are completely flat, as they should be in a Beveridgean system, the index is 100. Belgium, Germany, and France have generous first pillars that are partially redistributive. The United Kingdom, the home of the Beveridgean concept, has a small first pillar, which is highly redistributive.[3] It follows from this diversity that the demographic crisis, which is by and large common to all of these countries, affects them in different ways.

As table I.3 shows, on the basis of existing systems, the burden of public pensions is expected to increase dramatically. The year at which the burden will reach its peak varies across countries. If the systems change, the budgetary burden of the demographic shock will also change. Not surprisingly, the impending budgetary burden tends to be greatest in the countries that rely the most on PAYG.[4]

However, the budgetary burden is not the only implication of the demographic crisis. Holland's funded, occupational second pillar offers beneficiaries defined benefits and suffers from the vulnerabilities inherent to those liabilities. In the United Kingdom, where a large number of second- and third-pillar funds are converting from a defined-benefit (DB) to defined-contribution (DC) basis, administrative costs weigh heavily on fund performance.

The Urgency of Scholarly Analyses of National Policies

Mindful of the importance of the pension crisis in Europe and of the intellectual challenge of designing solutions, we organized a conference on "Strategies for Reforming Pension Schemes" in Munich in the fall of

Table I.4
Life expectancy and effective age of retirement (2001)

	Age of Retirement, Effective (standard)		Life Expectancy at Age 65 in 2040	
	Women	Men	Women	Men
Belgium	55.9 (62)	57.8 (65)	87	84
Denmark	60.4 (65)	60.9 (65)	87	83
France	58.0 (60)	58.2 (60)	88	84
Italy	59.2 (65)	59.6 (65)	87	83
Netherlands	60.3 (65)	61.1 (65)	—	—
United Kingdom	61.0 (60)	63.1 (65)	86	83
European Union 15	59.1	60.5	87[a]	83[a]

Source: European Commission (2003), OECD (2005).
Note:
a. Average life expectancy B for OECD.

2004 with the support and sponsorship of CESIfo. The papers selected were mostly by European authors,[5] and the range of the issues addressed in this volume indeed reflects the diversity of the problems faced in Europe. Although every study addresses a problem of general significance, all of them focus on issues that are particularly relevant for some European country or important for them all.

This volume is divided into three parts. The chapters in the first part focus on the reform of key structural features of existing pay-as-you-go systems. The chapters in the second part address the sustainability of PAYG systems in a democratic context, in which reforms have to be voted and pension plans face the pressures of systems competition. The third section analyzes policy issues that are specific to the private, funded systems, which increasingly are perceived to supply necessary compensation for the diminishing benefits of PAYG systems.[6]

Part I, Pay-as-You-Go Pension Systems

All three of the chapters in the first part of this book deal with a feature of pay-as-you-go systems of particular importance in continental Europe—the choice of the statutory retirement age and the effective retirement age. One of the important factors leading to the financial crisis of social security in countries such as France, Germany, and Italy is that the rate of activity of elderly workers has been steadily decreasing despite increasing longevity. The current average effective rate of retirement in these three countries is about fifty-nine. Table I.4 shows that by 2040 these diverging trends imply that in some countries (notably Belgium) the average female worker's retirement will be almost as long as her working life. Social security is not the only culprit. Other social insurance schemes such as unemployment and disability insurance and early retirement schemes explain why so many workers retire before the normal age of retirement (sixty-five in Germany and Italy and sixty in France).

A natural presumption and a frequent recommendation of policy critics is that the treatment of early (or delayed) retirement in a pay-as-you-go system should be actuarially fair. Workers who retire early should see their expected pensions reduced by an amount equal in present discounted value to the contributions they do not make into the system. In circumstances where early retirement is encouraged, returning to an actuarially fair treatment would in itself entail significant tightening. In "Optimum Delayed Retirement Credit" (chapter 1), Eytan Sheshinski uses a simple but powerful model to demonstrate that such a move is not likely to go far enough. If different elderly workers experience, in unobservable ways, a different disutility of work, the fact that the government can not distinguish between them creates a problem of adverse selection. If the actuarial penalty for early retirement is zero, then workers who experience more than the average aversion to work will retire early anyway and pay less for the opportunity to do so than they would have been willing to pay. Consequently, there will be less money available to encourage others to retire late. As a result, the number of workers extending their active years is less than optimal. Sheshinski's lucid analysis adds to a growing consensus in the literature that delayed retirement credits should be more than actuarially fair and should favor longer working lives.

In 1993, the Balladur government implemented a major reform of the French pay-as-you-go system, one of whose objectives was to extend the length of the average worker's active years. In "How Elastic Is the Response of the Retirement-Age Labor Supply? Evidence from the 1993 French Pension Reform" (chapter 2), Antoine Bozio presents the first econometric analysis of those Balladur initiatives.

In France, debate about retirement provisions has long focused on the statutory age of retirement. One of President François Mitterand's first decisions when elected in 1981 was to lower the statutory retirement age from sixty-five to sixty. Twelve years later when the Balladur government undertook partially to restore the length of working lives, it did not do so by raising the statutory age. Rather, it lengthened the number of years of work required to entitle an individual to a full pension—from 37.5 to 40 years for workers in the private sector. In 2003, the Rafarin government applied this extension to large segments of the previously exempted public workforce.

Some critics argued, both in 1993 and in 2003, that most workers were not medically capable of working longer and that the extension would simply drastically reduce their benefits. Bozio uses newly available panel data on retirement histories to perform econometric tests of the quantitative effects of the Balladur reforms. He uses a difference-in-difference technique to control for the influence of other factors on the retirement decision. His conclusion, at the end of an extensive evaluation of the evidence, is that workers did, in fact, respond to the incentives in the 1993 reform by extending their active years. He estimates that every additional year of required work history generated six months of effective additional work.

In "Optimal Response to a Transitory Demographic Shock" (chapter 3), Juan C. Conesa and Carlos Garriga provide further evidence of the magnitude of the economic inefficiency entailed by rigid determination of the statutory retirement age. They estimate the magnitude of the welfare gains that can be realized by eliminating features of pay-as-you-go systems, which they identify as responsible for large deadweight losses. Foremost among these is the rigidity of the statutory retirement age.[7] The startling message of their chapter is that in the United States, at least, elimination of these three inefficiencies is sufficiently welfare improving to make it possible to adapt to a transitory demographic shock without either lowering promised pension benefits or raising average taxes.

The Conesa and Garriga study is an exercise in optimal tax design in the Ramsey tradition. The authors examine a hypothetical thirty-year transient demographic shock in which the demographic dependency ratio rises progressively from 33 percent to 40 percent during the first fifteen years and then falls back to its initial level. They suppose that in response to this hypothetical shock, the government redesigns key features of its PAYG system:

• It allows workers freely to choose their retirement age,

• It permits the social security administration to borrow against general tax receipts to cover temporary shortfalls, and

• It designs a new labor tax schedule, which varies with the worker's age, according to a bell-shaped curve.

The first reform permits older workers to continue earning the wages to which their productivity entitles them. The second reform allows the government to smooth the tax consequences of the demographic shock over time. The third one replaces a hypothetical, constant, proportional tax with one that rises and falls with age according to a different bell-shaped curve.[8] This provision allows the government to take advantage of the fact that retirement income taxation becomes increasingly similar to lump-sum taxation as workers advance in age. Together, these three reforms generate sufficient welfare gains to offset the burden of the authors' hypothetical demographic shock.

Conesa and Garriga calibrate their analysis to U.S. data. It is not clear that their optimistic conclusion would carry over to the large, continental European countries most affected by the current pension crisis. Three considerations suggest caution: (1) the demographic shock in continental Europe is greater than in their hypothetical example, and it is permanent; (2) existing tax rates are higher in Europe than the United States; and (3) existing debt levels in some European countries are so high as to preclude the temporary 60 percent increase advocated by the authors in their optimal scenario. Nonetheless, Conesa and Garriga's calculations do suggest that the efficiency gains derived from allowing free choice of retirement and from optimal tax reform are substantial.

Part II, Democratic Sustainability

In modern democracies, economic policies are created not by fiat but by political processes. Reforms that may be in the long-run interest of society have to pass immediate and recurrent electoral tests if they are to be implemented and sustained. Theodore C. Bergstrom and John L. Hartman explore the implications of this condition for pension reform in "Demographics and the Political Sustainability of Pay-as-You-Go Social Security" (chapter 4).

As the population ages, the internal rate of return of a pay-as-you-go system falls, and society must choose between reducing pension benefits and increasing social security taxes. However, the same aging of the population will also affect the choice that voters make between these two options. If individuals vote their self-interest, young voters will want to reduce pension benefits, and old voters will want to raise social security taxes. Bergstrom and Hartman analyze the U.S. pension system and compute the pivotal age at which the median voter switches from preferring pension reduction to preferring tax increases.

They find, on the basis of demographic projections of aging in the United States, that the median voter will continue to prefer higher taxes for forty more years. One cannot help but note that it would be interesting to apply the Bergstrom and Hartman voting calculus to the Conesa and Garriga reforms.[9]

Gabrielle Demange looks at the question of sustainability in broader terms and in an explicitly European context. "Free Choice of Unfunded Systems: A Preliminary Analysis of a European Union Challenge" (chapter 5) is a provocative and original analysis of the potential competition between national retirement systems that the European single market is capable of generating. Demange starts from the observation that the intragenerational distributional characteristics of a pension system are as critical to its sustainability as its internal rate of return. She points out that European pay-as-you-go systems vary widely in the degree of this intragenerational redistribution, with Bismarkian contributory systems at one end and Beveridgean fixed-pension systems at the other. In their purest form, Bismarkean systems provide no redistribution, and Beveridgean systems equalize pension benefits.

Demange treats a simple, two-country model in which the countries A and B are economic clones one of the other but have pension systems that differ in two critical parameters—the contribution rate and the degree of redistribution (represented by a parameter α, which equals 1 in a Bismarkian system and 0 in a Beveridgean system). She then supposes that individuals in the two countries are free to choose pension system A or pension system B. The argument suggests migration, but she supposes that it is possible for workers to join one or the other system without physically moving (as if they were joining alternative clubs).

The dynamics are complicated, since the adherence of different income groups changes the distributional aspects of the two systems. But under some conditions, strong conclusions can be drawn. If the underlying economies are dynamically efficient, efficiency considerations argue in favor of the system with the lower tax rate. Suppose that the system in country A is Beveridgean and has a lower tax rate and the system in country B is Bismarkian with a higher tax rate. (A can be viewed as a stylized representation of the United Kingdom, and B as a stylized representation of France.) If dynamic efficiency is strongly present, everyone will eventually choose the Beveridgean system—the rich because it provides the lowest social security burden and the poor because it is the most redistributive.

The Demange model is a model of individual choice. But it is suggestive of the kind of results that one might obtain if whole countries collectively chose their system through voting. One can conjecture that in such a model, the stylized British system might again be chosen over the stylized French system. This British and French comparison also suggests the potential importance of the private saving decision—an aspect of behavior that is assumed away in most of the chapters of the first two parts of this volume.

Part III, Funded Pension Systems

Although the governments of several large European countries have, in recent years, simultaneously scaled back public retirement benefits and developed and subsidized new channels for private retirement savings, the Thatcher, Major, and Blair governments in the United Kingdom have gone the furthest in this direction.

In a series of Social Security and Pension Acts from 1980 onward, the Thatcher and Major governments reversed a trend of steady growth of benefits and taxes in what had come to be an increasingly Bismarckian system.[10] One of the highlights of that process was the introduction of a personal pension scheme in 1988. A central characteristic of the scheme was that it allowed and encouraged workers who were entitled to benefit from the state's contributory system—State Earnings-Related Pension Scheme (SERPS) (see note 10)—to opt out and direct their and their employer's national insurance contribution instead to an approved, defined-contribution personal pension. The incentives to make the change were so attractive that more than 5 million employees had switched within two years. Critics argued that insufficient public supervision led to overselling, excessive transfers, and the charging of excessive fees by the private fund providers (see Blake, 2002).

Partly in reaction to these charges, the Blair government introduced in 2001 a new Stakeholders Pension Scheme, designed to offer middle-income working people a less expensive, more carefully regulated access to private pension funds. In the new scheme, administrative fees were capped, and workers signed up collectively as part of a group in a manner intended to reduce the risks of uninformed and individual behavior.[11] It was noteworthy, however, that the Blair government maintained what was perhaps the central feature of the Thatcher and Major reforms—the opportunity for workers to opt out of the state's earnings-related pay-as-you-go system and direct their social security tax payments and those of their employers to private funds. Outside of Holland and Switzerland, no other country in Western Europe has as yet introduced such an opt-out provision.[12] It is helpful, in evaluating the significance of this feature, to realize that, in a sense, it institutes a kind of mandatory private saving regime. Workers may choose to opt out or not, but they cannot escape the social security tax. The best they can do is direct it to a retirement fund. Elsewhere in Europe, incentives in favor of retirement-savings schemes are limited to subsidies and tax deductions earned when workers make additional contributions that are above and beyond their PAYG tax liability.

While the budgetary costs of the British reforms have indeed been large and excessive fees have indeed been charged (and subsequently partially rebated), it is nonetheless notable that, as a result of these reforms, state liabilities for future pensions have been substantially reduced. As table I.3 above shows, eighteen years after the introduction of personal pensions and five after the creation of the Stakeholders Pension Scheme, Britain can anticipate substantially lighter budgetary costs of the demographic crisis than many of its neighbors.

In "Public Policy and Retirement Savings Incentives in the United Kingdom" (chapter 6), the first chapter of the section of this book that is related to funded pensions, Woojen Chung, Richard Disney, Carl Emmerson, and Matthew Wakefield start by tracing the history of U.K. policy in this area over the last twenty years. The body of the chapter then focuses on a comparison of the personal pension and the Stakeholders Pension Scheme. As the authors point out, at first glance, the patterns seem very different in these two important episodes. Aggregate enrollment was much greater than expected in the case of personal pensions and much less than expected (near zero) in the Stakeholders Pension Scheme case. At both times, the authorities were concerned that the affected population might, out of myopia or limited rationality, not respond in a manner consistent with its best interests. Considerable attention was devoted to devising incentives that would compensate for this anticipated limited rationality. The question remains: does the fact that results diverged so substantially from expert predictions confirm the financial naiveté of the targeted workers, or or does it say something about the public-policy process? At the end of their thorough review, Chung, Disney, Emmerson, and Wakefield propose a novel and provocative conclusion.

The growing shift from defined-benefit to defined-contribution pension plans in the United Kingdom and many other countries is causing attention to focus on a topic that had until recently been the forgotten child of pension reform—the annuitization of savings. When things work as they are intended to, neither the beneficiary of a defined-benefit plan nor the recipient of a pay-as-you-go pension have to concern themselves with the financial implications of the retirement income that they have been promised. When retirement is financed by savings accumulated in defined-contribution plans, annuitization becomes critically important. In "Personal Security Accounts and Mandatory Annuitization in a Dynastic Framework" (chapter 7), Luisa Fuster, Ayşe İmrohoroğlu, and Selahattin İmrohoroğlu place the welfare implications of annuitization at the center of their analysis.

It is well known that the risk of outliving their savings weighs heavily on the well-being of individuals who do not have access to an efficient annuity market or to some alternative mechanism for annuitization. Mitchell, Poterba, Warshawsky, and Brown (1999) estimate that as of 1998, an average individual on the threshold of retirement in the United States, with no other source of retirement income, would be willing to give up 25 percent of his or her accumulated savings (and therefore 25 percent of expected retirement income) to be insured against that risk.[13]

The Mitchell, Poterba, Warshawsky, and Brown (1999) estimate is a partial equilibrium estimate of the value of access to fair annuitization, computed at the end of the active life of the individual concerned. It assumes that there is nothing further that the individual can do regarding the absence of annuitization. But if individuals become aware early in their lives of the fact that they will face longevity risk, they can plan to work longer and save more to offset some of the cost of this risk. If all individuals facing the same dilemma make similar adjustments, aggregate employment, aggregate savings, domestic capital, and GDP will be higher than they otherwise would have been.[14] Under such circumstances, measuring the welfare implications of access to fair annuitization requires a general-equilibrium approach.

In their chapter, Fuster, İmrohoroğlu, and İmrohoroğlu provide the first dynamic, general-equilibrium, empirical analysis of the value of access to fair annuitization. Their estimates are embedded in an overall evaluation of one of the partial-privatization proposals made in the United States in 2001 by the President's Commission to Strengthen Social Security. They use a general-equilibrium model of overlapping generations, calibrated to the U.S. economy, to compare the welfare of different categories of families on alternative steady-state paths with either partial privatization, no privatization, or full privatization. The partial-privatization scenario is one in which five percentage points of social security taxes are mandatorily deflected into private savings accounts (PSAs). Accordingly, the authors measure the average, steady-state level of welfare associated with the PSA reform under two alternative assumptions regarding annuitization: (1) longevity insurance is not available (and individuals know this when they start working), and (2) longevity insurance, in the form of standard annuitization, can be purchased on actuarially fair terms. The difference between the two measures provides a general-equilibrium estimate of the value of access to fair annuitization.

In table 7.3 of their chapter, Fuster, İmrohoroğlu, and İmrohoroğlu report that the benefit of access to fair annuitization is 0.7 percent of the total expected utility of an average family.[15] Though this measure seems small at first, it must be noted that the denominator includes the sum of the lifetime utilities of families that may encompass several generations of altruistic individuals. It is thus not directly comparable to the estimate of Mitchell, Poterba, Warshawsky, and Brown, who relate the cost of longevity risk exclusively to the expected welfare of a single individual during his retirement years. Deriving a precise bridge between the two measures is a complex matter, but simply multiplying the Fuster, İmrohoroğlu, and İmrohoroğlu estimate by four may provide a reasonable first approximation. (This would roughly convert, in each generation, a policy effect computed as a percentage of lifetime welfare into the same effect computed as a percentage of welfare during the retirement years.) Thus adjusted, the Fuster, İmrohoroğlu, and İmrohoroğlu estimate is still small (2.8 percent). However, this does appear to represent, in their model, the general-equilibrium cost of the absence of annuity markets. In table 7.5, they present a partial-equilibrium estimate of this cost of 5 percent. If we use the same rule of thumb to adjust that estimate, we find a measure (20 percent) comparable in magnitude to the Mitchell, Poterba, Warshawsky, and Brown (1999) estimate.

Our authors' estimates depend on many of the assumptions of their analysis. Two of their assumptions are that (1) all individuals are subject to a zero borrowing constraint and (2) all are totally altruistic toward living parents or living children. The second assumption, which implies that family support can provide for formal longevity insurance, may diminish the welfare benefit of access to annuitization.

The occupational pension system of the Netherlands—in other words, the Dutch "second pillar"—is the most established, compulsory-funded system on the continent. Its current structure was essentially established immediately at the end of World War II. If an employer offers a pension plan, membership by all employees is obligatory. Employers may offer schemes administered by an insurance company, or they may adhere to an industrywide pension fund in whose governance employers and employees are represented equally. Participation in an industrywide scheme may be made compulsory by the Minister of Social Affairs at the request of the relevant associations of employers and unions (90 percent of all employees are covered by this occupational pension system, and 77 percent of them belong to mandatory industrywide funds).

As table I.2 reports, in 2000 the assets of the many plans in the system were 111 percent of Dutch GDP. Because these plans are defined-benefit systems, the demographic shock impacting all of Europe has disrupted the balance between assets and liabilities. The retirement of baby boomers and the unexpected increase in longevity are increasing the future obligations of the plans at the same time as unexpectedly lower birth rates are reducing the size of the working population, on whose present and future premium payments their financial viability depends. As A. Lans Bovenberg and Thijs Knaap point out in "Aging, Funded Pensions, and the Dutch Economy" (chapter 8), the dilemmas faced by Holland's defined-benefit plans have features that are similar to those faced by PAYG systems elsewhere on the continent.

To analyze these dilemmas, Bovenberg and Knaap use a general-equilibrium, overlapping-generations model, in which households with different productivities, belonging to different cohorts, maximize their lifetime utilities by choosing optimal paths of labor, leisure, and consumption.[16] They calibrate the model to the Dutch economy. One of the important features of the Dutch economy that the model captures is its financial openness. Domestic savings are largely invested in world markets and consequently do not have a significant effect on the domestic capital stock and domestic GDP. On the other hand, interest rates on world markets—which are exogenous in their model—influence domestic investment and real GDP with a lag and have a direct and immediate effect on the financial balance of pension funds.

Bovenberg and Knaap use their model to analyze alternative approaches to closing the financial shortfalls faced by the Dutch defined-benefit system. All of their proposals entail either raising contributions (the premiums that workers pay into the plans), reducing benefits (by lowering the indexation corrections applied to pensions), or increasing subsidies financed by general taxation. In this regard, they parallel the analogous proposals made by governments in countries with pay-as-you-go systems.[17]

One reform that could radically change the financial balance of Holland's funded occupational system would be a shift from a defined-benefit structure to a defined-contribution structure. Occupational plans in the United Kingdom and the United States have been progressively implementing this shift for a number of years. The change need not imply reduced expected benefits for current workers. If current assets are too low given expected returns to provide future pensions equal to anticipated defined-benefit payments, the shift could be accompanied with an infusion of additional funds into the pension plans. The change in formula would not eliminate current financial problems. But it would eliminate unexpected financial imbalances— not in the present but in the future.

The capacity of forward-looking individuals to adjust retirement savings plans to different anticipated risks is also discussed in "Optimal Portfolio Management for Individual Pension Plans" (chapter 9) by Christian Gollier. As European citizens become increasingly skeptical of the promised benefits of their pay-as-you-go systems, Gollier argues that the financial management of the pension funds with which they seek to protect their retirement years becomes an increasingly crucial feature of their life-cycle plans. The chapter provides an elegant survey of a growing literature on pension-fund management, to which Gollier has himself contributed. To the central question of whether younger households should invest a larger portion of their pension wealth in risky assets, Gollier answers, "It depends." The balance of the evidence is that wealthy, well-informed households who are not liquidity constrained should weight stocks more heavily when they are young than when they are old. But liquidity-constrained households with less information, whose labor earnings are volatile (perhaps because of the risk of being unemployed), should do the opposite. These qualified conclusions are important in societies where PAYG pensions are expected to diminish and households of all kinds are likely to allocate more of their income to retirement savings.

Working Lives and Personal Savings: Policy Proposals

As the populations of the developed world age, differentially but ever more rapidly, their governments are being forced to reevaluate the retirement systems that were put into place or expanded in the aftermath of World War II. In spite of the diversity of old-age income provisions across countries, common themes recur. All the chapters of this book emphasize two in particular—the implications of extending working lives and the importance of increasing personal savings. Both issues loom large in ongoing policy developments. In the United States, the press of other issues has frozen the debate. But in Europe, where the problems are more urgent, the option of delay is less viable, and new strategies are emerging.

We choose to conclude this introduction with a brief discussion of the importance of these two themes in the reform strategy of successive German governments since 2001 and in the new direction proposed by the Blair government in the United Kingdom in its May 2006 White Paper, "Security in Retirement: Towards a New Pensions System" (United Kingdom, Department for Work and Pensions, 2006).

Pension Reform in Germany, 2001 to 2006

In Germany, the aging of the population and the collapse of the birth rate have taken crisis proportions. Given current fertility rates, life expectancies, and immigration policies, the Germany population is expected to decline by 25 percent from 2000 to 2050. Sensitized by extensive debate and by numerous expert reports on the need for additional saving to compensate for the future pay-as-you-go shortfalls implied by these trends, the Schroeder government introduced in 2001 a new voluntary but subsidized vehicle for retirement. Workers were encouraged to contribute a portion of their gross pay (programmed to rise to 4 percent by 2008) to approved, individual accounts managed by authorized banks or insurance companies. The accounts are called "Riester" accounts after the name of the then Minister of Labor and Social Affairs.[18] To date, workers and their employers continue to be obligated to pay statutory social security taxes of 19.5 percent of gross wages, but the replacement rate of future pension claims was reduced from 70 to 67 percent. Voluntary Riester savings were intended to fill this gap. This private investment in old-age provision is heavily subsidized by direct public allowances to the amount of the worker's Riester contribution or a tax deduction to the extent of contributions.[19] Thanks to these subsidies, the total budgetary cost of the annual state promotion of these accounts is expected to be 10 billion euros in 2008.

At the start, this reform did not succeed in attracting young individuals to build up a funded supplement to their reduced nonfunded pension claims. In 2003, 30 million people were eligible for the Riester subsidy, but only 3.8 million people had a private insurance contract. Studies suggest that the low enrollment was partly due to aversion against more risky investment in old-age provision (magnified by contemporaneous market declines) and partly due to confusing regulations regarding which products were eligible for subsidization. In time, some regulations were clarified and simplified, markets recovered, and the demand for Riester pensions increased to 5.6 million contracts by 2006.

In the policy debate that preceded their introduction, some experts had advocated that Riester accounts should be mandatory. One of the arguments was that only mandatory provision would obviate the moral hazard that was inherent in the simultaneously maintained guarantee of old-age assistance for lower-income groups. The concern expressed was that workers at the bottom of the wage distribution might, if given the choice, decide not to contribute to their retirement and to free-ride on promised welfare support instead. In 2001, the mandatory option was not chosen, but the government was legally obligated to track the demand for Riester savings and to review regularly the advisability of the option to make them compulsory.

Another controversial set of issues in the 2001 debate concerned the statutory retirement age and the regulatory replacement rate in the pay-as-you-go system. Intense opposition to raising the first or lowering the second blocked substantial change at that time. The statutory retirement age remained sixty-five for men and women.

In 2004, a further structural reform within the PAYG system altered the likely future course of the replacement rate in an important manner. The reform consisted in the introduction of the so-called sustainability factor in the pension formula. The pension formula mandates that yearly adjustments to pension benefits be linked to the yearly growth rate of wage income net of pension contributions and Riester savings. The introduction of this "sustainability factor" into the pension formula makes yearly benefit adjustments contingent on the ratio of pensioners to contributors. It is so constructed that an increase of this dependency ratio diminishes the pension adjustments and vice versa. This factor constitutes an automatic stabilizer of the pension budget. The aim is that the statutory contribution rate should not increase above 20 percent until 2020 and not increase above 22 percent until 2030.

The retirement-age issue has, in turn, been addressed by Chancellor Angela Merkel's coalition government. In 2006, the new government resolved to increase the statutory age from sixty-five to sixty-seven. Between 2012 and 2035, it will be raised one month every year. Some commentators have noted that few people work until the age of sixty-five today because the labor market is tight for older employees. As table I.2 in this introduction shows, the effective retirement age at the turn of the century was roughly five years younger than the statutory age at that time. Hence, the critics argue that this 2006 reform is, in effect, a hidden pension reduction. To counter this criticism, the German government has also introduced initiatives to improve labor-market conditions for older workers. A package of measures called Initiative Fifty Plus, entailing regulatory changes plus tax reductions and subsidies, is expected to reverse previous provisions that created strong incentives for early retirement.

Extending working lives and increasing personal savings—two central themes of this volume—turn out to have been central preoccupations of the pension-reform strategies of the German government in the first years of the twenty-first century. They are also the headline features of the White Paper of May 2006 in which the British government outlined its future strategy.

"Security in Retirement"

The 2006 White Paper issued by Blair government devotes one chapter to each of the five principal features of its new pension strategy:

• The introduction as of 2012 of a new, automatic system of low-cost personal saving accounts. Contributions are to be set at 8 percent of wages—4 percent from the employee, 3 percent from his or her employer, and 1 percent from tax relief. Collections, distributions, and other movements in the system are to be centralized in a national "non-departmental public body." This feature, along with stricter limits on investment choice, is expected to keep administrative and management costs below standard practice in private markets.

• The abolition, simultaneous with the introduction of these new accounts, of all existing subsidies to workers "opting out" of the state contributory system into defined-contribution funds, whether they are personal or occupational.[20] Workers who had previously opted out into these defined-contribution funds (and their employers) would simply be required to pay the full statutory contribution to the state contributory pay-as-you-go system.

• Again beginning in 2012, wage indexation of the basic state pension—which the Thatcher government had replaced with price indexation in 1980—is to be restored. Far from being a technical change, this is a change with major budgetary implications. It has been estimated that the Thatcher decision had saved the state 2 percent of GDP in the 1980s. At the same time, the contributory part of the state PAYG system is to be progressively transformed into a flat addition to the already flat basic state pension. By 2030, the contributory elements in the state system are to be eliminated, and the system is to basically return to its Beveridgean structure.

• Minimum length of contribution to ensure entitlement to the full, flat state pension is to be reduced to thirty years. Special provisions reducing this minimum for women, in general, and for individuals caring for children and elderly persons are to be introduced.

• The statutory retirement age for women is to be raised to parity with men at age sixty-five by 2020 and then raised for both sexes to age sixty-eight by 2046.

There are elements in the White Paper that will increase public pension expenditures. The indexation of the state pension to the general wage level is the most salient, but reductions in required contribution periods can also, by making more people eligible for full pensions, lead to increased public expenditures. By and large, however, the general thrust of the document goes in the direction of budgetary consolidation and calls for increased sacrifices. The raising of the retirement age is a case in point. Individuals may stop working before age sixty-five (eventually age sixty-eight) and still receive a full state pension if they have satisfied the minimum contributory requirement, but they will not begin receiving it until they reach age sixty-five (eventually age sixty-eight). Postponement reduces the actuarial value of total expected payments. To the criticism that this measure is unduly restrictive, the authors of the White Paper answer that it divides the benefits of greater longevity between longer working years and longer retirement. It would be unnatural if great longevity were to lead exclusively to longer retirement and the budgetary cost of the greater pension expenditures were to fall entirely on a shrinking active labor force.[21]

The most salient features of the White Paper are its proposals regarding personal savings accounts. The fact that employees will no longer be able to opt out of national insurance contributions into defined-contribution funds closes the door on what was a major channel for savings between 1986 and 2006. That channel is replaced by the new personal savings accounts. They are supposed to be simpler, more transparent, and less costly. In principal, they are not mandatory, but enrollment is automatic, and workers lose their employer's 3 percent contribution if they decide not to accept the account. The contributions to these accounts that the White Paper proposes are, in addition to the other, the standard required contributions to the state system.

The entire package implies a dramatic increase in payments by employees and employers. National insurance contributions that could previously be transferred to private defined-contribution funds must instead be paid to the state in full in exchange for a state pension that will eventually be completely flat. Contributions to the new personal accounts are to be paid on top of those NICs.

As they are designed, the White Paper provisions clearly provide much more forceful support for private saving than their German counterpart, the Riester accounts. The magnitude of the proposed forced savings are double the recommended level of contributions to Riester funds (8 percent as compared to 4 percent).[22]

It is interesting to compare the terms of the debate over the voluntary and automatic options in the two countries. In Germany, where a mandatory option never went beyond the status of possible alternative choice, the supporters of compulsion reasoned in terms of the moral hazard facing rational actors at the low end of the income scale. In the United Kingdom, moral hazard appears nowhere as an argument in the White Paper. Rather, its authors draw on the new field of behavioral economics and appeal to known patterns of inconsistency of economic reasoning by modest actors, who may prefer to be constrained to do what they know they ought to do but will not do of their own accord.

In both countries, there appears to be a consensus in favor of enhancing personal saving. But the leadership in one has proposed policies that, if enacted, will go much further than the reforms in place in the other. Why did the British government propose an 8 percent mandatory saving scheme, whereas the German government—which faces a stiffer demographic and budgetary challenge (see tables 1.1 and

1.4 of chapter 1)—adopted a 4 percent voluntary scheme? In a binary comparison, there are only conjectures, not proofs. But one possible conjecture relates the answer to initial policy conditions. Germany's pay-as-you-go system is, not surprisingly, quintessentially Bismarckian. Britain's is, also not surprisingly, Beveridgean.[23] Nor is it surprising that the contributory public system is the more generous of the two. The conjecture is that the difference of degree that one observes between Germany and Britain may reflect a tension between personal saving and generous, contributory public pension schemes. The same logic that suggests that a generous PAYG provision tends to displace private saving (see Feldstein and Lieberman, 2002) also suggests that there may be more political resistance to public policies that encourage private saving in countries with generous contributory PAYG systems.

The policy experiences of Germany and Britain illustrate the centrality of efforts to prolong working lives and to encourage private savings in developed countries faced with demographic pressures. They also provide an example of the way in which different initial conditions and different shocks tend to lead to different approaches to these common problems. In today's integrated world, in which countries like Germany and Britain compete and compare their social systems on a daily basis (perhaps in ways modeled in Gabrielle Demange's essay in chapter 5 of this book), we should expect that such experiences will subtly influence one another.

Notes

1. The relationship of pay-as-you-go to underdeveloped annuities markets is the subject of chapter 8 in this volume.

2. Chapter 4 examines, under simplifying assumptions, the conditions for the existence of such majority support.

3. Italy is a special case. Its public pension system is generous, but the notional, individual account system introduced in 1995 is, by its nature, not redistributive. This is one among other distributive indexes. The figure quoted for the Netherlands is a bit surprising; it may refer to all three pillars, not just the first-pillar pension benefits.

4. The notional account system introduced in Italy in 1995 protects it somewhat from the budgetary implications of aging, though it does not provide as much protection as does the United Kingdom's emphasis on funding. Notional account versions of the first-pillar provision have also been introduced in Poland and Sweden.

5. Fourteen papers were presented at the conference. Independent referees selected eight for inclusion in this volume, and the editors added another, written after the conference was over, that addresses a missing aspect of the reform debate.

6. All three parts include a mixture of theoretical and empirical studies. Three of the book's chapters are essentially theoretical, two are based on econometric evaluations of important policy initiatives, and four others rely on quantitative calibration of general-equilibrium models to test hypotheses about system design and sustainability.

7. Their calibrations treat the retirement age as a fixed number and do not allow for the early retirement penalties and delayed retirement credits that are the focus of chapters 1 and 2. Their estimates of the dead-weight loss entailed by the rigidity of the retirement age must therefore be viewed as upper limits.

8. This differs from studies that conclude that the tax rate should decrease at old age (see, e.g., Lozachmeur, 2006).

9. The Conesa and Garriga reforms would first have to be mapped into a unidimensional index to avoid circular voting dilemmas.

10. Originally, the British pay-as-you-go system remained largely shaped by Beveridgean principles and had as its central feature a flat basic state pension. But the introduction of the supplementary State Earnings-Related Pension Scheme (SERPS) in the late 1970s gave it an indelibly Bismarckian character.

11. See House of Commons Library (2001) for a description of the Stakeholders system.

12. In Eastern Europe, Hungary instituted a similar opt-out system in 1997, and Poland a fully mandatory second pillar in 1999.

13. The calculation is based on an assumed relative rate of risk aversion of 3.

14. The effect on the capital stock assumes that savings are at least partially invested at home. Fuster, Imrohoroglu, and Imrohoroglu, in fact, assume that the U.S. economy is financially closed.

15. The same table reports that the private savings accounts reform without annuitization raises average total, steady-state, expected utility by 0.6 percent and that full privatization raises it by 0.5 percent.

16. They introduce health care into the labor-leisure choice by assuming that health care requires an investment in time on the part of the recipient. The additional assumption that the complementary inputs from health-care professionals are nontraded means that aging tends to generate inflationary pressures in nontraded goods and services in an otherwise largely open economy.

17. A significant difference, which remains implicit in the analysis, is that increasing contributions to Holland's pension plans increases national wealth, whereas increasing contributions to a pay-as-you-go system only redistributes national income.

18. Riester's structural reform constituted a departure from the parametric adjustments of the previous two decades, which had seen both social security tax rates and the public subsidy from general funds frequently adjusted upward. In 2001, more than 35 percent of pension expenditures were financed by public subsidy.

19. The tax office checks which option is more favorable for the insured individual. When the worker retires, his or her pension is then also based on the cumulative value of earnings net of Riester contribution.

20. For technical reasons having to do with the complexity of their forward-looking nature, tax subsidies for workers "opting out" into occupational defined-benefit funds (a disappearing breed) are to be maintained.

21. The increases in retirement age proposed in the White Paper are similar in nature and magnitude to those announced by the Merkel government, but they are phased in more than ten years later (2046 as compared to 2035). On this score, the Merkel provisions are the more forceful of the two.

22. Not enough is yet known about the institutional structure of the proposed U.K. funds to compare it with the institutional structure of the Riester funds. Both are conceived as being tightly regulated.

23. In the 1970s, the state system became more contributory and lost some of its Beveridgean character. However, since the mid-1980s, the tendency has been toward restoration of the original focus on a flat, basic pension.

References

Blake, D. (2002). "The United Kingdom: Examining the Switch from Low Public Pensions to High-Cost Private Pensions." In M. Feldstein and H. Siebert, eds., *Social Security Pension Reform in Europe*. Chicago: University of Chicago Press.

European Commission. (2003). *Adequate and Sustainable Pensions*. Employment and Social Affairs. Retrieved from ⟨http://ec.europa.eu/employment_social/publications/2004/ke5303483_en⟩.

Feldstein, M., and J. Lieberman. (2002). "Social Security." In A. Auerbach and M. Feldstein, eds., *Handbook of Public Economics* (vol. 4). Amsterdam: North-Holland.

House of Commons Library. (2001). "Stakeholder Pensions." Research Paper 01/69.

Kotlikoff, L. (1992). *Generational Accounting*. New York: Free Press.

Kremers, J. J. M. (2001). "Pension Reform: Issues in the Netherlands." In M. Feldstein and H. Siebert, eds., *Social Security Pension Reform in Europe*. Chicago: University of Chicago Press.

Lozachmeur, J.-M. (2006). "Optimal Age-Specific Income Taxation." *Journal of Public Economic Theory*, 8, 697–711.

Mitchell, O., J. M. Poterba, M. J. Warshawsky, and J. R. Brown. (1999). "New Evidence on the Money's Worth of Individual Annuities." *American Economic Review*, 89(5), 1299–1318.

Organization for Economic Cooperation and Development (OECD). (2005). *Pensions at a Glance*. Paris: OECD.

United Kingdom, Department for Work and Pensions. (2006). "Security in Retirement: Towards a New Pensions System." Retrieved from ⟨http://www.dwp.gov.uk⟩.

I

Pay-as-You-Go Pension Systems

1

Optimum Delayed Retirement Credit

Eytan Sheshinski

A central question for pension design is how benefits should vary with the age of retirement beyond the earliest eligibility age.[1] For examples of widely varying pension benefits designs in many countries, see Gruber and Wise (1999). In the United States, retirement ahead of the normal retirement age (NRA), currently age sixty-five but being raised to sixty-seven by the year 2011, reduces benefits by 5/9 of one percent per month (about 6 percent annually) up to the early eligibility age of sixty-two. This is called the *actuarial reduction factor* (ARF). Similarly, benefits increase for retirement beyond the NRA up to age seventy. This is called *delayed retirement credit* (DRC). Figure 1.1 describes this pattern in the United States.

Workers vary in many ways—in life expectancy, income levels, and the degree of difficulty in continuing work. A good system needs to have flexibility in retirement ages to accommodate this diversity (see Diamond (2003, lecture 3). It is often argued that it is desirable that the system be neutral with respect to individual retirement decisions, implying that the incentive design should be actuarially fair on average. That is, the present value of additional contributions due to postponed retirement should equal the expected present discounted value of additional benefits.

The implicit assumption is that neutrality will preserve otherwise optimal individual decisions. We shall argue, however, that under asymmetric information, this is not the case. Certain individual attributes relevant to retirement decisions, such as labor disutility, are not observable by pension suppliers (government or private pension firms) and therefore pension schemes cannot depend on such attributes. Consequently, when individuals *self-select* their optimal retirement age based on their personal characteristics, the ensuing equilibrium is socially suboptimal: benefits to retirees are constrained by the need to provide sufficient incentives to continue work. A delayed retirement

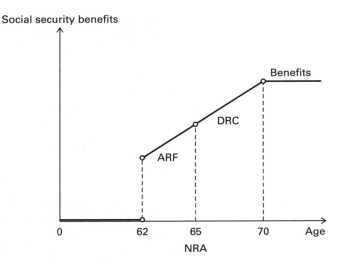

Figure 1.1

credit, by providing an incentive to continue to work, alleviates this constraint and leads to a better allocation of resources. This result holds even when all individuals have the same life expectancy (see Diamond and Mirrlees, 1978; Diamond, 2003, lectures 6–7).

In a recent paper, Cremer, Lozachmeur, and Pestieau (2004) analyze the shape of the optimal income tax and retirement benefit functions. In their model individuals differ by productivity (observable) and health, that is, labor disutility (nonobservable). Although our self-selection and moral-hazard conditions are different, it is notable that they also observe that in the second-best optimum there is a tax on continued labor and a positive relation between retirement benefits and the age of retirement.

This chapter presents a simple model of self-selection and retirement. On the basis of this model, I examine the desirability of providing incentives for continued work and the dependence of the optimum incentives on longevity.

The Model

Consider three different consumption levels—c_a for active workers, c_b^0 for early retirees, and c_b^1 for normal (or delayed) retirees. Utility of consumption and labor disutility are additively separable. The utility function for a worker with labor disutility level θ is written $u(c_a) - \theta$. We assume that θ is nonnegative and distributed in the population with distribution $F(\theta)$ (and density $f(\theta)$). For convenience, we assume that $f(\theta)$ is continuous and positive for all nonnegative θ. The utility function of nonworkers is $v(c)$, where c will take the values of c_b^0 or c_b^1, depending on the age at retirement.

We assume that the marginal product of workers is equal and normalize it to one. Thus, the only difference among workers is in the level of labor disutility.

Let T_0 be the age at which individuals have to make a decision whether to take early retirement or postpone retirement to age T_1, $T_1 > T_0$. With a certain life span of $T > T_1$, the length of retirement time is either $T - T_0$ for early retirees or $T - T_1$ for delayed retirement.

Normalizing the length of maximum retirement to one, delayed retirement entails additional work for a period of length $\alpha(= (T_1 - T_0)/(T - T_0))$, $0 < \alpha < 1$, and retirement for a period of length $1 - \alpha(= (T - T_1)/(T - T_0))$, while early retirement is for a period of one. For simplicity, further assume a zero subjective discount rate and zero rate of interest.[2]

If all those with labor disutility below a certain level θ_0 work while the others take early retirement, social welfare W is

$$W = \alpha \int_0^{\theta_0} (u(c_a) - \theta)\, dF(\theta) + (1 - \alpha) \int_0^{\theta_0} v(c_b^1)\, dF(\theta)$$

$$+ \int_{\theta_0}^{\infty} v(c_b^0)\, dF(\theta). \tag{1.1}$$

The budget constraint for the system is

$$\alpha \int_0^{\theta_0} (c_a - 1)\, dF(\theta) + (1 - \alpha) \int_0^{\theta_0} c_b^1\, dF(\theta) + \int_{\theta_0}^{\infty} c_b^0\, dF(\theta) = R, \tag{1.2}$$

where R are the resources available to the economy.

When $c_b^1 - c_b^0$ is positive, we call this difference the *delayed retirement credit (DRC)*. Our objective is to analyze whether such credit is optimal and examine the dependence of its level on exogenous factors.

First-Best: Labor Disutility Observable

To ensure that the maximization of (1.1) s.t. (1.2) entails that some individuals work, we assume that when no one works, those with the least disutility of labor prefer to work for an additional consumption equal to their marginal product:

$$u(R+1) > v(R) \tag{1.3}$$

When nobody works, consumption equals R. The assumption is that an individual with no labor disutility, $\theta = 0$, will find it advantageous to work and consume $R + 1$. This condition is called the *poverty condition* (Diamond and Sheshinski, 1995).

When labor disutility is observable, it is possible to determine the optimum consumption levels and the cutoff θ to maximize (1.1) s.t. (1.2). Optimum consumption $(c_a^*, c_b^{0*}, c_b^{1*})$ is allocated to equate marginal utilities of consumption:

$$u'(c_a^*) = v'(c_b^{0*}) = v'(c_b^{1*}). \tag{1.4}$$

All nonworkers enjoy the same level of consumption $c_b^{0*} = c_b^{1*} = c_b^*$. Consequently, the first-best entails no delayed retirement credit.

All individuals with disutility levels below a cutoff θ^*, $\theta^* > 0$, work and the rest retire. Assuming an interior solution, the cutoff is determined by equating the utility gain from extra work $u(c_a^*) - \theta^* - v(c_b^*)$ to the value of extra consumption as a consequence of work $u'(c_a^*)(c_a^* - 1 - c_b^{0*})$.

By (1.4), this condition becomes

$$u(c_a^*) - \theta^* - v(c_b^*) = u'(c_a^*)(c_a^* - 1 - c_b^*). \tag{1.5}$$

The first-best allocation (c_a^*, c_b^*, θ^*) is determined by (1.4), (1.5), and the resource constraint (1.2).

Second-Best: Self-Selection Equilibrium

Suppose now that labor disutility is not observable. Consequently, the cutoff θ is determined by individuals: given the alternative consumption levels, those with disutility above the level that equates the utility of continued work and delayed retirement to that of early retirement will prefer working and *vice-versa*. Thus, the threshold θ, denoted $\hat{\theta}$, is determined by

$$\alpha(u(c_a) - \hat{\theta}) + (1 - \alpha)v(c_b^1) = v(c_b^0)$$

or

$$\hat{\theta} = \frac{1}{\alpha}[\alpha u(c_a) + (1 - \alpha)v(c_b^1) - v(c_b^0)]. \tag{1.6}$$

A sufficient condition to make a retirement program socially desirable is that the marginal utility of nonworkers exceeds that of workers with the least disutility of work. This condition—

$$u(x) = v(y) \quad \text{implies} \quad u'(x) < v'(y) \tag{1.7}$$

—is termed the *moral-hazard condition* (Diamond and Mirrlees, 1978). By (1.3), there is some work at the optimal allocation. Thus, the worker with least labor disutility $\theta = 0$ must work, implying $u(c_a) > v(c_b^0)$ and so, by (1.7), $u'(c_a) < v'(c_b^0)$.

Maximization of (1.1) s.t. (1.2), with θ_0 replaced by $\hat{\theta}$ (which, by (1.6), is a function of c_a, c_b^0, and c_b^1) yields the following first-order conditions:

$$\alpha(u'(c_a) - \lambda)\int_0^{\hat{\theta}} dF = \lambda A u'(c_a), \tag{1.8}$$

$$\alpha(v'(c_b^0) - \lambda)\int_{\hat{\theta}}^{\infty} dF = -\lambda A v'(c_b^0), \quad \text{and} \tag{1.9}$$

$$\alpha(v'(c_b^1) - \lambda)\int_0^{\hat{\theta}} dF = \lambda A v'(c_b^1), \tag{1.10}$$

where

$$A = [\alpha(c_a - 1) + (1 - \alpha)c_b^1 - c_b^0]f(\hat{\theta}). \tag{1.11}$$

We have used (1.6) to obtain the derivatives of $\hat{\theta}$ w.r.t. c_a, c_b^0, and c_b^1. The right-hand side of these equations are the social values of resource savings from induced changes in labor supply due to altered benefits. The private return to working is $\alpha c_a + (1 - \alpha)c_b^1 - c_b^0$. Comparing this with the additional output α, we see that there is an implicit tax on work when $\alpha c_a + (1 - \alpha)c_b^1 - c_b^0 < \alpha$. As seen from (1.9), this is the case if at the optimum there are some nonworkers and $v'(c_b^0) > \lambda$. When $\hat{\theta}$ from (1.6) is an interior solution, then (1.7) ensures that this condition is satisfied.

Conditions (1.8) to (1.10) and the resource constraint (1.2) solve for optimum consumption and the corresponding Lagrangean, denoted $\hat{c}_a$, $\hat{c}_b^0$, $\hat{c}_b^1$, and $\hat{\lambda}$, respectively.

From (1.8) and (1.10), we see that $u'(\hat{c}_a) = v'(\hat{c}_b^1)$. Optimum delayed retirement benefits provide the same marginal utility as workers' consumption.[3]

Dividing (1.8) and (1.9) by the respective marginal utilities and adding, we see that the inverse of the Lagrangean equals the average of the inverses of the marginal utilities:

$$\hat{\lambda}^{-1} = u'(\hat{c}_a)^{-1} \int_0^{\hat{\theta}} dF + v'(\hat{c}_b^0)^{-1} \int_{\hat{\theta}}^{\infty} dF. \tag{1.12}$$

Proposition 1.1   When the optimum allocation has workers and non-workers, it has a positive delayed retirement credit (DRC) and an implicit tax on work.

Proof   With $u'(\hat{c}_a) = v'(\hat{c}_b^1)$, we have from (1.6) and (1.7) that $u'(\hat{c}_a) < v'(\hat{c}_b^0)$. Hence, from (1.12), $u'(\hat{c}_a) < \hat{\lambda} < v'(\hat{c}_b^0)$ and $v'(\hat{c}_b^1) < v'(\hat{c}_b^0)$ or $\hat{c}_b^0 < \hat{c}_b^1$.   ∎

The explanation of this result is straightforward. From the moral-hazard condition (1.6) we know that an attempt to implement the first-best allocation (1.4) is impossible because nobody will work. Any feasible policy that increases the benefits of retirees without reducing workers' welfare is desirable. In the absence of a delayed retirement credit $c_b^1 = c_b^0$, the cutoff $\hat{\theta}$ is determined by the condition

$$\alpha(u(\hat{c}_a) - \hat{\theta}) + (1 - \alpha)v(\hat{c}_b^0) = v(c_b^0)$$

or

$$u(\hat{c}_a) - \hat{\theta} - v(\hat{c}_b^0) = 0. \tag{1.13}$$

Now introduce a small delayed retirement credit, raising retirement benefits for workers by $\Delta/(1 - \alpha)$. Since these higher benefits apply for a period of $(1 - \alpha)$, total costs for each worker increase by Δ and utility increases by $v'(c_b^0)\Delta$. Similarly, reducing workers' consumption by Δ/α saves Δ over the working period α and decreases utility by $u'(c_a)\Delta$. By the moral-hazard condition, $v'(c_b^0) - u'(c_a) > 0$, and hence workers' utility increases. Furthermore, the following inequality holds for the marginal worker:

$$\alpha(u(\hat{c}_a) - \hat{\theta}) + (1 - \alpha)v(\hat{c}_b^0) + (v'(\hat{c}_b^0) - u'(\hat{c}_a))\Delta > v(\hat{c}_b^0), \tag{1.14}$$

implying that labor supply increases (by $f(\hat{\theta})$). Since there is a tax on labor, $\hat{c}_a - 1 - \hat{c}_b^0 < 0$, this enables an increase in benefits for early retirees, c_b^0.

No Early Retirement

Suppose that θ has a finite upper bound $\bar{\theta} > 0$. The *poverty-condition* (1.3) ensures that the optimum involves some work. At the other end, suppose that the optimum allocation involves no nonworkers—that is, $\hat{\theta} = \bar{\theta}$. This means that the consumption of nonworkers $\hat{c}_b^0$ is set at a level (possibly zero) that ensures that nobody chooses early retirement. From (1.12), it follows that in this case, $\hat{\lambda} = u'(\hat{c}_a) \; (= v'(\hat{c}_b^1))$.

From (1.8) (or (1.10)) and (1.11)[4] we now obtain the condition $\alpha(\hat{c}_a - 1) + (1 - \alpha)\hat{c}_b^1 - \hat{c}_b^0 \geq 0$. Since there are no nonworkers to support, there is no implicit tax on work.[5]

Two-Class Case: Comparative Statics

Delayed Retirement Credit
Consider an economy with two types of individuals—those with labor disutility θ_1 and those with $\theta_2(\theta_1 < \theta_2)$. Population weights of these groups are f_1 and $f_2 = 1 - f_1$, respectively. We assume that the first-best has the form that the θ_1 types work while the θ_2 types take early retirement.

Social-welfare optimization now takes the form

$$\underset{c_a, c_b^*, c_b^1}{Max} \{[\alpha(u(c_a) - \theta_1) + (1 - \alpha)v(c_b^1)]f_1 + v(c_b^0)(1 - f_1)\}, \tag{1.15}$$

subject to the resource constraint

$$[\alpha(c_a) - 1) + (1 - \alpha)c_b^1]f_1 + c_b^0(1 - f_1) = R \tag{1.16}$$

and to the moral-hazard condition

$$\alpha(u(c_a) - \theta_1) + (1 - \alpha)v(c_b^1)] \geq v(c_b^0) \geq \alpha(u(c_a) - \theta_2) + (1 - \alpha)v(c_b^1). \tag{1.17}$$

Condition (1.17) ensures that individual behavior coincides with that described in the objective function and the resource constraint (1.16). The moral-hazard condition and (1.17) imply that

$$\alpha(u(c_a) - \theta_1) + (1 - \alpha)v(c_b^1) = v(c_b^0). \tag{1.18}$$

Performing the maximization of (1.15) subject to (1.16) to (1.18), we obtain that at the optimum $u'(\hat{c}_a) = v'(\hat{c}_b^1) < v'(\hat{c}_b^0)$. Hence, $\hat{c}_b^1 - \hat{c}_b^0 > 0$.

Longevity and Delayed Retirement

We can use this example to analyze the effect on the optimal configuration of a decrease in α. The decrease in α can be interpreted either as an increase in longevity (given the age of early eligibility for retirement and normal retirement age, a rise in longevity implies that workers spend a larger fraction of time in retirement) or as an institutional change reducing the time between early and normal retirement.

Differentiating (1.16) and (1.18) totally with respect to α, viewing $\hat{c}_b^1$ as dependent on $\hat{c}_a$ through the relation $u'(\hat{c}_a) = v'(\hat{c}_b^1)$, yields

$$\frac{d\hat{c}_b^1}{d\alpha} = \frac{-\beta}{u'(\hat{c}_a)(1 - f) + v'(\hat{c}_b^0)f_1}[(u(\hat{c}_a) - \theta_1 - v(\hat{c}_b^1))(1 - f_1)$$

$$+ (\hat{c}_a - 1 - \hat{c}_b^1)v'(\hat{c}_b^0)f_1 \tag{1.19}$$

$$\frac{d\hat{c}_b^0}{d\alpha} = \frac{-1}{u'(\hat{c}_a)(1 - f_1) + v'(\hat{c}_b^0)f_1}[(\hat{c}_a - 1 - \hat{c}_b^1) - (u(\hat{c}_a) - \theta_1 - v(\hat{c}_b^1))]f_1,$$

$$\tag{1.20}$$

where

$$\beta = \frac{u''(\hat{c}_a)}{\alpha v''(\hat{c}_b^1) + (1 - \alpha)u''(\hat{c}_a)} > 0.$$

From (1.12) and (1.18), $u(\hat{c}_a) - \theta_1 - v(\hat{c}_b^1) = (1/\alpha)(v(\hat{c}_b^0) - v(\hat{c}_b^1)) < 0$. Also, from (1.8) to (1.12), $\hat{c}_a - 1 - \hat{c}_b^1 < (1/\alpha)(\hat{c}_b^0 - \hat{c}_b^1) < 0$. It follows from (1.19) that $d\hat{c}_b^1/d\alpha > 0$, while the sign of $d\hat{c}_b^0/d\alpha > 0$ is ambiguous.

By (1.19) and (1.20), the effect on the delayed retirement credit is

$$\frac{d\hat{c}_b^1}{d\alpha} - \frac{d\hat{c}_b^0}{d\alpha} = \frac{-1}{u'(\hat{c}_a)(1 - f_1) + v'(\hat{c}_b^0)f_1}[\beta(u(\hat{c}_a) - \theta_1 - v(\hat{c}_b^1))$$

$$+ (1 - \beta)(u(\hat{c}_a) - \theta_1 - v(\hat{c}_b^1))f_1$$

$$+ (\hat{c}_a - 1 - \hat{c}_b^1)(v'(\hat{c}_b^0) - u'(\hat{c}_a))f_1]. \tag{1.21}$$

A sufficient condition for (1.21) to be positive is that $\beta \leq 1$. This condition holds when $v''(\hat{c}_b^1) \leq u''(\hat{c}_a)$ or, in terms of coefficients of risk aversion (since $v'(\hat{c}_b^1) = u'(\hat{c}_a)$), $v''(\hat{c}_b^1)/v'(\hat{c}_b^1) \leq u''(\hat{c}_a)/u'(\hat{c}_a)$.[6] A reduction in α reduces total output and consequently the consumption of workers.

The change in consumption of nonworkers depends on the magnitude of the change in output relative to the change in consumption of workers. The above condition implies that to maintain equal marginal utility of workers before and after their (delayed) retirement, the reduction in workers' retirement consumption $\hat{c}_b^1$ is not larger than the reduction in their consumption while working $\hat{c}_a$.

In the special case where $u(c) = v(c)$ and consequently $\hat{c}_a = \hat{c}_b^1$, equations (1.19) to (1.21) take the simple form:

$$\frac{d\hat{c}_b^1}{d\alpha} = \frac{\theta_1(1 - f_1) + v'(\hat{c}_b^0)f_1}{u'(\hat{c}_a)(1 - f_1) + v'(\hat{c}_b^0)f_1} > 0$$

$$\frac{d\hat{c}_b^0}{d\alpha} = \frac{u'(\hat{c}_a) - \theta_1}{u'(\hat{c}_a)(1 - f_1) + v'(\hat{c}_b^0)f_1} > 0 \qquad (1.22)$$

$$\frac{d\hat{c}_b^1}{d\alpha} - \frac{d\hat{c}_b^0}{d\alpha} = \frac{(v'(\hat{c}_b^0) - u'(\hat{c}_a))f_1 + \theta_1}{u'(\hat{c}_a)(1 - f_1) + v'(\hat{c}_b^0)f_1} > 0.$$

The sign of the last expression is unambiguous due to the moral-hazard condition. An increase in longevity (or shortening of the time span between early and normal retirement), leads to a decrease in the gap between benefits to normal compared to early retirees.

Conclusion

When the population is heterogeneous with respect to labor disutility, efficiency dictates that some should retire early and others should continue working. Consumption levels of workers and nonworkers should be such as to equate all marginal utilities. When retirement decisions are made by individuals, these conditions cannot be satisfied, and incentives should be provided to reduce the tendency to retire early. This is the reason behind the delayed retirement credit. It has been shown that when some should retire and some should work, it is always desirable to provide a DRC. Because retirees have a higher marginal utility of consumption, the private return to postponing retirement falls short of the additional output produced by additional work. This is called a tax on labor at the margin.

Notes

1. Earliest eligibility age is designed to strike a balance between those who would, in the absence of such threshold, erroneously retire too early and others who have health or other reasons to retire earlier and for whom this imposes a liquidity constraint. One would like to know how this balance changes with increased life expectancy and morbidity. Social security reforms in the United States and Sweden left the earliest eligibility age intact.

2. The results carry over, with changes, to the case with positive subjective discount and interest rates.

3. If $u(c)$ is a constant shift function of $v(c)$, then $\hat{c}_a = \hat{c}_b^1$.

4. Modified (Kuhn-Tucker) conditions for a boundary solution.

5. There is another way to see this. From the resource constraint (1.2), when $\hat{\theta} = \bar{\theta}$, $\alpha(\hat{c}_a - 1) + (1 - \alpha)\hat{c}_b^1 = R$. Hence, $\hat{c}_b^0 \leq R$ (in particular, with no exogenous resources, $R = 0$, $\hat{c}_b^0 = 0$). None of the output of workers α is allocated to nonworkers.

6. This holds, for example, when $u(c)$ is a constant shift of $v(c)$.

References

Cremer, H., J.-M. Lozachmeur, and P. Pestieau. (2004). "Social Security, Retirement Age and Optimal Income Taxation." *Journal of Public Economics*, 88, 2259–2281.

Diamond, P. A. (2003). *Taxation, Incomplete Markets, and Social Security*. Cambridge, MA: MIT Press.

Diamond, P. A., and J. A. Mirrlees. (1978). "A Model of Social Insurance with Variable Retirement." *Journal of Public Economics*, 10, 295–336.

Diamond, P. A., and E. Sheshinski. (1995). "Economic Aspects of Optimal Disability Benefits," *Journal of Public Economics*, 57, 1–23.

Gruber, J., and D. Wise, eds. (1999). *Social Security and Retirement Programs around the World*. NBER Conference Report. Chicago: Chicago University Press.

2

How Elastic Is the Response of the Retirement-Age Labor Supply? Evidence from the 1993 French Pension Reform

Antoine Bozio

One key issue in pension-reform debates is the labor-supply elasticity of older workers. To what extent are older workers able or willing to work longer careers as full retirement age and marginal incentives to work increase? In this chapter, we estimate this key parameter using the 1993 French pension reform as a natural experiment and draw implications for the likely long-run effects of the 1993 and 2003 reforms.

To face the approaching demographic shock (baby boomers, who were born between 1945 and 1961, are expected to start retiring in 2005, and life expectancy increases currently at a rate of a quarter a year), governments have only three ways to secure the solvency of the public pension schemes—lower pensions levels, increase contribution rates, or increase retirement age. The 1993 pension reform, which was implemented by Edouard Balladur's government, is the first reform in France that has aimed at restricting the conditions for obtaining a full pension. It was designed to reduce the amount of pensions by increasing the period taken into account to compute the reference wage (from the best ten years to the best twenty-five years). But it was also supposed to give incentives to delay retirement by increasing the length of contribution necessary to get the full replacement rate from 150 to 160 quarters—or from 37.5 to 40 years.

Opponents of the 1993 reform argued that it was illogical to encourage workers to retire later while there was still a lot of unemployment and while the job market for those over fifty-five years old was almost nonexistent. Some have predicted that the low labor demand at older ages would lead the reform to have no net effect: workers would just remain longer in unemployment or in early retirement schemes. Another argument was that most workers were unable to work past age sixty for health reasons and would be physically forced to leave jobs at sixty with a lower pension. As a result, increasing contribution length would lead to lower pensions and not to a higher retirement age. In the current debate, which was reactivated by new reform measures in 2003 (which intensified the 1993 reform and extended it to the public sector), accurate estimates of behavioral parameters are key elements.[1]

From a scholarly point of view, this study provides an opportunity to confirm or invalidate results concerning the impact of social security on labor-force participation discussed in the theoretical and empirical literature.[2] Theoretical analyses of optimal retirement have stressed the role of heterogeneity and older labor-supply elasticities, among other factors (Sheshinski, 1978; Diamond, 2003). There is considerable controversy, however, about estimates of these elasticities. Studies with cross-sectional data (Gruber and Wise, 2004; Johnson, 2000; Duval, 2003) show a strong correlation between the development of social security programs and the decrease in labor-force participation at older ages. However, studies on panel data that use exogenous changes in social security wealth show very little or no impact of social security on labor-force participation (Krueger and Pischke, 1992; Costa, 1998; Baker and Benjamin, 1999), and they stress alternative explanations like the secular increase in income, the development of a society based on leisure, or the low labor demand at older ages. Baker and Benjamin (1999) emphasize the differentiated effects that reforms can have on the retirement age and on the labor market. They show that the introduction of early retirement in Canada has had a considerable impact on the retirement age but almost none on the labor market: the individuals who retired earlier would otherwise have had limited labor participation. The true variable of interest for the economist, as well as for the decision maker, is the elasticity of labor supply (and labor demand) to the incentives of social security. This literature has rightly stressed the fundamental problem of identification of the true impact of social security when all the reforms (which consisted, in the 1970s and 1980s, in expanding the generosity of social security) were collinear with the secular trend of increasing leisure time and income (Krueger and Pischke, 1992). Worse, the analysis of those earlier pension reforms was particularly susceptible to endogeneity bias: with higher income, voters would push to expand the generosity of the pension system because in all cases they wanted to retire earlier. Another identification problem underlined by Krueger and Pischke is the fact that social security benefits are a function of past earnings and retirement behavior is likely also to be correlated with past earnings. Reforms that have gone in the opposite direction and have tended to restrict access to pension programs are recent and therefore have not yet been extensively studied. Krueger and Pischke (1992) provide an evaluation of the social security notch[3] but show no reversal in the decline of labor supply, while others (Snyder and Evans, 2002) have suggested that this natural experiment could have led to increased postretirement work. Johnson (2000) put forward the case of New Zealand to show that the recent reform led to a significant increase in labor-force participation at older age levels.

Concerning the 1993 French pension reform, there has been, to this date, no ex-post empirical study. The only papers that are available are microsimulation studies developed around the model Destinie (INSEE, 1999). In the first versions (Pelé and Ralle, 1997, 1999), simulations were conducted with the assumption of a unitary response coefficient. Individuals retire from the labor force as soon as they get the "full rate," so any increase in the length of contribution required to get the full rate results automatically in the same increase of the retirement age. They stress therefore that only a fraction of the French workers are affected by the 1993 reform and that more will be as new cohorts begin to retire. Recent cohorts have started their careers later due to increased schooling and are more likely to be affected by an increase in the required length of contribution to obtain full pensions.

Recent simulations (Mahieu and Sedillot, 2000; Bardaji, Sedillot, and Walraet, 2002, 2003) adopt a more sophisticated approach by assuming that people choose their retirement age following a Stock and Wise (1990) model. They choose the date that maximizes expected utility of income and pension benefits as a function of preferences for leisure, risk aversion, and time preference. To calibrate preferences in the model, the authors use the parameters that can best replicate current behavior. These microsimulations must use as inputs hypotheses concerning behavioral preferences. To date, the best estimate of preferences of French individuals concerning retirement comes from a study by Mahieu and Blanchet (2001, 2004), who estimated an option value model following Stock and Wise (1990) using cross-sectional data. They remained cautious about the robustness of their results as they had data on only one generation (the 1930 cohort). Their estimates are dependent on the low variations within a generation that are the results of the strength of current incentives. They have no data on changes in behavior introduced by the 1993 reform.

The goal here is to use the variations introduced by the 1993 reform to identify more precisely the incentives of the French pension system and to estimate ex post the impact of the 1993 reform on the retirement age. My identification strategy relies on the progressive implementation of the reform, which creates many control groups not affected by the reform. The interaction between the generation and the length of the career at age sixty allows a clear-cut identification of the effect of the reform on the retirement age. One additional quarter of necessary contribution led to an increase of 1.5 months of the age of retirement, which implies a coefficient of response of 0.54. Moreover, the reform has led to a disclosure effect, which encourages individuals to claim more disability pensions and to find additional quarters of past contributions.

This chapter confirms for the first time, with national micro data, the strong correlation between social security parameters and labor-force participation displayed with cross-country data. However, results also underline the fact that a large minority of the population prefers, even with a high penalty, to leave work early. First, the features of the 1993 pension reform are recalled, and some suggestive graphical evidence of the likely impact of the reform is offered. Then I describe my identification strategy and present empirical estimates. Finally, the net impact of the 1993 French pension reform is assessed.

The 1993 French Pension Reform

The French Pension System
The French pension system is complex and is characterized by numerous schemes with different ways of computing pensions.[4] Self-employed workers have their own schemes, civil servants have pensions that are paid by the state budget, workers in special public services (train, subway, electricity) benefit from special and generous schemes, and the majority of wage earners in the private sector (68 percent of French workers in 2002) contribute to the *régime général* and receive pensions from the Caisse Nationale d'Assurance Vieillesse (CNAV). The 1993 reform aimed only at the *régime général*.[5] Beside these basic pension schemes, there is a second pillar, which consists of mandatory complementary schemes: for the private sector, Association pour le Régime de Retraite Complémentaire (ARRCO) and Association Générale des Institutions de Retraite des Cadres (AGIRC) (for nonexecutives and executives) are financed in a pay-as-you-go manner. They

were affected by the reform as the full rate in the complementary schemes is conditioned on obtaining the full rate in the basic pension scheme of the *régime général*.

Appendix 2A presents a brief overview of the rules that determine pensions in the *régime général* before the 1993 reform. It provides readers who are not familiar with the French pension system with some institutional details.

The 1993 Reform

In July 1993, the Balladur government made changes in some of the rules for calculating first-pillar pensions. This chapter estimates the effects on the retirement age of one of these parameter changes—an increase in the length of contribution needed to obtain a full pension.

As appendix 2A explains in detail, ever since 1945 the basic formula for calculating first-pillar pensions in the *régime général* has been

$$P = \tau * PC * W_{ref},$$ (2.1)

with $MIN \leq P \leq MAX$,

where P is the annual pension, τ is the pension rate, and W_{ref} is the reference wage. PC is a proportionality coefficient (not affected by the 1993 reform), which is generally close in value to 1.[6] Between 1983 and 2003, the rule defining the pension rate τ could be summarized as follows:

$$\tau = 0.50 * \left[1 - \delta * \max\left\{ 0, \min\left[(65 - AGE), \frac{N_1 - D_1}{4} \right] \right\} \right],$$ (2.2)

with δ the penalty fixed at 10 percent, N_1 the necessary length of contribution in quarters in all schemes, and D_1 the actual length of contribution in all schemes (also called the length of career). In practice, this rule of a penalty either relative to quarters of contribution or to age sixty-five offers a minimum rate τ at age 60 of 25 percent, whatever the length of contribution, and a maximum rate of 50 percent at any age between sixty and sixty-five, when the length of contribution is the "necessary" length.

The Balladur reform left these two formulas unchanged but modified three significant parameters. The first modification, which is the focus of this chapter, was an increase in N_1 (the length of contribution necessary to obtain the full rate) from 37.5 years (150 quarters) to 40 years (160 quarters). The reform was phased in at a rate of one additional quarter per year of birth from 1934 to 1943. As a result, individuals born in 1933 or before continued to need only 150 quarters to obtain a full pension. Workers born in 1943 and after needed 160 quarters. Therefore, the reform was fully phased in as of January 1, 2003, since it is impossible to retire prior age sixty. The fact that the reform was phased in by year of birth rather than year of retirement is a key element of our identification strategy.

The second change was the computation of the reference wage, W_{ref}. The 1993 reform defined it as the best twenty-five years of wages instead of the best ten years. This measure was also phased in with one additional year in the reference wage calculation by year of birth from the 1934 cohort to the 1948 cohort. Therefore, individuals born in 1933 or before computed their reference wage with their best ten years, whereas the 1948 cohort calculated on the basis of the best twenty-five years. This reform will be fully implemented on January 1, 2008.

The third and last change in the 1993 reform was to increase pensions each year with inflation and not according to wage growth. This measure legalized a practice existing since 1987.

The direct impact of the new formula for computing the reference wage was to lower pension levels. Indeed, the average of the twenty-five best years has to be lower than the average of the ten best years. The amount of the decrease depends on the steepness of the wage curve. The CNAV (2002) has computed pensions with the rules prereform and postreform to evaluate the reduction in pensions. It amounts to between 1 percent and 6 percent for the cohorts from 1934 to 1940.

The implementation of the change in the reference wage concerned all the individuals of each generation whatever their retirement age. This means, for example, that within the 1934 cohort everyone was affected by the change of the reference wage.[7]

The change of N_1 in the pension formula did not affect everyone uniformly. Because the reform is being phased in, it creates a differentiated impact according to the generation and to the number of quarters of contribution at age sixty. The two dimensions of the variations introduced by the reform are the year of birth (cohort effect) and the age of entry (in quarters) into the labor market.

To summarize, those who were not affected by the reform included the cohorts born in 1933, individuals with fewer than 130 quarters of contribution and those with more than N_1 at age sixty at retirement.[8] The wage earners affected by the increase in N_1 belong to the 1934

Table 2.1
Changes in the replacement rate ($\tau * PC$), in percentage points, following the 1993 reform: Generation 1934.

Quarters of Contribution at Retirement	Retirement Age					
	60	61	62	63	64	65
≤130	0	0	0	0	0	0
131	−1.09	0	0	0	0	0
133	−1.11	0	0	0	0	0
135	−1.12	−1.12	0	0	0	0
137	−1.14	−1.14	0	0	0	0
139	−1.16	−1.16	−1.16	0	0	0
141	−1.17	−1.17	−1.17	0	0	0
143	−1.19	−1.19	−1.19	−1.19	0	0
145	−1.21	−1.21	−1.21	−1.21	0	0
146	−1.22	−1.22	−1.22	−1.22	0	0
147	−1.22	−1.22	−1.22	−1.22	−1.22	0
148	−1.23	−1.23	−1.23	−1.23	−1.23	0
149	−1.24	−1.24	−1.24	−1.24	−1.24	0
150	−1.25	−1.25	−1.25	−1.25	−1.25	0
≥151	0	0	0	0	0	0

Note: Following the 1993 pension reform, the replacement rate of workers born in 1934 and retiring at age sixty-four with 150 quarters of contribution was cut by 1.25 percentage points, from 50 percent to 48.75 percent. The replacement rate of workers born in 1934 and retiring at age sixty-two with 139 quarters of contribution was cut by 1.16 percentage points, from 50 percent to 48.84 percent.

generation and have between 131 and 150 quarters of contribution, to the 1935 generation with 131 to 151 quarters of contribution, to the 1936 generation with 131 to 152 quarters of contribution and so on. Tables 2.1 and 2.2 describe for generations 1934 and 1936 the drop in the replacement rate due to the 1993 reform for different quarters of contributions. Later in this chapter, I describe the identification strategy, but these tables show which group was affected by the reform and which is going to be the control group.

Suggestive Graphical Evidence of the Effect of the 1993 Reform

The Available Data
The dataset that is most commonly used to study retirement in France is a specific panel, the Échantillon Interrégime de Retraités (EIR). This is a panel of 20,000 people selected by date of birth.[9] It reports all

Table 2.2
Changes in the replacement rate ($\tau * PC$) in percentage points following the 1993 reform: Generation 1936.

Quarters of Contribution at Retirement	Retirement Age					
	60	61	62	63	64	65
≤130	0	0	0	0	0	0
131	−1.09	0	0	0	0	0
133	−3.32	0	0	0	0	0
135	−3.37	−1.12	0	0	0	0
137	−3.42	−3.42	0	0	0	0
139	−3.75	−3.75	−1.58	0	0	0
141	−3.52	−3.52	−3.52	0	0	0
143	−3.57	−3.57	−3.57	−1.19	0	0
145	−3.62	−3.62	−3.62	−3.62	0	0
146	−3.65	−3.65	−3.65	−3.65	0	0
147	−3.67	−3.67	−3.67	−3.67	−1.22	0
148	−3.70	−3.70	−3.70	−3.70	−2.47	0
149	−3.72	−3.72	−3.72	−3.72	−3.72	0
150	−3.75	−3.75	−3.75	−3.75	−3.75	0
151	−2.50	−2.50	−2.50	−2.50	−2.50	0
152	−1.25	−1.25	−1.25	−1.25	−1.25	0
≥153	0	0	0	0	0	0

Note: Following the 1993 pension reform, the replacement rate of workers born in 1936 and retiring at age sixty-four with 150 quarters of contribution was cut by 3.75 percentage points, from 50 percent to 46.25 percent.

information about each retiree's pension entitlements in all pension schemes, using administrative data from the basic schemes (*régime général* and public pension schemes) and from more than 180 different complementary schemes. The drawbacks of the EIR are that it is limited to a selection of generations, that it has few observations for each cell, and that it has a rather long periodicity—once every four years. In the 2001 version, the only generations entirely affected by the 1993 reform are the 1934 and 1936 cohorts. They saw an increase in N_1 of, respectively, only one and three quarters (Coeffic, 2003). Because individuals are observed only when they have retired, younger generations affected by the 1993 reform are not included in the EIR 2001.

In this chapter, I use a different database (which to my knowledge has never been used by economists)—namely, the administrative and comprehensive data collected by the CNAV while managing the files of every would-be pensioner of the private-sector pension scheme.[10]

Since 1977, the CNAV has produced files on the retirees in the *régime général*. Starting in 1982, length of contribution was added to the basic variables of the file, and starting in 1994 the year of birth of the retirees was also added. The data are derived from exhaustive tabulations of all incoming retirees. The tabulations of the CNAV give the exact number of pensioners in each possible cell,[11] and I have turned those tabulations into a simple database. The data do not cover a large number of variables (gender, type of pension, length of contribution, year of submission of the retirement claim, age of retirement, year of birth), but they have the enormous advantage of being comprehensive, annual, and very recent. Thus, information is available on all pensioners in the private sector who have retired up to December 31, 2003.[12] Those who have completely retired were born in 1934, 1935, 1936, and 1937. Those born in 1938 can also be used as they have already reached age sixty-five, the second peak of retirement in France. Another advantage of this dataset is that age is coded in quarters. The only drawback of the base is that it is impossible to use generations before the reform as control groups. To do so would require the use of the EIR data.

Before developing my identification strategy, I first present some graphical evidence of the likely impact of the 1993 French pension reform. The strongest heuristic evidence comes from administrative data on the retirement age and work history of new retirees.

Average Retirement Age and Years of Contribution

The evolution of the average retirement age provides a hint of the possible effects of the 1993 reform. Publicly available data on average retirement age from the *régime général* are reproduced in figure 2.1. The series shows that average retirement age declined until 1994, when it reached a floor. This suggests an effect of the 1993 reform. However, it is impossible to draw firm conclusions concerning the increase of the retirement age since 1994, as this increase might be due to purely demographic changes. The average retirement age computed every year is in practice similar to the average age of the sixty to sixty-five age group (the minimum retirement age is sixty, and there is no incentive to retire after sixty-five). So if a smaller generation starts retiring at age sixty, then the average retirement age of this particular year will be higher.[13]

More suggestive of the effect of the 1993 reform is the fact that average age at retirement by generation declined constantly until generation 1932, when it stabilized and then increased slightly. Figure 2.2,

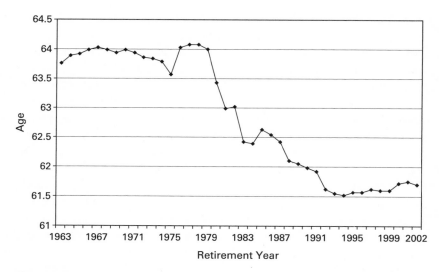

Figure 2.1
Average retirement age in the French private sector.
Source: Administrative CNAV data.

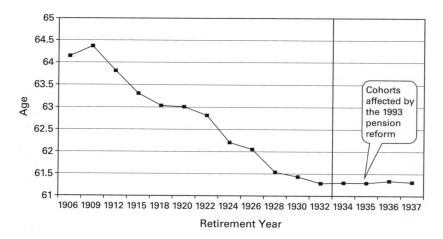

Figure 2.2
Average retirement age in the French private sector by generation.
Note: We exclude the individuals who retired after age sixty-six. For the cohorts born from 1909 to 1934, average retirement age was computed with EIR 2001, and for younger cohorts (born from 1935 to 1937), it was computed with administrative data from the CNAV (1994 to 2003). The sample is not quite comparable in both datasets because EIR 2001 has data only on the retirees alive in 2001. Differential mortality might play a role for older cohorts.

which is based on EIR 2001 data until generation 1934 and then uses the CNAV dataset, describes the evidence.[14] The small increase in average retirement age since generation 1934 does not suggest a large impact of the 1993 reform (around 0.03 year increase in the average age). But this may be misleading. The counterfactual hypothesis is one of a continuing secular decline in the average retirement age. Most important, the progressive implementation of the reform suggests an initially small and progressively increasing impact.[15]

Fortunately, there also is more direct and unambiguous information on the length of contribution by generation. Figure 2.3, based on both EJ' ، 2001 and the administrative data of the CNAV, is strongly sugges-t ،e of the impact of the 1993 reform. The figure depicts simple histo-،rams with the distribution of length of contribution at retirement for ،he various generations affected. Cohorts not affected by the reform (born in 1928, 1930, and 1932) show a huge peak at 150 quarters of contribution, the exact number required to receive a full-rate pension. The peak moves to 151 quarters for the 1934 generation, to 153 for the 1936 generation, and to 155 for the 1938 generation, following the way the reform was phased in.

In the light of those figures, there is no doubt that the 1993 reform has had some impact on the retirement age of wage earners in the private sector.

Identification Strategy

The first part of the analysis consists in applying a difference-in-difference methodology using the different impacts of the reform for persons who were just above and just below the moving threshold of N_1 $(150, 151, 152, \ldots)$ quarters of contribution. Then this methodology is generalized to a fixed-effect regression to make the best use of all the variations in the data.

The Difference-in-Difference Approach Applied to Adjacent Cohorts

The objective here is to estimate the degree to which the increases in the required quarters of contribution mandated by the 1993 reform led to increases in the age of retirement. However, an estimation of the effects of a longer required contribution period for a full-rate pension is subject to two identification problems. First, the increase is highly

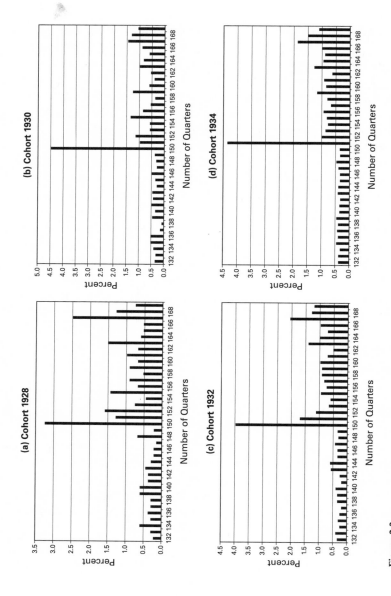

Figure 2.3
Distribution of the number of quarters of contribution at retirement by cohort (pensioners of *régime général*).
Source: Échantillon Interrégime de Retraités (EIR) 2001 for cohorts 1928 to 1934; administrative data of the CNAV for cohorts 1935 to 1938.

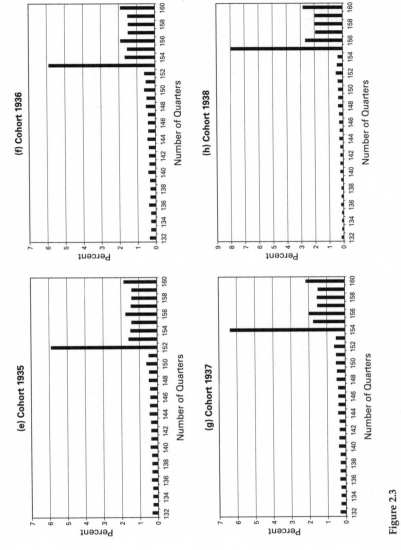

Figure 2.3
(continued)

correlated with a reduction in the replacement rate (due to changes in the reference wage formula) and with the secular trend in a declining retirement age. A simple time difference estimation would lead to biased estimates of the elasticity. Second, the length of contribution is itself an endogenous variable: persons who have started to work early in life are more likely to retire early. The progressive implementation of the 1993 reform offers a double variation to identify the pure impact of the reform, which depends on both year of birth and quarters of contribution. The strategy of the difference-in-difference approach relies simply on instrumenting the variation in pension wealth due to the increase in the length of contribution necessary to get the full rate by an interaction between date of birth and quarters of contribution at age sixty. This interaction clearly identifies the increase in the age required to get the full rate. One can thus consider the following equation for retirement age:

$$AGE_{ijk} = \alpha + \beta_j GEN_j + \gamma_k QUA_k + \eta_{j,k} GEN_j * QUA_k + v_i + \varepsilon_{ijk}. \qquad (2.3)$$

The retirement age AGE_{ijk} of an individual i from cohort j and with k quarters of contribution at age sixty depends on the identity of the cohort GEN_j (secular trend), its length of work QUA_k (contribution length),[16] and an individual fixed effect. The effect of the reform is captured by the interaction term $GEN_j * QUA_k$. The AGE and QUA variables are all expressed in quarters.

To identify the effect of the 1993 reform, I make the hypothesis that it has had no effect on the number of quarters of contribution at age sixty. I then estimate equation (2.3) for each change at the margin in the contribution length required to get the full rate. For example, a difference-in-difference regression can be done between individuals born in 1934 with 151 and 152 quarters of contribution at age sixty and those born in 1935. With 151 and 152 quarters of contribution at age sixty, those born in 1934 can retire with the full rate at age sixty. Neither category is affected by the 1993 reform. On the other hand, those born in 1935 who have only 151 quarters of contribution at age sixty must wait one more quarter to retire with the full rate. This last group is the only one to face the leisure-income tradeoff—retire at age sixty with a lower pension or delay retirement by one quarter for a full-rate pension.

The estimates of the difference-in-difference (DD) regression are as follows:

$$DD_{estimates} = [E[AGE_{ijk}|j = 1935 \ \& \ k = 151]$$

$$- E[AGE_{ijk}|j = 1935 \ \& \ k = 152]]$$

$$- [E[AGE_{ijk}|j = 1934 \ \& \ k = 151]$$

$$- E[AGE_{ijk}|j = 1934 \ \& \ k = 152]]. \tag{2.4}$$

Using equation (2.3), one can rewrite the DD estimates in the following way:

$$DD_{estimates} = [(\alpha + \beta_{1935} + \gamma_{151} + \eta_{1935, 151}) - (\alpha + \beta_{1935} + \gamma_{152})]$$

$$- [(\alpha + \beta_{1934} + \gamma_{151}) - (\alpha + \beta_{1934} + \gamma_{152})]. \tag{2.5}$$

$$DD_{estimates} = \eta_{1935, 151}. \tag{2.6}$$

Thus, the true impact is shown for the increase of length of contribution for the 1935 cohort that had only 151 quarters of contribution at age sixty. The same methodology can be replicated for the cohorts 1935 and 1936 with 152 to 153 quarters at age sixty, for cohorts 1936 and 1937 with 153 to 154 quarters at sixty, and so on.

To have a clearer view of this estimation strategy, it is helpful to look at figure 2.4, which depicts the average retirement age by cohort and quarters of contribution at age sixty. The individuals affected by the reform have between 131 and N_1 quarters of contribution at age sixty. The schedule of average retirement shifts toward the northeast of the graph, as cohorts are increasingly affected. This figure is another graphical proof of the clear impact of the reform. This difference-in-difference strategy measures the vertical difference between the schedules at the (increasing) required contribution length (N_1).

A More General Approach to Difference-in-Difference Estimation
The difference-in-difference estimation procedure I have just introduced is straightforward, but it loses some of the information provided by the phasing in of the 1993 reform. Younger generations are not only affected by the reform at higher contribution lengths (up to 160), but they are also affected in stepped degrees of intensity. For example, an individual with 150 quarters of contribution at age sixty would need to delay retirement by one quarter if she were born in 1934 and by four quarters if born in 1937. To face one or ten quarters of necessary contribution to reach the full rate should lead to different delays of

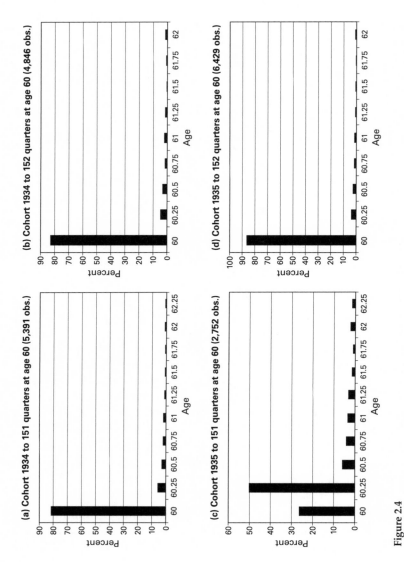

Figure 2.4

Distribution of the retirement age by generation and by the number of quarters of contribution at age sixty (normal pensions only).

Sources: Administrative data of the CNAV. The number of quarters of contribution at age sixty is computed from the number of quarters at retirement, supposing that each quarter past sixty led to one quarter of contribution.

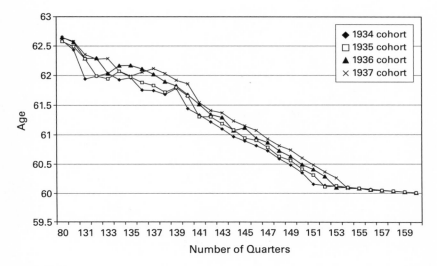

Figure 2.5
Average retirement age by cohort and quarters of contribution at age sixty.
Note: Administrative data of the CNAV. We have excluded individuals with quarters of contribution at the retirement age above 160.

retirement and possibly to different elasticities. These different intensities can be properly seen in figure 2.5, and a general framework needs to be developed to estimate them.

To pool individuals with one, two, or three missing quarters of contribution in a single test of the relationship between quarters of missing contribution and increased age of retirement, I extend the sample to all possible pairs of affected and unaffected cohorts and recompute difference-in-difference estimates in this larger universe. As shown above, in comparisons of adjacent years cohort effects cancel out. They do not automatically cancel out in comparisons of nonadjacent years. The application of my method, is therefore valid only if cohort effects are not significant. The results reported below suggest that that is true:

$$AGE_{ijk} = \alpha + \gamma_k QUA_k + \eta_{j,k} GEN_j * QUA_k + v_i + \varepsilon_{ijk}. \qquad (2.7)$$

Figure 2.6 plots the interaction coefficients $GEN_j * QUA_k$ for each cohort. Two main elements are of interest: the intensity of the reform is clearly captured by these interaction terms, and individuals not affected by the reform (those with more than N_1 quarters of contribution) have null coefficients on these interaction terms. This last fact gives

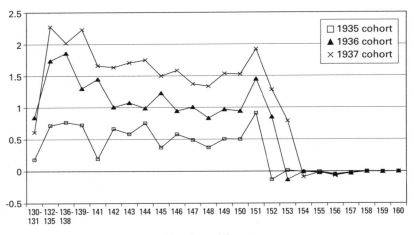

Figure 2.6
Interaction quarters times cohort coefficients.
Note: For each cohort, quarters of contribution at age sixty dummies are interacted with cohort dummies in equation (2.7) for the retirement age (in quarters). Simple quarter dummies QUA_K were also included in the regression.

even more credibility to my estimation strategy and to the claim that it has eliminated cohort effects.

Equation (2.7) can be estimated without specifying all possible interaction dummies. We can simplify these interaction terms and replace them with dummy variables corresponding to the number of quarters that an individual has to postpone retirement to benefit from a full pension. The logic of this simplification is as follows: a person born in 1936 with 152 quarters at age sixty is affected by the reform with one quarter, with 151 quarters at sixty she is affected by two quarters, and with between 133 and 150 quarters she is affected by three quarters. Create a set of variables R_n, where n is the number of quarters the individual has to postpone retirement to have the full rate. For instance, R_2 equals 2 if the individual has to postpone retirement of two quarters to obtain the full rate.

Difference-in-difference can then be used to estimate:

$$AGE_{ijk} = \alpha + \gamma_k QUA_k + \eta_n R_n + v_i + \varepsilon_{ijk}. \tag{2.8}$$

The η_n coefficient can be interpreted as the effect of an increase in additional quarters of contribution length necessary to get the full rate.

From Response Coefficients to Elasticities

The η_n coefficient is a response coefficient—that is, the average increase in retirement age following the increase of one or more quarters of required contribution length. The elasticity—that is, the average increase in percent of length of career following a 1 percent increase in required contribution length—can be computed simply as follows:

$$\text{Elasticity} = \eta_n \times \frac{\text{Average required length of contribution}}{\text{Average actual length of career}}. \tag{2.9}$$

This ratio is usually very close to 1, especially for individuals affected by the reform. Therefore, I use the term *elasticity* in a way equivalent to *response coefficient*, as these two measures are in effect very close.

Empirical Estimates

In this section, baseline estimates are presented from the regressions described previously, the negative hypotheses that the reform did not influence first the treatment group and then the control group are tested, and the reform effect is estimated with the EIR data.

Baseline Estimates

Table 2.3 presents three successive estimates based on one-year-apart differences in differences. The sample is restricted to normal pensioners. For each pair of cohorts, the average retirement age for each group is computed, and equation (2.4) is applied to compute the double-difference estimates.

Figure 2.4 depicts the corresponding histograms. Each histogram displays the distribution of effective retirement age by generation and by contribution length at age sixty. The double-difference strategy simply consists in computing the difference of the average retirement age for each group. Table 2.3 is the numerical equivalent of those histograms.

The result is that the 1993 reform has had a dramatic impact on the retirement age. Response coefficients are always close to 1: it amounts to 1.04 for the 1934 and 1935 double difference, 1.12 for the 1935 and 1936 double difference, and 1 for the 1936 and 1937 double difference. An increase of one quarter in the necessary length of contribution led to a postponement of one quarter of the retirement age.

Column 4 of table 2.4 presents difference in difference estimates obtained from the pooled sample of all cohorts affected by the reform.

Table 2.3
Average retirement age: Difference-in-difference estimates with normal pensions

Panel A. Natural experiment 1

	Length of Contribution at Age 60		
Cohort	151	152	Difference
1935	241.54	240.44	1.100
	(0.038)	(0.020)	(0.036)
1934	240.630	240.569	0.06
	(0.025)	(0.024)	(0.032)
Difference	0.911	−0.130	**1.040*****
	(0.042)	(0.028)	(0.049)

Panel B. Natural experiment 2

	Length of Contribution at Age 60		
Cohort	152	153	Difference
1936	241.420	240.372	1.048
	(0.033)	(0.018)	(0.031)
1935	240.44	240.516	−0.076
	(0.019)	(0.020)	(0.026)
Difference	0.981	−0.144	**1.125*****
	(0.034)	(0.024)	(0.041)

Panel C. Natural experiment 3

	Length of Contribution at Age 60		
Cohort	153	154	Difference
1937	241.291	240.326	0.965
	(0.028)	(0.015)	(0.027)
1936	240.37	240.408	−0.036
	(0.016)	(0.016)	(0.022)
Difference	0.920	−0.08	**1.001*****
	(0.029)	(0.021)	(0.035)

Note: Computations with administrative data from the CNAV. Excluded are individuals who have retired after age sixty-eight for the first experiment, after sixty-seven for the second one, and after sixty-six for the third one. Also excluded are individuals who retired with more than 160 quarters. Individuals retiring with disability pensions, unfitness for work pensions, and war pensions were similarly excluded. Standard errors are reported in brackets, and interaction coefficients are in bold type. The retirement age is in quarters.
***Significance level is 1 percent.

Table 2.4
The response of retirement to the full-rate contribution length: Baseline estimates

Variable	Coefficient (standard error)				
	(1) 1934–1935	(2) 1935–1936	(3) 1936–1937	(4) All	(5) All
R linear					0.610*** (0.015)
R_1	1.040*** (0.049)	1.125*** (0.041)	1.001*** (0.035)	0.687*** (0.042)	
R_2				0.633*** (0.021)	
R_3				0.601*** (0.016)	
Quarters dummies	Yes	Yes	Yes	Yes	Yes
Cohort dummies	Yes	Yes	Yes	No	No
Sample	1934–1935 cohorts with 151 and 152 quarters at age 60	1935–1936 cohorts with 152 and 153 quarters at age 60	1936–1937 cohorts with 153 and 154 quarters at age 60	All cohorts with all quarters at age 60	All cohorts with all quarters at age 60
N	19,418	20,265	19,791	811,605	
R^2	0.07	0.06	0.05	0.494	
F	314.49	426.52	504.21	23,277.23	24,731.10

Source: Computations with administrative data from the CNAV.
Note: The first three columns are limited to the double-difference samples. For the cohorts 1934 and 1935, the sample is restricted to individuals with 151 and 152 quarters at age sixty; for the cohorts 1935 and 1936, the sample is restricted to individuals with 152 and 153 quarters at age sixty; for the cohorts 1936 and 1937, the sample is restricted to individuals with 153 and 154 quarters at age sixty. The coefficient of the interaction term dummies (cohort times quarters) is then R_1.

The last two columns use all individuals who retired with normal pensions born from 1934 to 1937. Excluded from the sample are observations where retirement age is above age sixty-six. RB_n variables are defined as the number of quarters n necessary to get the full rate after the reform. For instance, R_2 equals 2 if the individual is born in 1935 with 133 to 150 quarters of contribution at age sixty, those born in 1936 with 151 quarters of contribution at age sixty and those born in 1937 with 152 quarters of contribution. In specification 5, we suppose a linear effect. Dummy variables are included for each quarter of contribution at age sixty possible. Standard errors are reported in brackets. Significance levels: *10 percent. **5 percent. ***1 percent.

Since the comparisons in this pooled sample are between cohorts two and three years apart, not just adjacent cohorts, three separate interaction dummies (R_1, R_2, and R_3) are allowed, as described above.[17] The response coefficients we get with this specification are all below 1, between 0.6 and 0.68 according to the magnitude of the change in required contribution implied by the reform. The larger the change in required contribution, the lower the response coefficient. The coefficient of R_1 is higher than the others but lower than in the adjacent double-difference estimates. Column 5 of table 2.4 restricts the relationship between number of quarters required and number of quarters postponement of retirement to be linear. This specification results in a response coefficient of 0.61, significant at the 1 percent level.

Finding a response coefficient of around 1 for the population at the margin (around N_1 quarters of contribution at age sixty) and a response coefficient of about 0.6 for the entire population (with quarters of contribution at age sixty between 131 and 153) is not surprising. It could be that individuals affected at the margin attenuate their response less than those who need to postpone retirement by a larger spell. There are, however, two other possible interpretations. First, the general regression might underestimate the response because of the omission of the cohort dummies. As has already been suggested, if this were true, then the interaction coefficients for people not affected by the reform should differ according to generation. Another look at figure 2.6 will convince the reader that these coefficients are truly equal to 0 for all generations. The second possibility is that this double-differences approach overestimates the response coefficients. This possibility is investigated further in the next section.

Checking for Various Biases

In the previous section, it was shown that difference-in-difference estimates are unbiased only if one condition is verified: the dividing line between control groups and treated groups is not itself affected by the reform. This can be assessed by checking two hypotheses—the assumption that the reform did not influence the contribution length at age sixty and the assumption that the reform did not lead individuals to retire with other types of pensions. Here those two possible sources of bias are checked.

While the assumption that the reform did not affect the contribution length at age sixty seemed at first a logical assumption, there are no data on the true contribution length at the time of the reform (which logically should be unaffected by the reform). Instead, as discussed above, a proxy is computed from the declared contribution length at the retirement age, from which is subtracted the quarters since age sixty. The dataset allows us to compare, from one cohort to the other, the number of individuals with a given number of quarters of effective contribution. In the 1934 cohort, we find 5,391 individuals retiring with 151 quarters of contribution and 4,846 retiring with 152 quarters. For them, one quarter more or less made no difference to their pension. In the 1935 cohort, 2,752 retire with 151 quarters, and 6,429 retire with 152 quarters. For that cohort, one quarter made a substantial difference in the pension. The comparison of declared cases of intracurb extra-marginal lengths of contribution is similar right through the 1937 cohort.

Two explanations can be given for this pattern. First, people might just have worked more before age sixty as a result of the reform. This would bias the measure of the true contribution length at the time of the reform. However, this hypothesis is not very credible, knowing that the first generation affected has had only a small amount of time to start working again and that the job market for those age fifty-eight and older is close to nonexistent. The second possibility is that the number of quarters of contribution declared can vary with the effort of the retiree to complete and possibly pad her file. Before the reform, a would-be pensioner would not care to look for proofs of an early age career if she had already 150 quarters of contribution with her main career. After the reform, the same person has high incentives to spend a weekend to find the small piece of paper proving that she has participated, at age fourteen in an internship for three months. This could bring her as much as a 2.5 to 3 percentage points increase of pension. To be fair, this active search might actually be undertaken by the individual's employer or the social security administration (CNAV). This would correspond to a *disclosure effect*.

This disclosure effect is more likely to have taken place at the margin. Those who had less than 150 quarters are likely to have already tried hard to look for additional quarters to be validated. Their incentives to look for some additional quarters of contribution is not changed by the reform. Hence the general regressions of table 2.4 (columns 4 and 5) are less affected by the disclosure bias, which is concentrated on a small part of the persons affected by the reform (those at the margin). The R_1 coefficient should be the one mostly affected. The analysis of the theoretical sign of this bias will be detailed in appendix 2B, while the results of corrected estimates will be described in the section on correction of the disclosure effect.

The second possible source of bias is the potential impact of the reform on disability pensions or unfitness for work pensions—other retirement routes that guarantee the worker a full-rate pension at age sixty. If the reform led individuals affected by the reform to retire with such pensions, then it means that our estimations based on normal pensions are biased as the extent of the treated group is affected by the reform. In this case, the true group affected by the reform would be not only those who have retired with normal pensions but all pensioners.

In the next section, the question of disability pensions is addressed, and a simple model is presented to explain the impact of this bias on our estimates.

Impact of the Reform on Disability Pensions
In theory, pensions granted for disability or unfitness for work should not be affected by the 1993 reform. Being deemed unfit for work or being disabled is based on a medical investigation and is independent, in principle, from the number of quarters of contribution. However, for pensions granted for unfitness for work, the number of quarters of contribution plays a role as people who can have already the full rate have no incentives to ask for such type of pension. A disclosure effect might also be at stake here. First to be checked is whether the reform has induced individuals to retire with disability pensions. In the first three columns of table 2.5, the same double-difference procedure is followed as before, this time letting the dependent variable be the fact of having been granted a disability pension or not. Disability pensions are granted more often to individuals affected by the reform. The impact is strong and very significant at the margin. The probability of having disability pensions or pensions for unfitness rises by as much as 13 to 15 percent when the individual is constrained by the reform.

The last two columns of table 2.5 are similar to the last two columns of table 2.4. Column 4, which distinguishes the effect according to the number of additional quarters needed for full pension, shows that the reform has increased the likelihood to receive a disability or unfitness pension from 2 to 4 percent. The effect is higher for those affected at the margin. This is not surprising, as the others had probably

Table 2.5
Impact of the reform on disability or unfitness pensions.

Variable	Coefficient (standard error)				
	(1) 1934–1935	(2) 1935–1936	(3) 1936–1937	(4) Disability	(5) Disability
R linear					0.019*** (0.001)
R_1	0.136*** (0.010)	0.132*** (0.010)	0.152*** (0.010)	0.042*** (0.002)	
R_2				0.021*** (0.002)	
R_3				0.020*** (0.003)	
Gender	−0.010** (0.0050)	−0.008* (0.0048)	−0.0006 (0.0047)	−0.030*** (0.001)	−0.030*** (0.001)
Quarters dummies	Yes	Yes	Yes	Yes	Yes
Cohort dummies	Yes	Yes	Yes	No	No
Sample	1934–1935 cohorts with 151 and 152 quarters at age 60	1935–1936 cohorts with 152 and 153 quarters at age 60	1936–1937 cohorts with 153 and 154 quarters at age 60	All cohorts with all quarters at age 60	All cohorts with all quarters at age 60
N	23,210	24,038	23,347	1,268,945	
R^2	0.01	0.01	0.02	0.04	
F	81.68	91.38	93.92	1,498.86	1,586.82

Source: Computations with administrative data from the CNAV.
Note: The specifications are identical to the one used in table 2.4, but the dependant variable is a dummy variable that takes the value 1 if the individual has retired with a disability pension or a pension for unfitness for work. The gender variable codes 1 for male. Standard errors are reported in parentheses.
Significance levels: *10 percent. **5 percent. ***1 percent.

already made efforts to retire at the full rate with other types of pension. In the second specification, the effect of additional required quarters is assumed to be linear.

A control experiment can be conducted using the pensions granted to former prisoners of concentration camps (children during the war), veterans (mostly from the Algerian war), or mothers working in factories. The possibility of claiming such pensions is much more reduced, and it is likely that even with more than N_1 quarters of contribution former prisoners of concentration camp or veterans would have

Table 2.6
Control experiment: Impact of the reform on war pensions.

Variable	Coefficient (standard error)				
	(1) 1934–1935	(2) 1935–1936	(3) 1936–1937	(4) War Pension	(5) War Pension
R linear					0.0002*** (0.00008)
R_1	0.0008 (0.0007)	−0.0004 (0.0005)	0.00002 (0.0004)	0.00009 (0.0002)	
R_2				0.00023** (0.0001)	
R_3				0.00026*** (0.00009)	
Gender	0.0011*** (0.00035)	0.0007*** (0.00028)	0.00035* (0.00019)	0.0056*** (0.00008)	0.0056*** (0.00008)
Quarters dummies	Yes	Yes	Yes	Yes	Yes
Cohort dummies	Yes	Yes	Yes	No	No
Sample	1934–1935 cohorts with 151 and 152 quarters at age 60	1935–1936 cohorts with 152 and 153 quarters at age 60	1936–1937 cohorts with 153 and 154 quarters at age 60	All cohorts with all quarters at age 60	All cohorts with all quarters at age 60
N	23,210	24,038	23,347	1,268,945	
R^2	0.0007	0.0004	0.0003	0.004	
F	3.98	2.17	1.56	151.34	160.49

Note: The specifications are identical to the one used in table 2.4, but the dependant variable is a dummy variable that takes the value 1 if the individual has retired with a war-related pension. Standard errors are reported in parentheses.
Significance levels: * 10 percent. ** 5 percent. *** 1 percent.

claimed such type of pension. Table 2.6 shows the same regressions as previously with the dependent variable being the fact of being granted such war pensions or not. The effect is generally nonsignificant.

Correction of the Disclosure Effect

The impact of the reform on disability pensions is also a disclosure effect similar to the one affecting declared length of contribution. The reform has strengthened the incentive to reveal information to retire as soon as possible with a full-rate pension. Once this effect is well identified, the sign of the resulting bias needs to be assessed and ways to correct it need to be considered. The analysis is presented in appendix

2B. A good correction appears to estimate our difference-in-difference excluding from the sample the individuals who have retired at least a quarter after gaining access to a full-rate pension.

Final results, corrected for these two disclosure biases, are presented in table 2.7. Difference in difference estimates based on comparisons of adjacent years appear in columns 1 through 3. Response coefficients are between 0.63 and 0.66, closer to the estimates of the general regression but nevertheless higher for those affected at the margin. The last two columns of table 2.7 present results from the pooled sample of comparisons of all affected cohorts. Excluded are individuals affected at the margin. These pooled results are not much affected by the disclosure effect. The coefficient in the linear specification drops from 0.610 to 0.596. The coefficient most affected is R_1, for the individuals affected only by an increase of one quarter in the required length of contribution. This is not surprising as these are the ones with the greatest incentive to move themselves from the treatment group to the control group.

The next section uses EIR 2001 data to check for the presence of any trend that might bias this estimate.

Robustness Checks with Échantillon Interrégime de Retraités (EIR 2001)

The administrative CNAV data have one shortcoming: they lack data before the reforms to control for a possible trend. Although imprecise (small sample, retirement age in years) and subject to unfortunate delays (in 2001 only the 1934 and 1936 cohorts were complete to test the impact of the 1993 reform), the EIR 2001 allows the control experiments that were lacking with previous estimates on the administrative data of the CNAV. The following tests are no real estimates of the reform and should not be compared quantitatively with the previous estimates. The sole purpose of this section is to check whether there do not exist earlier trends that could throw doubt on our estimates.

Table 2.8 uses the same double-difference methodology that was used with CNAV data. This allows control experiments to be run on previous generations, like 1930 to 1932. The interaction coefficients that show a positive effect are quite imprecise. Because of the lack of precision in the data, the standard errors should be bigger than in the CNAV dataset. The coefficients of the natural experiment are positive (significant in one case), whereas those of the control experiment are all null or nonsignificant. This confirms that we are indeed

Table 2.7
The response of retirement age to the full-rate contribution length: Corrected estimates.

	Coefficient (standard error)				
Variable	(1) 1934–1935	(2) 1935–1936	(3) 1936–1937	(4) All	(5) All
R linear					0.596*** (0.017)
R_1	0.655*** (0.057)	0.626*** (0.057)	0.664*** (0.056)	0.613*** (0.050)	
R_2				0.610*** (0.025)	
R_3				0.588*** (0.018)	
Quarters dummies	Yes	Yes	Yes	Yes	Yes
Cohort dummies	Yes	Yes	Yes	No	No
Sample	1934–1935 cohorts with 151 and 152 quarters at age 60	1935–1936 cohorts with 152 and 153 quarters at age 60	1936–1937 cohorts with 153 and 154 quarters at age 60	All cohorts with all quarters at age 60	All cohorts with all quarters at age 60
N	16,099	17,095	16,874	763,307	
R^2	0.62	0.59	0.63	0.455	
F	8,855.58	8,294.41	9,653.24	20,549.04	21,965.53

Source: Computations with administrative data from the CNAV.
Note: The first three columns are limited to the double-difference sample, where individuals who have retired more than one quarter after having the right to a full-rate pension are excluded.

In the last two columns, all individuals with normal pensions born from 1934 to 1937 are included. Excluded from the sample are observations where retirement age is above age sixty-six and individuals are at the margin (individuals that have at age sixty between 151 and 153 quarters of contribution). RB_n variables are defined as previously. Included are dummy variables for each quarter of contribution at age sixty. Standard errors are reported in parentheses.
Significance levels: * 10 percent. ** 5 percent. *** 1 percent.

Table 2.8
Average retirement age: Difference-in-difference estimates (EIR)

Panel A: Natural experiment 1

	Contribution Length at Age 60		
Cohort	Affected	Control	Difference
1934–1936	244.659	241.111	3.547
	(0.166)	(0.041)	(0.113)
1930–1932	244.225	241.420	2.804
	(0.175)	(0.055)	(0.146)
Difference	0.434	−0.309	**0.743*****
	(0.248)	(0.060)	(0.180)

Panel B: Control experiment 1

	Contribution Length at Age 60		
Cohort	Affected	Control	Difference
1930–1932	244.225	241.420	2.804
	(0.175)	(0.055)	(0.146)
1926–1928	244.96	242.060	2.899
	(0.256)	(0.076)	(0.203)
Difference	−0.734	−0.640	**−0.095**
	(0.314)	(0.088)	(0.251)

Panel C: Natural experiment 2

	Contribution Length at Age 60		
Cohort	Affected	Control	Difference
1934	246.706	245.992	0.713
	(0.265)	(0.109)	(0.348)
1932	245.907	246.007	−0.100
	(0.339)	(0.152)	(0.487)
Difference	0.799	−0.014	**0.813**
	(0.435)	(0.185)	(0.580)

Panel D: Control experiment 2

	Contribution Length at Age 60		
Cohort	Affected	Control	Difference
1932	245.907	246.007	−0.100
	(0.339)	(0.152)	(0.487)
1930	246.474	246.697	−0.223
	(0.380)	(0.156)	(0.517)
Difference	−0.567	−0.690	**0.123**
	(0.520)	(0.222)	(0.710)

Note: Computations with data from EIR 2001. Excluded are individuals who retired after age sixty-six. The sample is also restricted to individuals who retired only through *régime général* schemes. A person is considered affected by the reform if she has at age sixty between 131 and 150 quarters of contribution and nonaffected otherwise. Standard errors are reported in parentheses, and elasticities in bold.
Significance level: *** 1 percent.

Table 2.9
The response of retirement age to the full-rate contribution length: Estimates with data
from EIR 2001.

Variable	Coefficient (standard error)
QUA*Generations affected	0.726*
	(0.376)
QUA	−0.264
	(187.395)
Trend*QUA	0.002
	(0.097)
Generation 1932	−0.458***
	(0.094)
Generation 1934	−0.528***
	(0.086)
Generation 1936	−0.603***
	(0.114)
N	13,072
R^2	0.091
$F_{(6.13065)}$	217.273

Note: Computations with EIR 2001 data. Excluded are individuals who retired at age
sixty-five or older. The sample is restricted to individuals who have retired only through
régime général schemes. The dependent variable, age at retirement, is in quarters. QUA
variable is equal to 1 if individuals have at age sixty between 131 and 152 quarters of contribution and is 0 otherwise. The trend is the year of birth. Standard errors are reported in
parentheses.
Significance levels: *10 percent. **5 percent. ***1 percent.

estimating the effect of the 1993 reform and not capturing other trend-
related effects.

Table 2.9 reports results of the estimate of the following equation:

$$AGE_{ij} = \alpha + \beta_j GEN_j + \gamma \overline{QUA} + \delta \overline{QUA} \times \text{Affected Generations}$$

$$+ \zeta \overline{QUA} \times \text{Trend} + \varepsilon_{ij}, \tag{2.10}$$

with AGE_{ij} the retirement age of an individual i and from cohort j,
GEN_j the cohort j, and $\overline{QUA}$ a new dummy variable that takes the
value 1 if the person has at age sixty between 131 and 152 quarters of
contribution and 0 otherwise. The impact of the reform for each generation is not estimated because the data are not precise enough to do so.
The $\overline{QUA} \times \text{Trend}$ variable controls for a possible trend specific to the
test group. This possibility is clearly rejected. The interaction coefficient
δ is statistically significant at 10 percent.

The importance of these EIR data results is that they provide control experiments with insignificant response coefficient estimates. Next discussed is how the particular patterns of early retirees and the unemployed affect our results.

How to Account for Early Retirees and the Unemployed?

The sample includes unemployed individuals and individuals in early retirement schemes. The available administrative CNAV data do not have information on the previous occupation before official retirement. Moreover, unemployment and early retirement schemes attribute free quarters of contribution to their beneficiaries, as part of the benefit package.

A large proportion of these people have, therefore, no incentive not to delay retirement: they face no leisure-income arbitrage.[18] The estimates so far include mechanical delays in retirement from this group.

According to previous studies (Colin, Iéhlé, and Mahieu, 2000), only 34 percent of the wage earners in the private sector were working just before retirement, and 47 percent were either unemployed or in early retirement schemes and had the possibility to receive additional quarters of contribution simply by remaining in those schemes. However, the proportion affected by these schemes varies greatly according to the length of contribution at age sixty.

A recent report (Bommier, Magnac, Rapoport, and Roger, 2006) that uses EIR matched with Déclarations Annuelles de Données Sociales (DADS)[19] and Union Nationale Interprofessionelle pour l'Emplois dans l'Industrie et le Commerce (UNEDIC) files (unemployment and early retirement schemes) offers more precise estimates of the status of individuals prior to retirement, by length of contribution. Thus, it allows us to compute the share of those theoretically affected by the 1993 reform who could escape the leisure-income tradeoff by remaining in their previous schemes. One difficult question is how to consider individuals who do not appear in the DADS file. One way is to treat them as inactive (Colin et al., 2000), but this misses the fact that the larger part of them are civil servants who worked, when young, in the private sector. Table 2.10 uses data from this report to compute the distribution of status prior to retirement, considering the last status available in the data (for the working period 1985 to 1996). These data confirm that large numbers of early retirees have had very long careers (much more than 165 quarters of contribution at age sixty) and were

Table 2.10
Distribution of status prior to retirement.

Cohort 1930	Length of Contribution					
	<150	150–154	155–159	160–164	>165	All
Missing	61.75%	36.80%	31.30%	33.25%	24.02%	41.37%
Employed	24.69	39.16	40.41	39.59	37.98	32.84
Unemployed	10.83	15.33	20.23	15.66	20.51	15.88
Early retirement	2.73	8.71	8.07	11.50	17.49	9.92
Total in contribution paying schemes	13.56%	24.04%	28.30%	27.16%	38.00%	25.80%

Source: EIR 1997 for the 1930 cohort; DADS and UNEDIC from Bommier et al. (2006, app. 3, table 4).
Note: The individuals missing were not found in either the DADS files or the UNEDIC files during the period 1985 to 1996. They are likely to be civil servants who started working at a younger age or inactive women. The status is the one just prior to retirement or, if missing, the last one registered.

therefore not affected by the 1993 reform. However, for the group with between 150 and 160 quarters of contribution at age sixty, we still count 23 to 28 percent not working and in early retirement or unemployment schemes. For the group with fewer than 150 quarters of contribution at age sixty, this percentage is around 13 to 14 percent. People in this group have delayed their retirement age, as they faced no tradeoff.

Two types of estimates of the response effect can be made. The first estimate is a net effect of the reform, given the institutional setting (early retirement schemes, unemployment scheme, possibility of manipulating a disability pension). The second one is a pure elasticity (or response coefficient) representing the tradeoff between leisure and income, computed only for those who have faced this tradeoff.

The first estimate measures the average amount of postponement related to a variation of the contribution length for the people theoretically affected by the reform (those with length of contribution between 131 and 160 quarters). One has also to make an hypothesis about whether people in early retirement schemes and unemployment had incentives to retire early with disability pension or to manipulate. For most schemes, retirement was a better deal than previous schemes but not by much and not for all. So we assume that they did not try to retire earlier. This assumption will lead to a lower bound estimate. With results from tables 2.7 and 2.10, one can compute this net response coefficient to be 0.47 (below 150 quarters) and 0.40 for those marginally affected (150 to 154 quarters). These strikingly low results show how many possibilities there were for individuals theoretically affected by the 1993 reform to escape the income-leisure tradeoff.

A second type of estimate is necessary to capture the true, economic response effect: What is the variation in retirement age for those truly affected by the reform (who had no other escape route)? These computations lead to response coefficient of 0.54 (below 150 quarters) and 0.53 (151 to 155 quarters).[20]

Summing Up: An Early Retirement Puzzle?

The Net Impact of the Increase of the Required Length of Contribution

It is worth recalling who was actually affected by the 1993 French pension reform and what was expected from it. The reform changed only the pension formula of the wage earners of the private sector (68 percent of French workers), and within this group it changed only incentives to retire for those who had at age sixty between 131 and 160 quarters of contribution (18 percent of a generation). Among this group, 66 percent retire with a normal pension and are truly affected by the reform. In effect, the increase of the contribution length in the 1993 reform affected only 8 percent of the French workers, and only the younger ones were more than marginally affected by the reform. The bulk of the effect of the 1993 reform on the projected deficit comes through the reduction in replacement rates induced by the change in computation of the reference wage. Not much was expected from increasing the contribution length. In simulations made in 2004, the 1993 pension reform is predicted to reduce the number of retirees by 180,000 in 2010 and by 390,000 in 2040.

Among those affected, some have been granted disability pensions or pensions for unfitness to work, some have tried and succeeded in finding the additional quarters of contribution to receive a full-rate pension, and some have not changed their retirement age as they were going to retire later in any case (the individuals with positive v_i who have been excluded in the final estimate). Finally, the proportion of the CNAV beneficiaries that are used for our estimate of the response effect is roughly 10 percent, which corresponds to 6.8 percent of all French workers. In the longer run, however, the proportion of individuals affected will increase substantially as the number of wage earners with more than the required length of contribution will decrease (people start their career later). Using predictions made with Destinie, we can estimate the proportion affected at 21 percent for the cohorts 1940 to 1944 and at 48 percent for the cohorts 1965 to 1974. The 1993 reform, once fully phased in, has led to an increase in the required length of contribution of 2.5 years. The 2003 reform applies this increase to the public sector and further extends the required length of contribution for both categories by a total of 4.5 years in 2020. Our response coefficient of 0.54 means that, on average, these increases will lead, respectively, to an increase of 1.35 years of work (1993 reform) and 2.43 years (2003 reform) for the generations fully affected. On average, those in the 1940 to 1944 cohort who will face only the 1993 reform will delay retirement from around 0.28 years (as few individuals of these cohorts are affected by the reform). With respect to 37.5 years of required contribution length, this represents an increase of 0.5 percent of the labor force (only the private sector is included). The average increase in the length of career following the 1993 and 2003 reform on the 1955 to 1964 cohorts is one year—an increase of 2.4 percent of the labor force (both public and private sectors are included).

If capital is elastic in the long run, the predicted growth of gross domestic product following the increase of the required length of contribution can then be roughly estimated at 0.5 percent following the 1993 reform in the private sector (in 2008) and 2.4 percent following both the 1993 and the 2003 reform (by the year 2020).

One would also have liked to know whether the 1993 reform has had any impact on the labor supply before retirement. Unfortunately, the available data do not allow an assessment of the impact of the 1993 reform on the labor supply of French workers before they retire. Moreover, the 1993 reform has not been the only policy change to affect early retirement. In December 1993, following the pension reform, conditions to enter early retirement schemes were tightened. Age limits to enter early retirement schemes were increased by a year (from age fifty-six to fifty-seven). On the other hand, in April 1993, the Ministry of Labor launched an information campaign to encourage unemployed persons to enroll in a special early retirement scheme, Dispense de Recherche d'Emploi (DRE). Both reforms are hard to disentangle from possible effects of the 1993 pension reform, and even with better data, it will be difficult to devise a robust strategy to estimate the net effect of increased contribution length on the labor supply of fifty-five- to sixty-year-olds.

Even when all other routes toward retirement are taken into account, the true elasticity (for those actually affected by the reform and who had no other choice but to face the tradeoff) is still not as high as theory would predict for as high a penalty as exists in the French pension system (10 percent per missing year). Our estimate of 0.54, though it is far from negligible, is also well below 1.

An Early Retirement Puzzle?
The fact that early retirement and unemployment schemes reduce the net impact on labor-force participation of any pension reform does not come as a surprise. However, the mere fact that a large minority of French workers have retired as soon as possible even with a very strong penalty (10 percent reduction of their benefit) is puzzling for an understanding of retirement behavior.

There are many possible explanations for the unpopularity of postponement. First, even if wage earners have no interest in retiring before they can obtain a full pension, they might have been forced to do so it by their employers. However, labor law provides substantial protection for workers who have not reached the full-rate pension age. Penalties for early layoffs in this case are very high. This explanation is thus unlikely.

A second class of possible explanations involves the supply side. Some workers may have strong preferences for leisure that lead them to retire as soon as possible. Others may lack information concerning pension formulas. As the computation of the pension is complex, it is possible that some people do not understand the importance of the penalty for early retirement and choose to follow a rule of thumb— for instance, either retiring as soon as possible or retiring with a full pension.

A third explanation may involve liquidity constraints for inactive people waiting for retirement. A recent study by statisticians of the social security administration (Briard, 2004) stresses liquidity constraints as the main reason people give to explain their decision to retire with a penalty. This is a reasonable explanation, as women are more likely to retire at age sixty with a penalty, and men more likely to go on working until they reach the full-rate pension age. Table 2.11 shows that this estimation strategy applied to the women subsample confirms this point. Women have effectively a lower general elasticity than men (0.51 versus 0.59 in the total sample), but their elasticity when they are

Table 2.11
The response of retirement age to the full-rate contribution length: Corrected estimates, women only.

	Coefficient (standard error)				
Variable	(1) 1934–1935	(2) 1935–1936	(3) 1936–1937	(4) All	(5) All
R linear					0.515*** (0.017)
R_1	0.704*** (0.009)	0.656*** (0.009)	0.727*** (0.009)	0.609*** (0.073)	
R_2				0.591*** (0.036)	
R_3				0.492*** (0.027)	
Quarters dummies	Yes	Yes	Yes	Yes	Yes
Cohort dummies	Yes	Yes	Yes	No	No
Sample	1934–1935 cohorts with 151 and 152 quarters at age 60	1935–1936 cohorts with 152 and 153 quarters at age 60	1936–1937 cohorts with 153 and 154 quarters at age 60	All cohorts with all quarters at age 60	All cohorts with all quarters at age 60
N	6,040	6,560	6,495	423,350	
R^2	0.67	0.62	0.69	0.41	
$F_{(3,N)}$	4,137.70	3,565.97	9,653.24	9,530.35	10,186.87

Source: Computations with administrative data from the CNAV.

Note: The first three columns are limited to the double-difference sample, where individuals who have retired more than one quarter after having the right to a full-rate pension are excluded.

The last two columns use all individuals with normal pensions born from 1934 to 1937. Excluded from the sample are observations where retirement age is above sixty-six and individuals are at the margin (individuals who have at age sixty between 151 and 153 quarters of contribution). RB_n variables are defined as previously. Included are dummy variables for each quarter of contribution at age sixty. Standard errors are reported in parentheses.

Significance levels: *10 percent. **5 percent. ***1 percent.

marginally affected is slightly higher than that of men (0.70 versus 0.65 on the total sample). This suggests than they are more likely to postpone retirement when they are employed but that, in general, they are more likely to have a low length of contribution and have to wait in inactivity before retiring.

This dataset, although rich, has not enough variables to allow us to discriminate between possible explanations. It may be, for instance, that heterogeneity among workers in terms of preferences might be much higher than is usually thought. Variances of the preference for leisure are low in most simulation models. This may explain why they tend to underpredict early retirement.

Another possible explanation for our unpopular postponement puzzle may involve heterogeneity of life expectancies. A penalty called *actuarially fair* is indeed computed using average life expectancy by cohort, whereas life expectancies vary considerably within each cohort. If some people know that their life expectancy is shorter than the average, they will retire as soon as possible even if the penalty is higher than actuarially fair.

Conclusion

This chapter offers the first ex-post evaluation of the incentive effects of the increase in required length of contribution that was one of the features of the 1993 French pension reform. This private-sector reform was meant both to reduce replacement rates and to increase retirement age. To induce later retirement, the government increased the number of quarters of contribution necessary to obtain a full-rate pension from 150 to 160 quarters. Both the Échantillon Interrégime des Retraités (EIR 2001) and comprehensive administrative data from the Caisse Nationale d'Assurance Vieillesse (CNAV) (1994 to 2003) are used to estimate the response of retirement age to the length of contribution necessary to obtain a full pension from the general retirement scheme (CNAV). The fact that different groups were affected differently by the reform (depending both on birth year and contribution length at age sixty) allows a precise identification of the behavioral impact of changed incentives, using a difference-in-difference approach. One additional quarter of necessary contribution is found to lead to an average increase of 1.5 months in retirement age, corresponding to an elasticity of 0.54. This fairly high response should be considered in the light of the high level of penalty associated with early retirement in the French pay-as-you-go scheme. In view of this high penalty, some authors have assumed that the response coefficient of retirement age should be equal to 1.

Possible explanations for this unpopular postponement puzzle could be the effect of the credit constraints on persons waiting for retirement or a greater heterogeneity in preferences for leisure than is generally assumed. Heterogeneity in life expectancy could also play a role if some individuals know that they are likely to die earlier than the cohort average.

In addition, when possible, workers used other possibilities to leave at age sixty, by either making efforts to produce evidence of longer carriers or asking more frequently for a disability pension. The 1993 reform has increased the probability of retiring with a disability pension by 2 to 4 percent, according to our estimates.

The fact that people in unemployment or early retirement schemes account for a large part of the would-be retirees (23 to 28 percent) suggests that the net response rate of those potentially affected could be as low as 0.4 for those marginally affected by the reform and 0.47 for those entirely affected. The noticeable gap between the true economic elasticity and the estimated net effect of the reform underlines the large escape route to retirement available in the French pension system. This escape route will undermine any attempt at increasing incentives for later retirement.

This study, which has been entirely positive, clearly calls for further research on the normative question of what the optimal required length of contribution should be in France and elsewhere.

Appendix 2A   The French Pension System before the 1993 Reform

The French pension system of the *régime général* dates back to 1945, but the rules to compute pensions were changed quite a number of times. The two main reforms of after the Second World War are the 1971 Boulin reform, which increased the replacement rate, and the 1983 reform, which reduced the retirement age from sixty-five to sixty. The basic formula to compute pensions in the *régime général* was nonetheless always based on three terms—τ the pension rate, PC the proportionality coefficient, and W_{ref} the reference wage. The level of the pension cannot fall below a floor MIN and is truncated by a ceiling MAX:

$$P = \tau * PC * W_{ref},$$ (2.11)

with $MIN \leq P \leq MAX$.

The following sections describe the terms of this formula.

The Pension Rate τ

The rule defining the pension rate τ became complex after the 1983 reform. Until 2003, the pension rate τ was 0 below age sixty (the minimum retirement age is sixty). This was changed by the 2003 reform, which allowed workers with very long careers to claim pensions at an early retirement age of fifty-six. Between 1946 and 1971, the pension rate was at 20 percent at age sixty and was increased by four percentage points for each year of contribution after sixty (without limit). Thus, at age sixty-five, τ was 40 percent, and at age seventy it was 60 percent. After 1971, the pension rate at age sixty was increased to twenty-five percentage points, and each year after sixty brought five percentage points to τ. Thus it was 50 percent at age sixty-five and 75 percent at age seventy. At that time, it was independent of the length of contribution and only age-related.

The 1983 reform entailed a change in the pension rate τ formula.[21] The reform increased the full pension rate at age sixty to fifty percentage points but introduced a required length of contribution to obtain it. It applied the same penalty for quarters missing from this required length of contribution and for quarters missing from age sixty-five. This penalty was 10 percent (or five percentage points) for each year of missing contribution or for each year before the individual reaches age sixty-five. The most advantageous solution for the pensioner is then chosen. The pension rate did not increase beyond the full rate of 50 percent, which all workers had the right to claim at age sixty-five. This rule can be summarized by the following formula:

$$\tau = 0.50 * \left[1 - \delta * \max\left\{ 0, \min\left[(65 - AGE), \frac{N_1 - D_1}{4} \right] \right\} \right],$$ (2.12)

with δ the penalty (fixed at 10 percent as of 1971), N_1 the necessary length of contribution in quarters in all schemes (150 quarters or 37.5 years), and D_1 the actual length of contribution in all schemes (called *length of career*). D_1 includes all the quarters worked in the *régime général* but also all quarters worked in other regimes, such as public sector, self-employed, or even periods of work outside France.

In practice, this rule of a penalty either relative to quarters of contribution or to age sixty-five offers a minimum rate τ at 60 of 25 percent, whatever the length of contribution. An example will help the reader figure out how the formula really works. A person age sixty-one with a career of 140 quarters (thirty-five years) needs ten additional quarters to reach N_1 (at 150) but needs sixteen quarters before turning sixty-five. If this person decides to retire at age sixty-one, she will compute her penalty by multiplying $\frac{10}{4}$ by five percentage points, so 12.5 percentage points. So she obtains a pension rate of 37.5 percent. If that same person worked one more year, she would get a pension rate of 42.5 percent.[22]

The Proportionality Coefficient *PC*

The proportionality coefficient *PC* depends on the length of contribution to the *régime général* D_2 and on the required contribution length in the *régime général* N_2:[23]

$$PC = \min\left\{1, \frac{\widetilde{D_2}}{N_2}\right\}. \tag{2.13}$$

Between 1983 and 1993, N_2 was equal to N_1. The 1983 reform introduced a change in the computation of D_2 after age sixty-five—the corrected contribution length $\widetilde{D_2}$. Between 1945 and 1982, $\widetilde{D_2} = D_2$. The change introduced in 1983 was designed to allow workers without the necessary quarters of contribution at age sixty-five to obtain more quickly a unitary proportionality coefficient. The idea was also to avoid having people working after age sixty-five. So for each year after age sixty-five, individuals would see their length of contribution increase by 10 percent until they reach the necessary 150 quarters. This can be sum up by the following formula:

$$\widetilde{D_2} = \min\left[N_2, D_2 * \left\{\max(AGE - 65, 0) * \frac{10}{100}\right\} + D_2\right]. \tag{2.14}$$

To give an example, a person age sixty-six and three months with thirty-four years of career (136 quarters) would have needed an extra 3.5 years of work to obtain an unitary proportionality coefficient *PC*. With the correction introduced, five quarters after age sixty-five increase her contribution length by 12.5 percent, which gives 153 quarters. That person can thus retire without more delay with a full pension.

The Reference Wage W_{ref}

The reference wage was defined between 1946 and 1971 as the average wage of the last ten years truncated at the ceiling and weighted to reevaluate past nominal wage. The 1971 Boulin reform changed the formula to cover the ten best years.

The weights to compensate for monetary depreciation are published by the government. During the 1970s, they were higher than actual monetary depreciation and were a way of increasing the generosity of the system. Since 1987, the coefficients used have simply offset inflation. The ceiling is the wage beyond which contributions to the basic social security system increase no further. Above it, additional contributions are paid to the mandatory complementary schemes.

Floor and Ceiling, *MIN* and *MAX*

Although France has had an old-age benefit scheme since 1956, a floor was introduced in the contributive *régime général* scheme in 1983. Since then, a minimum pension is available for workers who fall below this floor and succeed in reaching the full rate. This minimum (€542 monthly from January 1, 2004) is therefore available, provided one has contributed N_1 quarters.

The pension ceiling is defined as 50 percent of the social security ceiling,[24] except for complementary provisions (increases for children or spouses).

Complementary Schemes

As the pensions from the CNAV could not be higher than 50 percent of the social security ceiling, mandatory complementary schemes were introduced. Initially, they were intended for executives and were distributed by a scheme called Association Générale des Institutions de Retraite des Cadres (AGIRC), created in 1947. Subsequently, the concept was extended to all workers through the Association pour le Régime de Retraite Complémentaire (ARRCO), created in 1962. Contributions to ARRCO became mandatory in 1972 and to AGIRC in 1974.

The complementary schemes are unfunded defined-contribution pension plans. Workers accumulate points in an account that entitles them to a pension at retirement age. The pension R is equal to the number of points NP multiplied by the value of the point V. The number of points corresponds to the product of the wage W by the contribution rate CR and divided by the reference wage fixed by the scheme P, which is a sort of price of the point. It is possible to receive a full pension at age sixty-five and a lower one at age fifty-five with a quasi-actuarial penalty $C(age, quarters)$. We can summarize this rule with the following formulas:

$$R = NP * V * C(age, quarters),\tag{2.15}$$

$$NP = \frac{(W * CR)}{P}.\tag{2.16}$$

The history of the parameters can be found in Bozio (2006). Here it is sufficient to note that the penalty is lower than in the basic pension of the CNAV, being closer to actuarial fairness. One important rule is that no penalty is applied if the applicant has reached the full rate in the *régime général*—that is, has N_1 quarters of contribution when retiring.

Appendix 2B   The Disclosure Bias and How to Correct It

Table 2.12 presents the theoretical difference in difference estimation of the disclosure effect to model two elements—the impact of the reform on disability pensions and the length of contribution disclosure effect. We distinguish cohorts, length of contribution at age sixty, and three types of individuals. The first type is a "normal" group of individuals who retire with a normal pension and who should be ideally our sample. Within the people retiring with a normal pension, however, there are "potentially disabled" individuals who could be granted a disability pension or a pension for unfitness for work if they have an incentive to claim such a pension. Finally, a group of normal would-be pensioners have 152 quarters of contribution effectively but declare only the number required to get the full rate (N_1), as effort is necessary to prove the last quarter of contribution. This group is named "uncertain length of contribution" as it is subject to a disclosure effect. The size of each group is respectively N_{34}, D_{34}, and K_{34} for the 1934 cohort and N_{35}, D_{35}, and K_{35} for the 1935 cohort. We note α a constant effect; β is a cohort effect (1935 cohort); γ is the length of contribution effect (151 quarters); v_i is an preference effect; and η is the true reform effect. All these parameters are expressed in quarters. The preference parameter v_i is different for every individual. For potentially disabled individuals and for the group with "uncertain length of contribution," v_i is close to 0. For normal people, v_i is on average positive, but its distribution is

Table 2.12
Theoretical bias on the retirement-age estimation following the disclosure effect.

	Length of Contribution at Age 60 in Quarters				
	151 Quarters		152 or 151 Quarters	152 Quarters	
Type	Potentially disable	Normal	Uncertain length of contribution	Normal	Potentially disable
Size	D_{cohort}	N_{cohort}	K_{cohort}	N_{cohort}	D_{cohort}
Cohort 1935	$\alpha + \beta + \gamma - d$	$\alpha + \beta + \gamma$ $+ v_i + \eta$	152 quarters $\alpha + \beta$	$\alpha + \beta + v_i$	$\alpha + \beta$
Cohort 1934	$\alpha + \gamma$	$\alpha + \gamma + v_i$	151 quarters α	$\alpha + v_i$	α

Note: This table reads as follows. It is similar to a classic 2×2 table representing a difference-in-difference estimation. However, here treated and control groups are divided in two subgroups—the normal group and those potentially disabled who could claim a disability pension if they had sufficient incentive to do so. Moreover, the "uncertain length of contribution" group has 152 quarters effectively but reveals before the reform only 151 quarters.

α is a constant effect, β is a cohort effect (1935 cohort), γ is the length of contribution effect (151 quarters), and v_i is an preference effect. Finally, η is the true reform effect. All parameters are in quarters. N_1 takes the value 151 for the 1934 cohort and 152 for the 1935 cohort. d is the disability pension effect.

The preference parameter v_i is different for every individual. For potentially disabled individuals and for the group with "uncertain length of contribution," v_i is close to 0. For normal people, v_i is on average positive, but its distribution is heterogeneous, with a minority of people with a large positive v_i.

heterogeneous with a minority of people with a large positive v_i (the individuals who have a low leisure preference and who will retire much after gaining access to a full pension).

Ideally, I would have liked to estimate double differences only on the sample of normal pensioners. If equation (2.4) is applied to the model to compute the difference-in-difference-estimate on the normal groups, we find the following:

$$DD = [(\alpha + \beta + \gamma + v_i + \eta) - (\alpha + \beta + v_i)]$$
$$- [(\alpha + \gamma + v_i) - (\alpha + v_i)] = \eta. \tag{2.17}$$

Unfortunately, normal individuals cannot be distinguished from the potentially disabled or the uncertain-length-of-contribution individuals when they are not affected by the reform. Hence, in practice, we compute the following double-difference estimate:

$$DD = \left[(\alpha + \beta + \gamma + v_i + \eta) - \left(\alpha + \beta + \frac{N_{35}}{K_{35} + N_{35} + D_{35}} v_i \right) \right]$$

$$- \left[\left(\alpha + \frac{N_{34} + D_{34}}{D_{34} + N_{34} + K_{34}} \gamma + \frac{N_{34}}{K_{34} + N_{34} + D_{34}} v_i \right) \right.$$

$$\left. - \left(\alpha + \frac{N_{34}}{N_{34} + D_{34}} v_i \right) \right],$$ (2.18)

which can be easily rewritten in the following way:

$$DD = \eta + \frac{K_{34}}{D_{34} + N_{34} + K_{34}} \gamma$$

$$+ \underbrace{\left[\frac{K_{35} + D_{35}}{K_{35} + N_{35} + D_{35}} + \left(\frac{N_{34}}{N_{34} + D_{34}} - \frac{N_{34}}{K_{34} + N_{34} + D_{34}} \right) \right]}_{>0} v_i. \quad (2.19)$$

Therefore, the double-difference estimates are different from the true reform effect η for two main reasons. First, the fact that the reform leads the uncertain-length-of-contribution group to reveal its true contribution length biases the double-difference estimate by the amount of the quarter effect γ times the share of individuals who have potentially the required length of contribution in the control group. We can estimate the coefficient γ. In the three regressions, it varies between -0.07 to 0.06, significant at the 10 percent level. The upper bound of the share of individuals affected by the disclosure effect is 20 percent, so this bias should be at most an underestimation or overestimation of the true η coefficient of 0.015. The second part of the bias is definitely positive and comes from an overweighting of normal individuals with a positive v_i in the treated group (or an underweighting in the control group) as a result of the disclosure effect.

To correct this bias, we estimate our difference in difference excluding from the sample the individuals who have retired at least a quarter after gaining access to a full-rate pension. These individuals have clearly a positive v_i. Then the DD estimates are as follows:

$$DD = \eta + \frac{K_{34}}{D_{34} + N_{34} + K_{34}} \gamma. \tag{2.20}$$

The results can be found in the first three columns of table 2.7. The bias corresponding to $(K_{34}/(D_{34} + N_{34} + K_{34}))\gamma$ is within the margin of error of the regression.

Notes

I was a PhD student at Paris School of Economics (PSE) when I wrote this chapter, and I am currently Research Economist at the Institute for Fiscal Studies (IFS) in London. I thank the Statistical Office of the Caisse Nationale d'Assurance Vieillesse (CNAV) for access to the database ACTIV5 and also thank the Direction de la Recherche, des Études, de l'Évaluation, et des Statistiques (DREES) for access to data from the Échantillon Interrégime de Retraité (EIR). I also gratefully acknowledge the helpful suggestions of Thomas Piketty, Didier Blanchet, Georges de Ménil, Jean-Olivier Hairault, Muriel Roger, Nicole Roth, and two anonymous referees. Special thanks also go to Benoit Rapoport, Gabrielle Fack, and Julien Grenet. All opinions expressed herein are those of the author and do not necessarily represent those of the CNAV or the DREES. None but the author bears any responsibility for the errors remaining in the chapter.

1. The 2003 reform still leaves two-thirds of the estimated future financial gap unfilled (Conseil d'Orientation des Retraites 2004).

2. For extensive surveys of the literature in this area, see Lumsdaine and Mitchell (1999), Bommier, Magnac, and Roger (2001), and Krueger and Meyer (2002).

3. The 1977 amendments to the Social Security Act in the United States created a substantial reduction (10 percent) in social security wealth for individuals born after 1916.

4. See Blanchet and Pelé (1999) and Bozio (2006) for an history of the legal changes of French social security, unemployment programs for older workers, and early retirement programs.

5. Besides the *régime général* of the CNAV, wage earners in the agricultural sector (Mutualité Sociale Agricole, or MSA), self-employed workers in industry and trade (ORGAnisation Nationale de l'Industrie et du Commerce, or ORGANIC), and craftsmen (CANCAVA) were also affected by the 1993 reform. These specific schemes joined the *régime général* in 1973 and 1974 and follow the same rules for the contributions paid after 1973.

6. The replacement rate is $\tau \times PC$. In the data sample, I do not be consider pensions at either the minimum threshold (MIN) or the maximum ceiling (MAX).

7. Except for the few persons who have fewer than ten years of contribution.

8. For both groups, before and after the reform, any pension penalty is affected only by age at retirement. For both categories, all possible "contribution" penalties are greater than age penalties, before and after the reform, and the reform did not change the age penalty.

9. The panel has been developed by the Direction de la Recherche, des Études, de l'Évaluation, et des Statistiques (DREES), a statistical and research unit under the supervision of both the Ministry for Social Affairs and the Ministry of Health. In its simpler version, it is based on information provided by all the French pension schemes; a matching is also possible with annual wage returns filed by firms (Déclarations Annuelles de Données Sociales, DADS) and the unemployment files of Union Nationale Interprofessionelle pour l'Emplois dans l'Industrie et le Commerce (UNEDIC). There exists an EIR for the years 1988, 1993, 1997, and 2001. The selection principle is that the panel consists of all

retirees born during the first six days of October of every other year. Thus, the 2001 panel contained retirees born every other year from 1906 to 1944.

10. The data used here come from the ACTIV5 files that are available on request at the Actuariat Statistique of the CNAV. They are published officially in a less detailed manner in CNAV circular letters, and some of their statistics are published under the yearly CNAV statistical book, the *Recueil Statistique*.

11. For example, there is a cell for a female who retired in 1995 at age 60.25 with 149 quarters of contribution on a disability pension and who was born in 1934.

12. In this dataset are all the French private-sector wage earners who retired between 1994 and 2003—1,241,400 different observations that correspond to information on exactly 5,273,827 retirees.

13. This explains why the average retirement age increases in 1975 and then decreases. The age group that was depleted by low birth rate during World War I (those born in 1915 to 1918) started to retire in 1975 at age sixty (Givord, 2002).

14. We exclude persons who have retired after age sixty-six to make the different data-sets comparable. The CNAV data for the generations 1935 to 1937 give information on all the persons who have retired and not (as in EIR 2001) on those who are alive in 2001. Differential mortality could distort the average age of an older generation.

15. The business cycle could possibly also have caused a temporary increase in retire-ment age.

16. Ideally, I would have liked to have the variable QUA_k measure the number of quar-ters of contribution at the date of the reform. As such a variable is not available, I use as proxy the number of quarters of contribution at age sixty computed supposing that all the quarters between age sixty and the retirement age have led to quarters of contribu-tion. Time spent in unemployment and early retirement schemes did generate quarters of contribution, but straight inactivity did not. Therefore, I underestimate the true length of contribution of persons who are inactive between age sixty and their effective retire-ment. Most persons in this condition are women, and they are very likely to retire at age sixty-five. Thus, I underestimate length of contribution in the lower range (less than 131 quarters at age sixty). This will not change my estimation as these people are not affected by the reform.

17. Columns 1, 2, and 3 of table 2.4 simply reproduce the results of table 2.3 for ease of comparison.

18. The reality is more complex, with benefits in some early retirement schemes being lower than the pension expected or higher for others.

19. Déclarations Annuelles de Données Sociales (DADS) is annual declaration of social data made each year by firms that provide information on the status of workers before they retire if the individuals were wage earners in the private sector.

20. The computation is straightforward. Subtract the share of early retirees and unem-ployed individuals from the response coefficient, and divide by the share of the pop-ulation that is truly affected by the reform. Respectively, $(0.6 - 0.13)/0.87 = 0.54$ and $(0.65 - 0.25)/0.75 = 0.53$.

21. The 1983 reform was perceived popularly, and mistakenly, to have lowered the retirement age to sixty. As the text explains, the reality was more complicated.

22. This 10 percent penalty is also designated in the literature as a five-percentage-point penalty. One can simply write the formula (2.12) in the following way: $\tau = 0.50 - \delta_2 * \max\{0, \min[(65 - AGE), (N - D_1)/4]\}$ with $\delta_2 = 0.5 * \delta = 5$ percentage points.

23. For example, a person who has worked four years for the public sector and thirty-five years in the private sector has a contribution length D_1 equal to thirty-nine years but has a contribution length to the *régime général* D_2 equal to thirty-five years. The distinction between N_1 and N_2 was introduced by the 1993 reform.

24. From January 1, 2005, onward, the social security ceiling is €30,192—which represents twice the full-time minimum wage—and the maximum pension in the basic scheme of the *régime général* is therefore €15,096 (so €1,258 monthly payment).

References

Baker, M., and Benjamin, D. (1999). "Early Retirement Provisions and the Labor Force Behavior of Older Men: Evidence from Canada." *Journal of Labor Economics*, 17(4), 724–756.

Bardaji, J., B. Sedillot, and E. Walraet. (2002). "Evaluation de trois réformes du Régime Général d'assurance vieillesse à l'aide du modèle de microsimulation Destinie." Working Paper (Document de travail), Institut National de la Statistique et des Études Économiques, Paris.

Bardaji, J., B. Sedillot, and E. Walraet. (2003). "Un outil de prospective des retraites: le modèle de microsimulation Destinie." *Economie et Prévision*, 160–161, 167–192.

Blanchet, D., and L.-P. Pelé. (1999). "Social Security and Retirement in France." In J. Gruber and D. Wise, eds., *Social Security and Retirement around the World*. Chicago: NBER/University of Chicago Press.

Bommier, A., T. Magnac, B. Rapoport, and M. Roger. (2006). "Etude de l'impact des politiques publiques sur l'offre de travail des travailleurs âgés." *Rapport à la DREES* (Direction de la Recherche des Etudes de l'Evaluation et des Statistiques).

Bommier, A., T. Magnac, and M. Roger. (2001). "Départs en retraite: évolutions récentes et modèles économiques." *Revue française d'économie*, 16(1), 79–124.

Bozio, A. (2006). "Réformes des retraites: estimations sur données françaises." PhD thesis, École des Hautes Études en Sciences Sociales, Paris.

Briard, K. (2004). "Carrières incomplètes et départ en retraite." *Les lundis de l'INED*.

Caisse Nationale d'Assurance Vieillesse (CNAV). (2002). *Réforme de l'assurance vieillesse: suivi du niveau des pensions*. Paris: Direction de l'Actuariat Statistique.

Coeffic, N. (2003). "l'âge de la liquidation des droits à la retraite de la génération 1934. *Etudes et Resultats*, DREES (Direction de la Recherche des Etudes de l'Evaluation et des Statistiques).

Colin, C., V. Iéhlé, and R. Mahieu. (2000). "Les trajectoires de fin de carrière des salariés du secteur privé." *Solidarité et Santé*, 3, 9–27.

Conseil d'Orientation des Retraites. (2004). *Retraites: les réformes en France et à l'étranger, le droit à l'information. Deuxième rapport*. Paris: La documentation française.

Costa, D. (1998). *The Evolution of Retirement*. Chicago: NBER/University of Chicago Press.

Cremer, H., J.-M. Loazchmeur, and P. Pestieau. (2004). "Social Security, Retirement Age and optimal income taxation." *Journal of Public Economics*, 88, 2259–2281.

Diamond, P. (2003). *Taxation, Incomplete Markets, and Social Security*. Cambridge, MA: MIT Press.

Duval, R. (2003). "The Retirement Effects of Old-Age Pension and Early Retirement Schemes in OECD Countries." Working Paper, Economics Department, Organization for Economic Cooperation and Development, Paris.

Givord, P. (2002). "Prévoir l'évolution des taux d'activité aux âges élevés: un exercice difficile." *Economie et Statistique*, 355–356, 105–121.

Gruber, J., and D. Wise. (2004). *Social Security Programs and Retirement around the World: Micro-simulation*. Chicago: NBER/University of Chicago Press.

Institut National de la Statistique et des Études Économiques (INSEE). (1999). "Le modèle de microsimulation dynamique Destinie." Working Paper (Document de travail), Institut National de la Statistique et des Études Économiques, Paris.

Johnson, R. (2000). "The Effect of Old-Age Insurance on Male Retirement: Evidence from Historical Cross-Country Data." Working Paper, Federal Reserve Bank, Kansas City.

Krueger, A., and B. Meyer. (2002). "Labor Supply Effect of Social Insurance." Working Paper, National Bureau for Economic Research, Cambridge, MA.

Krueger, A., and J.-S. Pischke. (1992). "The Effect of Social Security on Labor Supply: A Cohort Analysis of the Notch Generation." *Journal of Labor Economics*, 10(4), 412–437.

Lumsdaine, R., and O. Mitchell. (1999). "New Developments in the Economic Analysis of Retirement." In O. Ashenfelter and D. Card, eds., *Handbook of Labor Economics* (vol. 3C, pp. 3261–3307) (Amsterdam: Elsevier).

Mahieu, R., and D. Blanchet. (2001). "Une analyse microéconométrique des comportements de retrait d'activité." In Dalloz, ed., *Epargne et Retraite* (pp. 9–31). Paris: Revue d'Economie Politique.

Mahieu, R., and D. Blanchet. (2004). "Estimating Models of Retirement Behavior on French Data." In J. Gruber and D. Wise, eds., *Social Security Programs and Retirement around the World: Micro-simulation* (pp. 235–284). Chicago: NBER/University of Chicago Press.

Mahieu, R., and B. Sédillot. (2000). "Microsimulation of the Retirement Decision: A Supply-Side Approach." Working Paper, Institut National de la Statistique et des Études Économiques, Paris.

Pelé, L.-P., and P. Ralle. (1997). "Âge de la retraite: les aspects incitatifs du régime général." Working Paper, Institut National de la Statistique et des Études Économiques, Paris.

Pelé, L.-P., and P. Ralle. (1999). "Les choix de l'âge de la retraite: Aspects incitatifs des règles du régime général et effets de la réforme de 1993." *Economie et Prévision*, 138–139, 163–177.

Sheshinski, E. (1978). "A Model of Social Security and Retirement Decisions." *Journal of Public Economics*, 10, 337–360.

Snyder, S., and W. Evans. (2002). "The Impact of Income on Mortality: Evidence from the Social Security Notch." Working Paper, National Bureau for Economic Research, Cambridge, MA.

Stock, J., and D. Wise. (1990). "Pensions, the Option Value of Work, and Retirement." *Econometrica*, 58(5), 1151–1180.

3 Optimal Response to a Transitory Demographic Shock

Juan C. Conesa and Carlos Garriga

The financial sustainability of the social security system is an important policy concern due to the aging of the U.S. population and in particular of the baby-boom generation. According to estimates of the Social Security Administration, the dependency ratio (measured as population age sixty-five or older over population between ages twenty and sixty-four) will increase from its present 21 percent to 27 percent in the year 2020, 37 percent in 2050, and 42 percent in 2080 under the scenario they call medium population growth (figure 3.1).

Under this demographic scenario, the social security system, which is a pay-as-you-go (PAYG) program, will face clear financial imbalances unless some reforms are introduced. In this chapter, we explore the optimal response to a transitory demographic shock that affects negatively the financing of retirement pensions.[1] In contrast to existing literature, we follow an approach that is similar to that used in Conesa and Garriga (forthcoming) and endogenously determine optimal policies rather than exploring implications of exogenous parametric policies. Our approach determines the optimal strategy of the Social Security Administration to guarantee the financial sustainability of current retirement pensions in the least distortionary way. Moreover, no cohort will have to pay the welfare cost of the demographic shock.

Notice that we are concerned only about efficiency considerations in the financing of retirement pensions rather than about the efficiency of their existence in the first place. Their existence might be justified on different grounds.[2] We do not model why social security was implemented in the first place or why social security benefits are provided through a potentially inefficient tax system.

We consider for our experiments an unexpected transitory demographic shock, even though these shocks are certainly predictable by

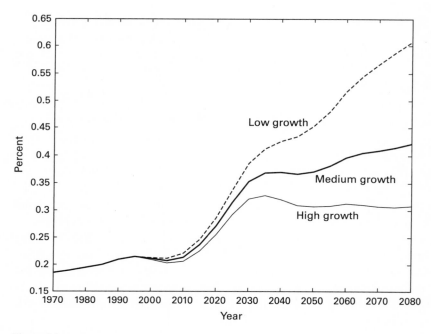

Figure 3.1
Population age 65 and older over population ages 20 to 64 (from SSA).

looking at figure 3.1. If the demographic shock is predictable, the fiscal authority should have reacted to it in advance. However, we believe it is more interesting to focus on what should be done from now on rather than on what should have been done. In this sense, prediction of a demographic shock without action is equivalent to the shock being unexpected. However, the transitory nature of the shock considered is a limitation of the analysis driven by computational tractability.

The quantitative evaluation of social security reforms has been widely analyzed in the literature.[3] Demographic considerations play an important role in the social security debate, but there are few quantitative studies of policy responses to demographic shocks and none to our knowledge from an optimal fiscal policy perspective. In particular, De Nardi, Imrohoroglu, and Sargent (1999) consider the economic consequences of different alternative fiscal-adjustment packages to solve the future social security imbalances associated with the projected demographics in the United States. They find that all fiscal adjustments impose welfare losses on transitional generations. In particular, policies that partially reduce retirement benefits (by taxing benefits, post-poning retirement, or taxing consumption) or that gradually phase out benefits without compensation yield welfare gains for future generations but make most of the current generations worse off. They conclude that a sustainable social security reform requires reducing distortions in labor supply or in consumption and saving choices and some transition policies to compensate current generations (issuing government debt). Our approach allows for the endogenous determi-nation of such policies in a way that nobody faces welfare losses. In other words, everybody will be guaranteed the same level of welfare as in the benchmark economy without a demographic shock. How-ever, for computational tractability we will substantially simplify the nature of the demographic shocks relative to De Nardi et al. (1999).

Jeske (2003) also analyzes payroll adjustments to demographic shocks in an economy similar to ours. He finds that in contrast with the benchmark economy not all cohorts are worse off due to the arrival of the baby boomers. The parents of baby boomers gain about 0.5 per-cent of average lifetime consumption, baby boomers lose 1 percent, the children of boomers gain 2 percent, and the grandchildren lose more than 2 percent. The intuition for this result comes from movements in factor prices implied by the demographic shock and the implied pay-roll taxes adjustment to balance the per-period government budget constraint.

In contrast to both of them, we do not analyze the different implica-tions of exogenously specified strategies to guarantee sustainability but instead optimize over this policy response to demographic shocks following the Ramsey approach. The quantitative analysis of optimal fiscal policy in overlapping generations economies was pioneered by Escolano (1992) and has been recently considered by Erosa and Ger-vais (2002) and Garriga (1999). Conesa and Garriga (forthcoming) used a similar framework to analyze the design of social security reforms, and therefore the focus was on efficiency considerations, abstracting from sustainability issues.

Our main conclusions indicate that the optimal strategy in absorbing a negative demographic shock consists of the following:

• Changing the age structure of labor-income taxation. In particular, labor-income taxes of the young should be substantially decreased.

• Eliminating compulsory retirement and allowing cohorts older than age sixty-five to supply labor in the market.

• Increasing the level of government debt during the duration of the demographic shock and then repaying it slowly.

We find that the welfare gains will be concentrated for generations born in the distant future after the demographic shock is over, while it does maintain the benchmark welfare level for existing cohorts and current newborns during the shock. Therefore, no generation is worse off along the fiscal-adjustment process implied by the demographic shock. This result contrasts with the findings of De Nardi et al. (1999) and Jeske (2003), where either current or future generations suffer important welfare losses. More important, we find that a sustainable social security reform does not necessarily require reducing distortions in consumption and saving choices. A reduction in labor supply distortions and the issuing of government debt are sufficient to compensate current generations.

In addition, we show that the welfare costs of distortionary taxation are quantitatively important right after the demographic shock but are relatively less important in the long run.

The distortionary impact of the financing of pensions in our artificial economy is assumed rather than endogenously determined. In our benchmark economy, pensions are financed through linear age-independent payroll taxes, and individuals do not establish a link between their individual contributions to the system and their future pensions. Hence, all the welfare gains obtained in our analysis are generated by the minimization of distortions and the redistribution of these additional resources. Indeed, it could not be otherwise since the possibility of Pareto improvements exists only because of the presence of distortions.

We also show that when the income from retirement pensions is not taxable, the government could use this fact to replicate lump-sum taxation and achieve first-best allocations. Yet since we want to focus on an environment where the government is restricted to distortionary taxation, we consider only an environment where the fiscal treatment of retirement pensions is constrained to be the same as that of regular labor income.

The rest of the chapter describes the benchmark theoretical framework used, our method of parameterizing our benchmark economy, the optimal fiscal policy problem using the primal approach, the experiment we perform, the demographic shock, and our analysis of the optimal response.

The Theoretical Environment in the Benchmark Economy

Households

The economy is populated by a constant measure of households who live for I periods. These households are forced to retire in period i_r. We denote by $\mu_{i,t}$ the measure of households of age i in period t. Preferences of a household born in period t depend on the stream of consumption and leisure this household will enjoy. Thus, the utility function is given by

$$U(c^t, l^t) = \sum_{i=1}^{I} \beta^{i-1} u(c_{i,t+i-1}, 1 - l_{i,t+i-1}). \tag{3.1}$$

Every period, each household owns one unit of time that they can allocate to work or leisure. One unit of time devoted to work by a household of age i translates into ε_i efficiency units of labor in the market, and these are constant over time.

Technology

The production possibility frontier is given by an aggregate production function $Y_t = F(K_t, L_t)$, where K_t denotes the capital stock at period t, and $L_t = \sum_{i=1}^{I} \mu_{i,t} \varepsilon_i l_{i,t}$ is the aggregate labor endowment measured in efficiency units. We assume the function F displays constant returns to scale, is monotonically increasing, is strictly concave, and satisfies the Inada conditions. The capital stock depreciates at a constant rate δ.

Government

The government influences this economy through the social security and the general budget. For simplicity, we assume that initially (before the demographic shock) these two programs operate with different budgets. Pensions (p_t) are financed through a payroll tax (τ_t^p), and the social security budget is balanced. On the other hand, the government collects consumption taxes (τ_t^c), labor-income taxes (τ_t^l), and capital-income taxes (τ_t^k) and issues public debt (b_t) to finance an exogenously given stream of government consumption (g_t).

Thus, the social security and government budget constraints are respectively given by

$$\tau_t^p w_t \sum_{i=1}^{i_r-1} \mu_i \varepsilon_i l_{i,t} = p_t \sum_{i=i_r}^{I} \mu_i, \quad \text{and} \tag{3.2}$$

$$\tau_t^c \sum_{i=1}^{I} \mu_i c_{i,t} + \tau_t^l (1 - \tau_t^p) w_t \sum_{i=1}^{i_r-1} \mu_i \varepsilon_i l_{i,t} + \tau_t^k r_t \sum_{i=1}^{I} \mu_i a_{i,t} + b_{t+1}$$

$$= g_t + (1 + r_t) b_t. \tag{3.3}$$

In response to the demographic shock, however, both budgets are integrated, and we allow the government to transfer resources across budgets to finance the retirement pensions.

Market Arrangements

We assume there is a single representative firm that operates the aggregate technology, taking factor prices as given. Households sell an endogenously chosen fraction of their time as labor ($l_{i,t}$) in exchange for a competitive wage of w_t per efficiency unit of labor. They rent their assets ($a_{i,t}$) to firms or the government in exchange for a competitive factor price (r_t) and decide how much to consume and save out of their disposable income. The sequential budget constraint for a working age household is given by

$$(1 + \tau_t^c) c_{i,t} + a_{i+1,t+1} = (1 - \tau_t^l)(1 - \tau_t^p) w_t \varepsilon_i l_{i,t} + (1 + (1 - \tau_t^k) r_t) a_{i,t},$$

$$i = 1, \ldots, i_r - 1. \tag{3.4}$$

On retirement, households do not work and receive a pension in a lump-sum fashion. Their budget constraint is

$$(1 + \tau_t^c) c_{i,t} + a_{i+1,t+1} = (1 - \tau_t^l) p_t + (1 + (1 - \tau_t^k) r_t) a_{i,t},$$

$$i = i_r, \ldots, I. \tag{3.5}$$

The alternative interpretation of a mandatory retirement rule is to consider different labor-income tax rates for individuals of ages above and below i_r. In particular, a confiscatory tax on labor income beyond age i_r is equivalent to compulsory retirement. Both formulations yield the same results. However, when we study the optimal policy, we prefer this alternative interpretation since it considers compulsory retirement as just one more distortionary tax that the fiscal authority can optimize over.

In the benchmark economy, a market equilibrium is a sequence of prices and allocations such that consumers maximize utility (3.1) subject to their corresponding budget constraints (3.4) and (3.5), given the equilibrium prices; firms maximize profits given prices; the government and the social security budgets are balanced, (3.2) and (3.3); and markets clear and feasibility.

Parameterization of the Benchmark Economy

Demographics
We choose one period in the model to be the equivalent of five years. Given our choice of period, we assume that households live for twelve periods, so that the economically active life of a household starts at age twenty, and we assume that households die with certainty at age eighty. In the benchmark economy, households retire in period 10 (equivalent to age sixty-five in years).

Finally, we assume that the mass of households in each period is the same. All these assumptions imply that in the initial steady state the dependency ratio is 0.33 rather than the 0.21 observed nowadays. The reason is that in our simple environment there is no lifetime uncertainty.

Endowments
The only endowment that households have is their efficiency units of labor at each period. These are taken from the Hansen's (1993) esti- mates, conveniently extrapolated to the entire lifetime of households (figure 3.2).[4]

Government
We assume that in the benchmark economy the government runs two completely independent budgets. One is a social security budget that operates on a balanced budget. The payroll tax is taken from the data and is equal to 10.5 percent, which is the Old-Age and Retirement In- surance (OASI). We exclude a fraction going to disability insurance; the OASDI is 12.4 percent. Our assumptions about the demographics together with the balanced budget condition directly determine the amount of the public retirement pension. It will be 31.5 percent of the average gross labor income.

The level of government consumption is exogenously given. It is financed through a consumption tax set equal to 5 percent, a marginal tax on capital income equal to 33 percent, and a marginal tax on labor income net of social security contributions equal to 16 percent. We have estimated these effective tax rates following Mendoza, Razin, and Tesar (1994). The effective distortion of the consumption-leisure

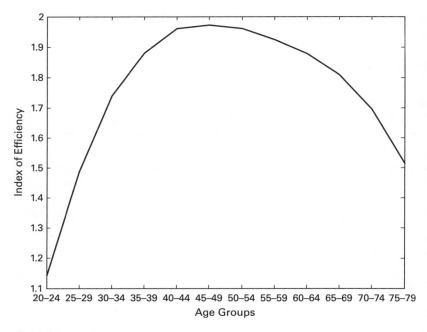

Figure 3.2
Age profile of efficiency units of labor (from Hansen, 1993).

margin is given by $(1 - \tau^1)(1 - \tau^P)/(1 + \tau^c) = 1 - 0.3$, yielding an effective tax of 30 percent.

The government issues public debt to satisfy its sequential budget constraint.

Calibration: Functional Forms
Households' preferences are assumed to take the form

$$\sum_{i=1}^{I} \beta^{i-1} \frac{(c_i^{\gamma}(1 - l_i)^{1-\gamma})^{1-\sigma}}{1 - \sigma}, \tag{3.6}$$

where $\beta > 0$ represents the discount rate, $\gamma \in (0, 1)$ denotes the share of consumption in the utility function, and $\sigma > 0$ governs the concavity of the utility function. The implied intertemporal elasticity of substitution of consumption is equal to $1/(1 - (1 - \sigma)\gamma)$.

Technology has constant returns to scale and takes the standard Cobb-Douglas form $Y_t = K_t^{\alpha} L_t^{1-\alpha}$, where α represents the capital-income share.

Table 3.1
Calibration targets and parameter values

Empirical targets	A/Y	IES	Average Hours	wN/Y	Dep./Y
Empirical values	3.5	0.5	1/3	0.7	0.12
Parameters	β	σ	γ	α	δ
Calibrated values	1.003	4	0.327	0.3	0.0437

Calibration: Empirical Targets

We define *aggregate capital* to be the level of fixed assets in the Bureau of Economic Analysis statistics. Therefore, our calibration target will be a ratio $K/Y = 3$ in yearly terms. Also, computing the ratio of outstanding (federal, state, and local) government debt to gross domestic product (GDP), we get the following ratio $B/Y = 0.5$ in yearly terms. Depreciation is also taken from the data, which as a fraction of GDP is 12 percent. Another calibration target is an average of one-third of the time of households allocated to market activities. We choose a curvature parameter in the utility function consistent with a coefficient of relative risk aversion in consumption of 2 (alternatively a consumption intertemporal elasticity of substitution of 0.5). Government consumption will be fixed at 18.6 percent of output as in the data. Finally, the capital-income share is taken to be equal to 0.3, as measured in Gollin (2002).

Calibration Results

To calibrate our economy, we proceed as follows. First, we fix the curvature parameter in the utility function to be $\sigma = 4$ and the capital share in the production function $\alpha = 0.3$. Then the discount factor $\beta = 1.003$ is chosen to match a wealth to output ratio of 3.5,[5] and the consumption share $\gamma = 0.327$ is chosen to match an average of one-third of the time devoted to working in the market economy. The depreciation rate is chosen so that in equilibrium depreciation is 12 percent of output. Notice that $\sigma = 4$ and $\gamma = 0.327$ together imply a consumption intertemporal elasticity of substitution of 0.5 (CRRA of 2). Table 3.1 summarizes the parameters chosen and the empirical targets that are more related to them.

Using the empirical tax rates and ratio of government consumption to gross domestic product, we derive from the government budget constraint an implied equilibrium government debt of 50 percent of output. This figure is consistent with the average figure in the data. Therefore, the capital-to-output ratio is 3 as desired.

Given this parameterization, social security annual payments in the benchmark economy amount to 7.35 percent of GDP, and the social security implicit debt is equal to 128 percent of annual GDP.

The Government Problem: The Primal Approach

We use the primal approach of optimal taxation as first proposed by Atkinson and Stiglitz (1980). This approach is based on characterizing the set of allocations that the government can implement with the given policy instruments available. A benevolent fiscal authority chooses the optimal tax burden, taking into account the decision rules of all individuals in the economy and the effect of their decisions on market prices.

Therefore, the government problem amounts to maximizing the social-welfare function over the set of implementable allocations together with the status quo constraints (that guarantee Pareto improvements).[6] From the optimal allocations, we can decentralize the economy, finding the prices and the tax policy associated with the optimal policy.

A key ingredient is the derivation of the set of implementable allocations. Effectively, it amounts to using the consumer's Euler condition and labor-supply condition to express equilibrium prices as functions of individual allocations and then substitute these prices in the consumer's intertemporal budget constraint. Any allocation satisfying the implementability condition by construction satisfies the household's first-order optimality conditions, with prices and policies appropriately defined from the allocation. See Chari and Kehoe (1999) for a description of this approach.

To illustrate this procedure, we derive the implementability constraint for a newborn individual. Notice that in our case the fiscal authority has to consider retirement pensions as given and that this is going to introduce a difference with Erosa and Gervais (2002), Garriga (1999), or Conesa and Garriga (forthcoming).

We distinguish two cases: first, retirement pensions are considered as regular labor income and are treated as such from a fiscal point of view; and second, retirement pensions are not subject to taxation. Both cases have different tax-policy implications.

Retirement Pensions as Taxable Labor Income

For clarity of exposition, we suppress the time subscripts. Consider the household maximization problem for a newborn individual facing equilibrium prices and individual specific tax rates on consumption, labor income, and capital income:

$$\max \sum_{i=1}^{I} \beta^{i-1} u(c_i, l_i)$$

$$\text{s.t. } (1 + \tau_i^c)c_i + a_{i+1} \le (1 - \tau_i^l)w\varepsilon_i l_i + (1 + (1 - \tau_i^k)r)a_i, \quad i = 1, \ldots, i_r - 1$$

$$(1 + \tau_i^c)c_i + a_{i+1} \le (1 - \tau_i^l)(w\varepsilon_i l_i + p) + (1 + (1 - \tau_i^k)r)a_i, \quad i = i_r, \ldots, I$$

$$a_1 = 0, \, a_{I+1} = 0, \, c_i \ge 0, \, l_i \in (0, 1).$$

Notice two important features of this formulation. The first one is that individuals of age i_r and older have a retirement pension denoted by p as part of their labor income (and it is taxed at the same rate as regular labor income). Second, on retirement individuals could still supply labor in the market.

Denoting by v_i the Lagrange multiplier of the corresponding budget constraint, the necessary and sufficient first-order conditions for an interior optimum are given by

$$[c_i] \quad \beta^{i-1} u_{c_i} = v_i(1 + \tau_i^c), \tag{3.7}$$

$$[l_i] \quad \beta^{i-1} u_{l_i} = -v_i(1 - \tau_i^l)w\varepsilon_i, \quad \text{and} \tag{3.8}$$

$$[a_{i+1}] \quad v_i = v_{i+1}[1 + (1 - \tau_i^k)r], \tag{3.9}$$

together with the intertemporal budget constraint.

Multiplying these conditions by the corresponding variable we get

$$\beta^{i-1} c_i u_{c_i} = v_i(1 + \tau_i^c)c_i, \tag{3.10}$$

$$\beta^{i-1} l_i u_{l_i} = -v_i(1 - \tau_i^l)w\varepsilon_i l_i, \quad \text{and} \tag{3.11}$$

$$v_i a_{i+1} = v_{i+1}[1 + (1 - \tau_i^k)r]a_{i+1}. \tag{3.12}$$

Let $p_i = p$ if $i = i_r, \ldots, I$, and zero otherwise. Adding up (3.10) and (3.11) over all i,

$$\sum_{i=1}^{I} \beta^{i-1}[c_i u_{c_i} + l_i u_{l_i}] = \sum_{i=1}^{I} \beta^{i-1} v_i[(1 + \tau_i^c)c_i - (1 - \tau_i^l)w\varepsilon_i l_i]$$

$$= \sum_{i=1}^{I} v_i(1 - \tau_i^l)p_i,$$

where the second equality comes from using (3.12) and the budget constraints. Finally, using (3.8) we get

$$\sum_{i=1}^{I} \beta^{i-1}[c_i u_{c_i} + l_i u_{l_i}] = -\sum_{i=1}^{I} \beta^{i-1} u_{l_i} \frac{p_i}{w\varepsilon_i}$$

or

$$\sum_{i=1}^{I} \beta^{i-1}\left[c_i u_{c_i} + u_{l_i}\left(l_i + \frac{p_i}{w\varepsilon_i}\right)\right] = 0, \tag{3.13}$$

where w denotes the marginal product of labor.

Any feasible allocation of consumption and leisure satisfying equation (3.13) can be decentralized as the optimal behavior of a consumer facing distortionary taxes. These distortionary taxes can be constructed by using the consumer's optimality conditions for the labor and leisure and for the consumption and savings margins. In particular, given an allocation and its corresponding prices, constructed from the marginal product of labor and capital, we can back out the optimal tax on capital and labor income by using the Euler and labor-supply conditions:

$$u_{c_i} = \frac{1 + \tau_i^c}{1 + \tau_{i+1}^c} \beta u_{c_{i+1}}[1 + (1 - \tau_i^k)r], \quad \text{and} \tag{3.14}$$

$$-\frac{u_{l_i}}{u_{c_i}} = \frac{1 - \tau_i^l}{1 + \tau_i^c} w\varepsilon_i. \tag{3.15}$$

Notice that in this case the optimal policy is not uniquely determined. Labor and consumption taxation are equivalent in the sense that they determine the same distortionary margin. Also, the taxation of capital income is equivalent to taxing consumption at different times at different rates. In practice, this implies that one of the instruments is redundant. For example, we could set consumption taxes to zero (or to any other constant) and decentralize the allocation using only labor- and capital-income taxes by solving a system of two equations (3.14) and (3.15) in two unknowns τ_i^k and τ_i^l.

Finally, directly using the consumer's budget constraints, we could construct the corresponding sequence of assets. That way we would have constructed an allocation that solves the consumer's maximization problem.

The primal approach of optimal taxation simply requires maximizing a social-welfare function over the set of implementable allocations— subject to the feasibility constraint, an implementability condition such as (3.13) for the newborn cohorts, and additional implementability constraints for each cohort alive at the beginning of the reform. We also impose that allocations must provide at least as much utility as in the initial steady state of our economy. The allocation implied by the optimal policy can be decentralized with distortionary taxes in the way we have just outlined.

Nontaxable Retirement Pensions

If pensions are not taxable, the maximization problem of the households is given by

$$\max \sum_{i=1}^{I} \beta^{i-1} u(c_i, l_i)$$

$$s.t. \quad (1 + \tau_i^c)c_i + a_{i+1} \le (1 - \tau_i^l)w\varepsilon_i l_i + (1 + (1 - \tau_i^k)r)a_i, \quad i = 1, \ldots, i_r - 1$$

$$(1 + \tau_i^c)c_i + a_{i+1} \le (1 - \tau_i^l)w\varepsilon_i l_i + p + (1 + (1 - \tau_i^k)r)a_i, \quad i = i_r, \ldots, I$$

$$a_1 = 0, \ a_{I+1} = 0, \ c_i \ge 0, \ l_i \in (0, 1).$$

Consequently, through the same procedure used as before we can obtain the expression

$$\sum_{i=1}^{I} \beta^{i-1} [c_i u_{c_i} + l_i u_{l_i}] = \sum_{i=1}^{I} \beta^{i-1} v_i [(1 + \tau_i^c)c_i - (1 - \tau_i^l)w\varepsilon_i l_i]$$

$$= \sum_{i=1}^{I} v_i p_i.$$

Substituting for the Lagrange multiplier, we get

$$\sum_{i=1}^{I} \beta^{i-1} \left[u_{c_i} \left(c_i - \frac{p_i}{1 + \tau_i^c} \right) + l_i u_{l_i} \right] = 0. \tag{3.16}$$

Notice that in this case the implementability constraint does include a tax term in it, τ_i^c. This did not happen before in expression (3.13). Hence, it is always possible to choose a particular taxation of consumption such that the implementability constraint is always satisfied. The reason is that now the fiscal authority could tax consumption at a high level but still compensate the consumer through other taxes. In the previous case, this strategy was not available since it was impossible to tax away the retirement pensions and compensate the consumers without introducing additional distortions in the system.

Another way to illustrate this simple intuition is by simply looking at the intertemporal budget constraint of the household:

$$\sum_{i=1}^{I} \frac{(1 + \tau_i^c) c_i}{R_i} = \sum_{i=1}^{I} \frac{(1 - \tau_i^l) w \varepsilon_i l_i}{R_i} + \sum_{i=1}^{I} \frac{p_i}{R_i}, \tag{3.17}$$

where $R_1 = 1$, $R_i = \prod_{s=2}^{i} [1 + (1 - \tau_s^k) r_s]$.

Let $\tau_i^c = \tau^c$. We impose the same taxation of consumption at each point in time of the lifetime of an individual. Then we could rewrite (3.17) as

$$\sum_{i=1}^{I} \frac{c_i}{R_i} = \sum_{i=1}^{I} \frac{1 - \tau_i^l}{1 + \tau^c} \frac{w \varepsilon_i l_i}{R_i} + \frac{1}{1 + \tau^c} \sum_{i=1}^{I} \frac{p_i}{R_i}.$$

Clearly, one could choose any desired level of taxation of τ^c and still introduce no distortion in the consumption-leisure margin by choosing $\tau_i^l = \tau^l = -\tau^c$. Effectively, τ^c would act as a lump-sum tax.

Therefore, under this new scenario the planner could decentralize a first-best allocation by strategically setting consumption taxes to replicate lump-sum taxation.

Notice that this strategy cannot be replicated for the case when retirement pensions are taxable as regular labor income, since the equivalent of (3.17) would be

$$\sum_{i=1}^{I} \frac{c_i}{R_i} = \sum_{i=1}^{I} \frac{1 - \tau_i^l}{1 + \tau^c} \frac{w \varepsilon_i l_i}{R_i} + \sum_{i=1}^{I} \frac{1 - \tau_i^l}{1 + \tau^c} \frac{p_i}{R_i}, \tag{3.18}$$

and hence the fiscal authority is forced to introduce a distortionary wedge in the consumption-leisure margin when trying to implement lump-sum taxation as before.

We are interested in distortionary tax responses to demographic shocks. Consequently, we focus on the scenario where the fiscal treatment of retirement pensions has to be the same as the one of regular labor income. However, we compare the outcomes, in terms of welfare, with the ones that could be obtained if the government could implement lump-sum taxation.

The Ramsey Problem
We assume that in period $t = 1$ the economy is in a steady state with a pay-as-you-go social security system and that no demographic shock or government intervention has been anticipated by any of the agents in the economy. The expected utility for each cohort remaining in the benchmark economy is given by

$$\bar{U}_j = \sum_{s=j}^{I} \beta^{s-j} u(\hat{c}_s, 1 - \hat{l}_s),$$

where $\hat{c}_s$, $\hat{l}_s$ are steady-state allocations of cohort s. At the beginning of period 2, the demographic shock is known, and then in response to it the optimal policy from then on is announced and implemented. We require that the fiscal authority guarantees to everybody at least the level of utility of the benchmark economy so that the resulting policy reform constitutes a Pareto improvement. This participation constraint will ensure that the optimal response to a demographic shock generates no welfare losses (neither for the initially alive or the unborn).

Notice that we are imposing a very strong participation constraint, since we require that nobody is worse off relative to a benchmark in which actual fiscal policies would have been sustainable forever (i.e., the initial steady state). Alternatively, we could have postulated different arbitrary policy responses to the demographic shock generating welfare losses for some generations and then improve on those. Clearly, our specification imposes stronger welfare requirements and is independent of any arbitrary nonoptimal policy we might have chosen instead. Besides, the main conclusion in the literature is that no matter what policy you choose, somebody will have to pay the cost of the demographic shock. We show this is not necessarily the case.

The government objective function is a utilitarian welfare function of all future newborn individuals, where the relative weight that the government places on present and future generations is captured by the geometric discount factor $\lambda \in (0,1)$, and $U(c^t, l^t)$ represents the lifetime utility of a generation born in period t.

Conditional on our choice of weights placed on different generations,[7] the Ramsey allocation is the one that solves the following maximization problem:

$$\max \sum_{t=2}^{\infty} \lambda^{t-2} U(c^t, l^t),$$

$$s.t. \quad \sum_{i=1}^{I} \mu_{i,t} c_{i,t} + K_{t+1} - (1-\delta) K_t + G_t \leq F\left(K_t, \sum_{i=1}^{I} \mu_{i,t} \varepsilon_i l_{i,t}\right) \qquad t \geq 2, \tag{3.19}$$

$$\sum_{i=1}^{I} \beta^{i-1} \left[c_{i,t+i-1} u_{c_{i,t+i-1}} + u_{l_{i,t+i-1}}\left(l_{i,t+i-1} + \frac{p_i}{F_{2,t+i-1}\varepsilon_i}\right)\right] = 0 \qquad t \geq 2, \tag{3.20}$$

$$\sum_{s=i}^{I} \beta^{s-i} \left[c_{s,s-i+2} u_{c_{s,s-i+2}} + u_{l_{s,s-i+2}}\left(l_{s,s-i+2} + \frac{p_i}{F_{2,s-i+2}\varepsilon_i}\right)\right]$$

$$= \frac{u_{c_{i,2}}}{1 + \tau_2^c} [(1 + (1 - \tau^k) r_2) \bar{a}_{i,2} + p_i], \quad i = 2, \ldots, I, \tag{3.21}$$

$$\sum_{s=i}^{I} \beta^{s-i} u(c_{s,s-i+2}, 1 - l_{s,s-i+2}) \geq \bar{U}_i, \quad i = 2, \ldots, I, \quad \text{and} \tag{3.22}$$

$$U(c^t, l^t) \geq \bar{U}_1, \quad t \geq 2. \tag{3.23}$$

Constraint (3.19) is the standard period resource constraint. Constraint (3.20) is the implementability constraint for each generation born after the reform is implemented and is exactly the one derived in (3.13). This equation reveals that the government faces a tradeoff when determining the optimal labor-income tax of the older generations. A higher labor-income tax is an effective lump-sum tax on social security transfers, but it also reduces the incentives of the older generations to supply labor in the market. The optimal policy will have to balance these opposite forces. Constraint (3.21) represents the implementability constraints for those generations alive at the beginning of the reform, where τ^k is the benchmark tax on capital income, which is taken as given, and $\bar{a}_{i,2}$ are the initial asset holdings of generation i. Notice that taking τ^k as given is not an innocuous assumption, since that way we avoid confiscatory taxation of the initial wealth. Finally, constraints (3.22) and (3.23) guarantee that the policy chosen makes everybody at least as well off as in the benchmark economy. In particular, given that the government objective function does not include the initial s generations equation (3.22) will be binding.

This formulation imposes some restrictions, since it rules out steady-state golden-rule equilibria. Also, the initial generations alive at the beginning of the reform are not part of the objective function and appear only as a policy constraint. An equivalent formulation would include the initial s generations in the objective function with a specific weight λ_s, where the weight is chosen to guarantee that the status quo conditions for each generation are satisfied.

The policy maker discounts the future at the exponential rate λ. The Pareto improving nature of the reform implies that the rate λ has to be big enough to satisfy the participation constraints of all future generations. In particular, if λ were too low, then the long-run capital stock would be too low, and future generations would be worse off than in the benchmark economy. That restricts the range of admissible values for λ.

Within a certain range, there is some discretion in the choice of this parameter, implying a different allocation of welfare gains across future generations. To impose some discipline, we choose λ so that the level of debt in the final steady state is equal to that of the benchmark economy and all debt issued along the transition is fully paid back before reaching the new steady state. Our choice of the planner's discount factor, the parameter $\lambda = 0.957$, implies the full repayment of the level of debt issued in response to the demographic shock. That does not mean that the ratio of debt to output will be the same in the final steady state, since output does change.

Further Constraints in the Set of Tax Instruments
We impose additional restrictions in the set of fiscal instruments available to the fiscal authority. This can be done by using the consumer's first-order conditions to rewrite fiscal instruments in terms of

allocations and then imposing additional constraints on the Ramsey allocations.

The regime we investigate is one in which capital-income taxes are left unchanged relative to the benchmark. Reformulating this constraint in terms of allocations, we need to impose

$$\frac{u_{c_{1,t}}}{u_{c_{2,t+1}}} = \frac{u_{c_{2,t}}}{u_{c_{3,t+1}}} = \cdots = \frac{u_{c_{I-1,t}}}{u_{c_{I,t+1}}} = \beta[1 + (1 - \tau^k)(f_{k,t+1} - \delta)], \quad t \geq 2. \quad (3.24)$$

We introduce this constraint since we want to analyze an environment in which the reforms involve only changing the nature of labor-income taxation so that welfare gains are accrued only because of the change in the nature of the financing of retirement pensions rather than a more comprehensive reform involving also changes in the nature of capital-income taxation. Moreover, as Conesa and Garriga (forthcoming) show, the additional welfare gain of reforming capital-income taxation is very small.

With such a constraint, the only instruments available to the fiscal authority will be the taxation of labor income and government debt.

A Transitory Demographic Shock
In our experiment, we introduce an unexpected transitory demographic shock, capturing the idea that an increase in the dependency ratio is going to break down the sustainability of the social security system we had in the initial steady state of our benchmark economy.

The reason that we want to model it as an unexpected shock is that we want to investigate the optimal response from now on, instead of focusing on what we should have done in advance to an expected shock.

Since introducing realistic demographic projections would imply having to change substantially the demographic structure of our framework, we choose a very simple strategy. We simply increase the measure of retiring individuals for three consecutive periods. Notice that the demographic shock is transitory, in the sense that for three periods (equivalent to fifteen years) we face raising dependency ratios, and then for another three periods the dependency ratio falls until reaching its original level and staying there forever. We chose this specification of the demographic shock for computational convenience, since otherwise the model would imply changes in the age structure over time. The alternative would have been an environment where at

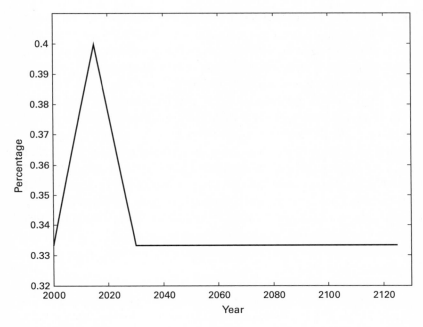

Figure 3.3
Evolution of the dependency ratio for simulated demographic shock.

some point the final age permanently increases reflecting an increase in life expectancy. This raises some computational problems, especially if individuals could forecast the demographic evolution and form expectations about future paths of government action. Hence, the benchmark economy would not be a steady state anymore, and the state of the economy at the benchmark date would be fully driven by arbitrarily chosen expectations. Figure 3.3 illustrates the evolution of the dependency ratio over time.

We have arbitrarily chosen to label the initial steady state in period 1 as the year 2000, and the demographic shock will be observed and fully predictable at the beginning of period 2 (the year 2005). Hence, the results that follow imply that the policy response from 2005 on is publicly announced and implemented at the beginning of 2005.

Notice that both individuals and the government are assumed to be surprised by the demographic shock. The government learns that given the demographic evolution the system is not sustainable and then implements a policy that rationalizes the financing of pensions.

Not only will the government optimally respond to the demographic shock guaranteeing the financial sustainability of pensions in a Pareto-improving way, but moreover the government will permanently change the financing scheme of pensions, hence generating long-run welfare gains relative to the benchmark economy. Our exercise is silent about the reasons why any collective decision process would have resulted in such a distortionary financing scheme in the first place. Indeed, the demographic shock in our exercise triggers the government response, but there is no clear reason why the government should not reform the system in the first place even in the absence of a demographic shock, purely for efficiency considerations. This is exactly what Conesa and Garriga (forthcoming) do in an environment where the government is not constrained to guarantee the pensions promised in the past.

Discussion of Results

The optimal reform is obtained by solving the maximization problem as stated in the previous section, with the only difference that we have introduced (3.24) as an additional constraint.

We find that the optimal financing scheme implies differential labor-income taxation across age. Why would the government choose to tax discriminate? The critical insight is that when individuals exhibit life-cycle behavior labor productivity changes with the household's age and the level of wealth also depends on age. As a result the response of consumption, labor and savings decisions to tax incentives varies with age as well. On the one hand, older cohorts are less likely to substitute consumption for savings as their remaining lifespan shortens. On the other hand, older households are more likely to respond negatively to an increasing labor-income tax than younger cohorts born with no assets, since the elasticity of labor supply is increasing in wealth. Therefore, the optimal fiscal policy implies that the government finds it optimal to target these differential behavioral elasticities through tax discrimination.

Figure 3.4 describes the evolution of the average optimal taxes along the reform. We decentralize the resulting allocation leaving consumption taxes unchanged, even though it is possible to decentralize the same allocation in alternative ways. In particular, we could set consumption taxes to zero and increase labor-income taxes so that they are consistent with the optimal wedge chosen by the government.

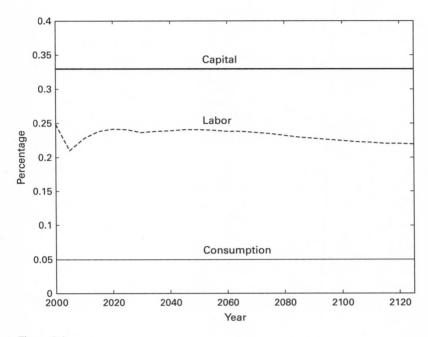

Figure 3.4
Evolution of average taxes.

In displaying the results, we arbitrarily label the year 2000 to be the steady state of the benchmark economy, and the reform is announced and implemented the following period (in 2005). Remember that a period in the model is five years.

Labor-income taxes are substantially lowered the first period following the reform (the combined impact of labor-income and payroll taxes was a 24.8 percent effective tax on labor in the benchmark), but then they are increased to repay the initial debt issued and reach a new long-run equilibrium around 22 percent on average.

Figure 3.5 displays its distribution across age at different points in time. The optimal labor-income tax rate varies substantially across cohorts. In the final steady state, the optimal labor-income tax schedule is concave and increasing as a function of age, up to the point at which individuals start receiving a pension. On retirement, the taxation of labor income (remember that retirement pensions are taxed at the same rate as regular labor income) is higher. This feature reflects the tension between the incentives for the fiscal authority to tax away the retirement pensions and the distortions that introduces on labor supply.

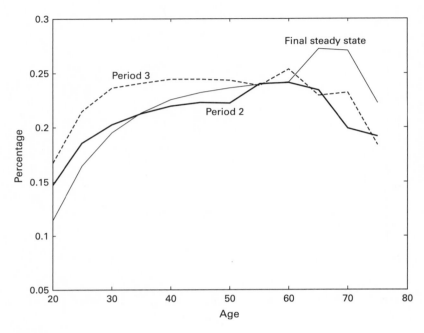

Figure 3.5
Labor income tax rates across different cohorts at different time.

Intuitively, the fiscal authority introduces such labor-income tax progressivity to undo the intergenerational redistribution in favor of the older cohorts that the social security system is generating.

As a result of this new structure of labor-income taxation, individuals will provide very little labor supply after age sixty-five and almost none in the last period, as shown in figure 3.6. Notice that the shape of labor supply is not dramatically changed with the reform, except for the fact that individuals would still provide some labor while receiving a retirement pension. However, the amount of labor supplied by the oldest cohorts is quite small.

The initial tax cuts, together with the increasing financial needs to finance the retirement pensions, necessarily imply that government debt has to increase in the initial periods following the reform.

Next, figure 3.7 displays the evolution of government debt over GDP associated with the optimal reform. To finance retirement pensions, government debt would increase up to 77 percent of annual GDP (relative to its initial 50 percent). Later on, this debt will be progressively repaid.

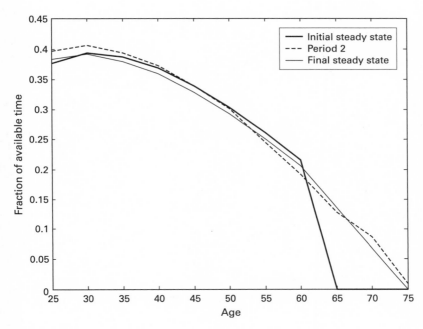

Figure 3.6
Labor supply across different cohorts at different time.

Overall, such a reform generates welfare gains only for those cohorts born once the demographic shock is over. However, the optimal response guarantees that the cohorts initially alive and those born during the shock enjoy the same level of utility as in the benchmark economy. Notice that by construction the initial old were not included in the objective function, and as a consequence the constraint to achieve at least the same utility level as in the benchmark economy has to be necessarily binding. This was not the case for new generations born during the demographic shock since they were included in the objective function of the fiscal authority. Yet the optimal policy response implies that the constraint will be binding, and only after the demographic shock is over will newborn cohorts start enjoying higher welfare. The welfare gains accruing to newborns are plotted in figure 3.8.

The optimal response associated with the sustainable policy contrasts with the findings where policies are exogenously specified as in De Nardi et al. (1999), where the initial cohorts are worse off, and Jeske (2003) where the baby boomers and the grandchildren of the baby boomers suffer welfare losses. In our economy, the cost of the shock is

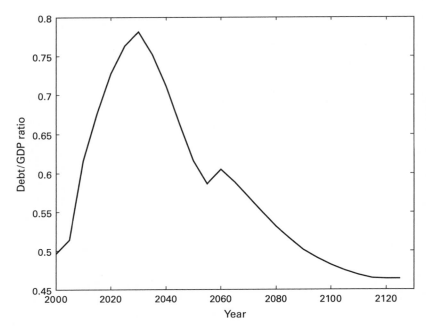

Figure 3.7
Evolution of debt to GDP ratio.

distributed over the cohorts initially alive and those generations born during the shock. Remember that the latter do enter the government's objective function, and hence the planner would be happy to allocate some welfare gains to these generations if it were possible.[8]

Notice that the welfare gains associated to the reform just discussed, labeled as "Ramsey" in figure 3.8, are much smaller than those associated to the first-best allocation, labeled as "Planner."

By construction, we have prevented the fiscal authority from lump-sum taxing the retirement pensions. If we were to allow the fiscal authority to tax differently retirement pensions from regular labor income, the fiscal authority would choose to do so imposing on pensions taxes higher than a 100 percent, effectively replicating a system with lump-sum taxes. Notice that the welfare gains from doing so (labeled as "Planner") would be much higher, especially for the initial generations. This comparison indicates that the welfare costs of having to use distortionary taxation are very high, especially at the initial periods of the reform.

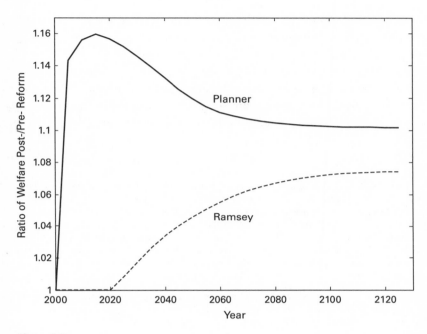

Figure 3.8
Welfare gains of newborn generations.

Conclusions

In this chapter, we have provided an answer to a very simple and policy relevant question: what should be the optimal response to an unanticipated transitory demographic shock in social security financing? To answer this question, we use optimal fiscal policy to determine the optimal way to finance some promised level of retirement pensions through distortionary taxation. In our experiment, the presence of a demographic shock renders the actual way of financing the social security system unsustainable, and our approach endogenously determines how to accommodate this shock, at the same time that the pension financing scheme is permanently changed to reduce distortions.

We find that the government can design a Pareto-improving reform that exhibits sizeable welfare gains in the distant future, after the demographic shock is over. This shows that the pressure induced by the demographic shock is substantial, since the reduction of the existing large distortions only prevents welfare losses but does not generate welfare gains until further away in the future. Our approach explicitly provides quantitative policy prescriptions toward the policy design of future and maybe unavoidable social security reforms.

The optimal response consists of the elimination of compulsory retirement, decreasing labor-income taxation of the young and a temporary increase of government debt to accommodate the higher financial needs generated by the increase in the dependency ratio.

Notes

We thank Mark Keightley, Georges de Ménil, Pierre Pestieau, and two anonymous referees for their very useful comments. Both authors acknowledge financial support from the Spanish Ministerio de Educación y Ciencia, SEJ2006-03879. Conesa also acknowledges support from the Barcelona Economics Program and Generalitat de Catalunya through 2005SGR00447. The authors can be reached via email at ⟨juancarlos.conesa@uab.es⟩ and ⟨Carlos.Garriga@stls.frb.org⟩. The views expressed are those of the individual authors and do not necessarily reflect official positions of the Federal Reserve Bank of St. Louis, the Federal Reserve System, or the Board of Governors.

1. In our artificial economy, we assume the transitory nature of the demographic shock for computational convenience, while figure 3.1 clearly shows the permanent nature of the future demographic shock faced by the U.S. population structure.

2. One basic reason could be dynamic inefficiencies (see Diamond, 1965, or Gale, 1973). Also, even in a dynamically efficient economy, social security might be sustained because of political economy considerations (see Grossman and Helpman, 1998; Cooley and Soares, 1999; or Boldrin and Rustichini, 2000). Also, social security might be part of some general social contract, as in Boldrin and Montes (2005).

3. Feldstein and Liebman (2002) summarize the discussion on transition to investment-based systems, analyzing the welfare effects and the risks associated with such systems.

4. To avoid sample selection biases, we assume that the rate of decrease of efficiency units of labor after age sixty-five is the same as in the previous period.

5. Notice that in a finite-life framework there is no problem with discount factors larger than 1, and in fact empirical estimates often take values as large.

6. Throughout the chapter, we assume that the government can commit to its policies. This is an important restriction that affects the results. The analysis of a time-consistent reform goes beyond the scope of this chapter.

7. We are identifying one Pareto improving reform, but it is not unique. Placing different weights on generations or the initial old would generate a different distribution of welfare gains across agents.

8. This result shows how large the pressure induced by the demographic shock is. This is specially important since our demographic shock is much less severe than expected even under the most optimistic scenario (compare figures 3.1 and 3.3) and the level of distortions present in our benchmark economy is very high. Hence, our exercise is biased toward generating large welfare gains.

References

Atkinson, A. B., and J. Stiglitz. (1980). *Lectures in Public Economics.* New York: McGraw-Hill.

Boldrin, M., and A. Montes. (2005). "The Intergenerational State: Education and Pensions." *Review of Economic Studies*, 72(3), 651–664.

Boldrin, M., and A. Rustichini. (2000). "Political Equilibria with Social Security." *Review of Economic Dynamics*, 3(1), 41–78.

Chari, V. V., and P. J. Kehoe. (1999). "Optimal Fiscal and Monetary Policy." In J. B. Taylor and M. Woodford, eds., *Handbook of Macroeconomics* (vol. 1C, pp. 1671–1745). Amsterdam: Elsevier.

Conesa, J. C., and C. Garriga. (forthcoming). "Optimal Fiscal Policy in the Design of Social Security Reforms." International Economic Review.

Cooley, T. F., and J. Soares. (1999). "A Positive Theory of Social Security Based on Reputation." *Journal of Political Economy*, 107(1), 135–160.

De Nardi, M., S. Imrohoroglu, and T. J. Sargent. (1999). "Projected U.S. Demographics and Social Security." *Review of Economic Dynamics*, 2(3), 576–615.

Diamond, P. (1965). "National Debt in a Neoclassical Growth Model." *American Economic Review*, 55(5), 1126–1150.

Erosa, A., and M. Gervais. (2002). "Optimal Taxation in Life-Cycle Economies." *Journal of Economic Theory*, 105(2), 338–369.

Escolano, J. (1992). "Optimal Taxation in Overlapping-Generations Models." Mimeo.

Feldstein, M., and J. B. Liebman. (2002). "Social Security." In A. J. Auerbach and M. Feldstein, eds., *Handbook of Public Economics* (vol. 4, pp. 2245–2324). Amsterdam: Elsevier.

Gale, D. (1973). "Pure Exchange Equilibrium of Dynamic Economic Models." *Journal of Economic Theory*, 6(1), 12–36.

Garriga, C. (1999). "Optimal Fiscal Policy in Overlapping Generations Models." Mimeo.

Gollin, D. (2002). "Getting Income Shares Right." *Journal of Political Economy*, 110(2), 458–474.

Grossman, Gene M., and E. Helpman. (1998). "Integenerational Redistribution with Short-Lived Governments." *Economic Journal*, 108(450), 1299–1329.

Hansen, G. D. (1993). "The Cyclical and Secular Behaviour of the Labour Input: Comparing Efficency Units and Hours Worked." *Journal of Applied Econometrics*, 8(1), 71–80.

Jeske, K. (2003). "Pension Systems and Aggregate Shocks." *Federal Reserve Bank of Atlanta Economic Review*, 88(1), 15–31.

Mendoza, E., A. Razin, and L. L. Tesar. (1994). "Effective Tax Rates in Macroeconomics: Cross-Country Estimates of Tax Rates on Factor Incomes and Consumption." *Journal of Monetary Economics*, 34(3), 297–323.

II   Democratic Sustainability

4

Demographics and the Political Sustainability of Pay-as-You-Go Social Security

Theodore C. Bergstrom and
John L. Hartman

The baby boom of the 1950s and the subsequent decline in the birth rate will produce a large increase in the proportion of retirees in the population over the next three decades. These demographic changes will greatly increase the tax burden imposed by the United States social security system. In 2001, there were about 5.3 people of working age for every one age sixty-six or higher. By 2020 this ratio will fall to 4.15, and by 2030 to about 3.2. Thus, over the next twenty-five years, the average cost per worker of maintaining social security benefits for the retired will increase by almost 70 percent.

Since 1986, social security tax revenue has significantly exceeded benefits paid out. The resulting surplus is used to purchase treasury bonds and is credited to a social security trust fund. Recent projections are that with no change in social security tax rates or in benefit schedules, benefits paid out will begin to exceed social security tax revenue in about 2018, and the trust fund will be depleted by about 2040.

Doubts have been raised about whether the social security trust fund provides a credible guarantee that current levels of social security benefits will be maintained, even until the fund is depleted. Feldstein (2005, 34) argues that since the excess of current social security tax receipts over current payments is simply loaned to the government to finance other government activities, the social security trust fund is "just an accounting mechanism for keeping track of past Social Security surpluses."

There is evidently no legal or constitutional requirement that money in the social security trust fund must be devoted to maintaining benefit levels for those who have paid into the fund. The U.S. Social Security Administration Web site[1] emphasizes that payment of Federal Insurance Contributions Act (FICA) payroll taxes does not entitle individuals to social security benefits "in a legal, contractual sense." According to the Web site, this issue was finally settled by a 1960 Supreme Court ruling, *Flemming v. Nestor*.

Miron and Murphy (2001, 2) observe that

The benefits a person receives depend on the law at the time the person receives benefits. They are not linked to the taxes this person paid during working life.... Congress has the power to increase or decrease benefits, even for those already retired, subject only to the political ramifications of so doing.

In the absence of a binding contractual obligation to maintain social security benefits, it is crucial to assess the likelihood that voter support for this system will be maintained through the anticipated demographic changes. Two countervailing forces are at work. As the population ages, an increasing proportion of voters will be at or near retirement age and thus will enjoy a high rate of return from maintaining at least the current level of benefits. But there is an opposing force. As the large baby-boom cohorts begin to collect benefits, the working population will have to be taxed more heavily to pay for these benefits. Therefore, the net present value of the social security program will decrease for young and middle-age workers.

This chapter investigates the balance of these two effects on political support for pay-as-you-go retirement plans in the United States. We estimate the impact of a small one-time change in social security benefits on the expected present value of taxes paid and benefits received for persons of each age and sex. For each sex, there is a pivotal age such that the expected net present value of an increase in social security benefits is positive or negative depending on whether one is older or younger than this age. For projected populations between now and the year 2050, we estimate the fraction of voters whose self-interest favors maintaining social security at least at current levels.

We also investigate the fractions of the population that would gain or lose from a change in the age at which people begin to receive social security benefits. This issue deserves separate attention because the age distribution of support for such changes is not the same as that for changes in benefits. Although currently retired persons have a strong financial interest in maintaining or increasing current benefit levels, they have no direct financial interest in a change in retirement age so long as it does not affect their own retirement status.

Political Support for Benefit Levels

Methods

We built an Excel spreadsheet[2] to calculate the net present value of social security taxes and benefits for U.S. voters by age and sex in 2001. To make these projections, we used U.S. census figures on the age distribution of the current population, along with age-specific birth and death rates to estimate future age distributions. We repeated this exercise to estimate present values to voters at the end of each decade from 2010 to 2050.

We made the following simplifying assumptions about the system. There is a predetermined age S (sixty-six years in our benchmark case)[3] at which workers begin to receive a constant pension level for the rest of their lives. In every year, the cost of current social security payments is collected through taxes that are divided equally among all persons of who are of ages between eighteen and S in that year.

A worker's expected present value of benefits from future social security payments must be discounted not only by the time discount rate r (assumed to be 5 percent in our benchmark case) but also by the probability that he or she will survive to receive them. Let $L_t(a, x)$ be the probability that someone who is of age a at time t will survive to age x. (To simplify calculations, we assume that nobody lives beyond age 100.) At time t, for a working person whose current age is $a < S$, the expected present value of the benefits resulting from a \$1 increase in annual social security payments is

$$B(a) = L_t(a, S)(1 + r)^{-(S-a)} \sum_{j=0}^{100-S} L_{t+S-a}(S, S + j)(1 + r)^{-j}. \tag{4.1}$$

We define the dependency ratio $D(\tau)$ to be the ratio of the number of retired persons to the number of workers in year τ. Since the cost of current social security payments is assumed to be collected in equal amounts from each current worker, the cost of social security to workers in year τ will be proportional to $D(\tau)$. For a working person of age a, the expected present value of the costs of a permanent \$1 increase in social security benefits is seen to be

$$C(a) = \sum_{j=0}^{S-a-1} L_t(a, a + j)D(a + j)(1 + r)^{-j}. \tag{4.2}$$

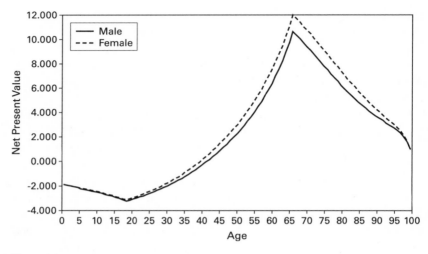

Figure 4.1
Net present values by age and gender.

Net present values of an increase in social security benefits are positive or negative for a person of age a, depending on the sign of $B(a) - C(a)$. We use sex-specific survival rates to construct separate estimates of age-specific expected benefit and cost functions for men and for women at each age between eighteen and the retirement age. Persons older than retirement age are assumed to collect benefits without paying social security taxes and thus will always gain from increased benefit levels.

Results

Figure 4.1 shows net present values of social security benefits under our benchmark assumptions for individuals of each age and sex, using projections from the year 2001.[4] We see that in 2001, the pivotal age at which voters' self-interest begins to favor increased social security is about forty-two for men and forty for women.

In 2001, the median age of the voting population in the United States was about forty-three years. If voters voted their self-interest and voter participation were the same for all ages, then about 55 percent of voters would favor maintaining at least the current level of social security benefits. But in the United States, voter participation increases sharply with age. The participation rate is about 36 percent for those under thirty years of age and 67 percent for persons over fifty. If we

Table 4.1
Social security dependency ratio, pivotal age, and median age.

	Year					
	2001	2010	2020	2030	2040	2050
Dependency ratio	0.19	0.19	0.24	0.31	0.33	0.33
Average pivotal age[a]	40	42	44.5	46	45.5	45.5
Median age of voting-age population	43	45	47	48	48	48
Median age of actual voters	47	50	52	53	53	53

Note:
a. The pivotal age for women is about two years less than that for men. These figures are the average of those for men and for women.

take account of age-specific voting rates, we find that under our benchmark assumptions, approximately 65 percent of voters would favor maintaining or increasing benefits.[5]

As the population ages over the next few decades, maintaining the social security system will become more expensive for working people. In our model, the annual social security tax paid by workers is proportional to the *dependency ratio*, which we define as the ratio of the number of persons over age sixty-six to the number of persons of ages eighteen to sixty-five. Table 4.1 shows how this ratio will increase over the next half century. As the dependency ratio rises and with it the tax burden of social security, so does the pivotal age at which one's expected present value of future social security benefits begins to exceed lifetime expected tax costs. This effect, in itself, reduces political support for social security. But over this period, the median age of voters rises at about the same rate as the pivotal age. Consequently, throughout the entire period, for more than half of voters the expected present value of social security benefits exceeds the expected present value of the taxes needed to sustain the social security program.

Table 4.2 shows that in 2001, under our benchmark assumptions, a substantial majority of voters stood to gain from maintaining or increasing the current level of social security benefits. Moreover, the size of this majority is not likely to change significantly over the next fifty years. Thus if current levels of social security benefits constitute a political equilibrium, there is little reason to expect that the expected aging of the U.S. population will result in political support for substantial changes in benefit levels.

Our conclusion that social security is likely to have strong political support is consistent with the results of public opinion polls. A recent

Table 4.2
Voters favoring higher social security benefits (benchmark assumptions).

	Year					
	2001	2010	2020	2030	2040	2050
Voters favoring higher benefits	65%	65%	63%	62%	64%	63%

survey by Shaw and Myseiewicz (2004) reports the results of a large number of public opinion polls over the course of the last decade. Interviewees were asked questions such as: "Is the US government spending too much, too little, or about the right amount on Social Security?" These polls have uniformly found a majority of respondents favoring an increase in social security benefits, while fewer than 10 percent favor a decrease. Even when polling questions emphasize that maintaining benefits is likely to require increased taxes, the results favor maintaining benefit levels. A recent survey conducted by the Pew Research Center (2005) asked, "When decisions about Social Security's future are being made, which do you think is MORE important?" The options offered were, "AVOIDING any tax INCREASES for workers and employees" and "AVOIDING any cuts in Social Security benefit amounts." About 60 percent of respondents thought that avoiding cuts in benefits was more important, while 30 percent thought avoiding tax increases was more important. A Gallup poll in April to May of 2005 offered respondents a choice between two options: increasing social security taxes or cutting social security benefits (Bowman, 2005). About 53 percent preferred increasing taxes, and 38 percent preferred reducing benefits.

Another interesting indicator is the experience of European democracies that have older populations than the United States has today but similar age ratios to those that the United States will experience in twenty years. The political balance in these countries has so far maintained high social security benefits, which has required high taxes on earnings. Boeri, Börsch-Supan, and Tabellini (2001) recently surveyed voters in France, Germany, Spain, and Italy, where they asked the following question:

In your opinion, should the state (a) reduce taxes and compulsory contributions, cutting pensions and/or transfers to households, (b) maintain taxes and compulsory contributions at current levels, or (c) increase pensions and/or transfers to households by raising taxes and/or compulsory contributions?

Table 4.3
Cross-country comparisons of attitudes toward social security benefits.

	Ratio of Age 65+ to Labor Force[a]	Social Security Tax Rate[b]	Favor at Least Present Benefits[c]
United States	.25	12.6%	60%
France	.38	14.75%	65%
Germany	.37	19.5%	73%
Spain	.37	28.3%	81%
Italy	.46	32.7%	56%

Notes:
a. OECD (2005).
b. Galasso and Profeta (2004).
c. For the United States, Pew Research Center (2005). For European countries, Boeri, Börsch-Supan, and Tabellini (2001).

In table 4.3, the first column reports ratios of the number of persons older than age sixty-five to the number in the labor force, the second column reports the social security tax rate, and the third column reports the percentage of those surveyed who prefer either constant or increased benefits.

By 2030, the ratio of persons over age sixty-five to those in the labor force in the United States will be very close to that currently found in France, Germany, and Spain. As table 4.3 shows, in all of these countries, despite the fact that social security tax rates are significantly higher than those in the United States, a majority of voters favor maintaining or increasing current levels of benefits.[6]

Excess Burden of Taxation   Our benchmark calculations do not account for the excess burden of taxation. Social security is financed by a tax on labor income.[7] If labor supply decreases in response to a tax on labor, then the actual cost to taxpayers of paying for benefits exceeds the amount of revenue collected. The excess burden of a tax is defined to be the amount by which the cost to taxpayers exceeds the revenue raised by the tax. If the ratio of excess burden to revenue collected is b, then to obtain a correct estimate of tax costs, we need to multiply the benchmark costs by $1 + b$.

The size of excess burden depends on the elasticity of labor supply. Although this issue has been much studied, there is wide divergence of opinion. Feldstein (1997) maintains that when one takes account of all the consequences of increased taxation for human-capital formation,

Table 4.4
Percent in favor of maintaining benefits.

	2001	2010	2020	2030	2040	2050
No excess burden	65	65	63	62	64	63
With 25% excess burden	58	60	58	57	58	58
With 66% excess burden	52	54	53	51	53	53
With 100% excess burden	47	49	50	50	50	51
With 150% excess burden	42	45	46	47	47	47

the labor-supply elasticity is very high, and the costs imposed by labor taxation are between two and two-and-one-half times as great as the amount of money raised. If this is the case, the ratio b of excess burden to benefits would be between 1 and 1.5. Feldstein's opinion does not seem to be widely shared. In a survey article, Slemrod (1998, 774) reports that "with some exceptions, the profession has settled on a value for [the labor supply] elasticity close to zero for prime-age males, although for married women, the responsiveness of labor force participation appears to be significant." A study by Ziliak and Kneiser (1999) concludes that when intertemporal effects are properly accounted for, labor supply is somewhat more elastic. Their results suggest that the excess burden ratio b is about 0.2. A recent study by Liu and Rettenmaier (2004) pays closer attention to the details of the social security tax, such as the fact that benefits received by individuals increase with the amount of taxes that they pay.[8] They arrive at an estimate of the excess burden ratio from the social security tax of approximately $b = .07$.

Table 4.4 indicates that even with excess burden as high as 66 percent, a majority of voters would benefit from increases rather than decreases in benefits. The majority in favor of higher benefits would disappear only if voters believed that the ratio of excess burden to benefits is close to 100 percent.

Alternative Discount Rates   For our benchmark calculations, we discounted future income flows at 5 percent. Workers cannot use their future social security benefits as collateral for loans. For those who are credit-constrained, the relevant discount rate is likely to be very high. Table 4.5 shows how estimated support for social security depends on the assumed discount rate. At a discount rate of 8.25 percent, support falls to 50 percent.

Table 4.5
Percent in favor of maintaining benefits.

	2001	2010	2020	2030	2040	2050
With 3% discount rate	81	78	74	74	75	75
With 5% discount rate	65	65	63	62	64	63
With 7% discount rate	55	57	56	55	56	56
With 8.25% discount rate	51	52	52	51	52	53

Doubts about Future of Social Security   Public opinion polls indicate that a significant number of voters believe that social security benefits will decline in the future. Shaw and Mysiewicz (2004) report on a survey that asked adults age twenty-five and older: "How confident are you that the Social Security system will continue to provide benefits of equal value to the benefits received by retirees today?" In 2003, 40 percent were "somewhat confident" or "very confident," 26 percent were "not too confident," and 26 percent were "not at all confident." While it is difficult to assign quantitative probabilities to adjectival responses like "somewhat confident" or "not too confident," there do appear to be significant doubts.

If voters do not believe that the present level of social security benefits will be available for their own generation, they are not likely to favor maintaining these benefits. The effect of voter doubts on voting outcomes depends on the age distribution of those who lack confidence in future benefits. While survey responses to this question were not reported by age, it is reasonable to assume that younger voters will be less confident than older voters that they will enjoy current levels of benefits when they retire.

Let us consider a simple model that reflects this assumption. Voters believe that social security benefits are subject to a constant hazard rate. Thus in any year in which benefits are still present, there is a probability h that they will disappear for the future. The effect of this hazard on expected present value of costs and benefits can be shown to be the same as an increase of h in the rate at which both future benefits and costs are discounted.

With an annual hazard of $h = .01$, the probability that benefits would still be present when a forty-five-year-old voter retires is about .8. If $h = .02$, this probability is about .67, and if $h = .0325$, it is about .5. From table 4.5, we see that under baseline assumptions, a majority of voters gain from a marginal increase in social security benefit levels so long as future benefits and costs are discounted at a rate less than .0825. Thus if the ordinary time discount rate is .05 and the annual hazard rate for social security benefits is less than .0325, a majority of voters will benefit from maintaining at least the current benefit level.

Voting on the Benefits Age

Suppose that self-interested voters select the age at which social security benefits begin. In the United States, workers who have reached the appropriate age can receive social security benefits regardless of whether they retire from the labor force.[9] In 2004, labor-force participation rates for persons age sixty-five to sixty-nine were about 28 percent, for persons age seventy to seventy-four, about 15 percent, and for persons older than age seventy-five, about 6 percent.[10] It is therefore important to distinguish the age at which benefits start (which we call the *benefits age*) from the *retirement age* at which people stop working.

There is an interesting theoretical difference between voting on the benefits *levels* and voting on benefit *ages*. There is a pivotal age at which voters' self-interests about benefit levels divide. Those older than the pivotal age gain from larger benefits and those younger gain from smaller benefits. The alignment of self-interest in voting over the benefits age is more complex. Typically, there is a coalition of young voters and some older voters who would benefit from increasing the benefits age and an opposing coalition of middle-age voters who would lose from such an increase.

Median voter models of political economy normally rely on the assumption of single-peaked preferences. Preferences over an issue are single peaked if policy alternatives can be arranged in a one-dimensional array so that each voter has a preferred point on the array and such that for any two points on the same side of his favorite point, a voter likes the one closer to his favorite at least as well as the other. An alternative that would win in pairwise majority voting against any other option is known as a *Condorcet winner*. If preferences of all voters are single-peaked, the median of the preferred points of all voters is the unique *Condorcet winner*.[11] The Condorcet winner is the predicted outcome for the usual median voter models.

Selfish voters' preferences on the benefits age are, not in general, single-peaked. For any selfish voter, the best social security plan is one in which benefits begin at exactly his own age. Consider a voter of age A who compares two alternative benefits ages x and y, where

$x < y < A$. This voter is older than either of the two proposed ages and hence will receive the same benefits under either alternative. If this voter is not in the labor force, she pays no social security taxes in either case and thus is indifferent between x and y. If she is still in the labor force, she will pay higher social security taxes with x than with y and hence strictly prefers y. In either case, her preferences are consistent with single-peakedness. Now suppose that $A < x < y$. A worker of age A will receive more benefits under x, but she will also pay more taxes since the earlier retirement age implies a larger retired population. Suppose that $A = 35$, $x = 65$, and $y = 100$. The most-preferred benefits age for a thirty-five-year-old worker is thirty-five years. Our earlier calculations show that in the United States, with a retirement age of sixty-five, the expected present value of future social security taxes and benefits for a thirty-five-year-old worker is negative. If the benefits age were 100, then the expected present value of social security taxes and benefits would both be approximately zero for a thirty-five-year-old worker. Thus the thirty-five-year-old would prefer benefits age A to age x and also prefer benefits age y to age x. This is inconsistent with single-peaked preferences.

In general, without single-peaked preferences, it may be that there is no Condorcet winner, so that repeated majority voting contests would lead to a cyclical outcome. Whether or not there is a Condorcet winner, it is interesting to determine whether now and in the future, majority voting by selfish voters is likely to favor small increases or decreases in the retirement age.

Table 4.6 shows the percentage distributions of voters who would gain, lose, or be indifferent about a one-year increase in the benefits age. Estimates are constructed for elections held in the years 2001, 2010, 2020, and 2030. (The benefits age in 2001 was sixty-five and is

Table 4.6
Voting blocks for and against increased benefits age.

| | Year and Change in Benefits Age | | | |
	2001 $65 \rightarrow 66$	2010 $66 \rightarrow 67$	2020 $66 \rightarrow 67$	2030 $67 \rightarrow 68$
Young and in favor	25%	30%	31%	30%
Old and in favor	3%	2%	3%	3%
Old and indifferent	16%	16%	19%	22%
Middle-age and opposed	55%	52%	47%	45%

currently mandated to be sixty-six in 2010 and 2020 and sixty-seven in 2030.) In each year, self-interest will divide voters into three groups— the young, the middle-aged, and those old enough to collect benefits even after the proposed increase. There will be a pivotal age such that those voters younger than this age will gain from an increased retirement age and those who are older than this age but not yet old enough to collect benefits will lose. Those who are old enough to receive benefits despite the proposed change will be indifferent about the change if they are retired but will gain if they are still in the labor force and paying taxes on earnings. In 2001, the pivotal age for this issue was 35.5. The pivotal age will be 39 in 2010, and 40.5 in 2020 and 2030.

Table 4.6 shows the fraction of all voters, weighted by age-specific voter-participation rates, who fall into each of the relevant groups. In table 4.6, we see that if old voters who are not in the labor force abstain or split their votes equally, then the selfish voter model predicts that a proposal to increase the retirement age would be defeated by approximately a two-to-one majority in 2001 and by about a four-to-three majority in 2030. It is possible, however, that a substantial fraction of retired individuals who have no direct stake in changing the benefits age could be persuaded that the alternative to an increase the benefits age would be reduced benefits. If so, their self-interest would favor an increased benefits age. By the year 2020, the group of middle-age voters opposing an increase falls short of a majority. After 2020, a reduction in retirement age could pass if it were able to attract a sufficiently large proportion of retired pensioners, who have no direct stake in the outcome.

Public opinion polls suggest that increases in the benefits age are not politically attractive. In a large number of polls over the past decade (Pew Research Center, 2005; Bowman, 2005; Shaw and Mysiewicz, 2004), when people are asked whether they favor or oppose an increased benefits age, about twice as many people are opposed as are in favor. The way that this question is usually asked, however, does not make it clear to voters that an increase in the retirement age might be an alternative to higher taxes or lower benefit levels. A result more favorable to increasing the benefits age comes from a 2004 poll (Bowman, 2005) that posed a more pointed question. Respondents were asked to choose between two alternatives for maintaining the social security system—an increase in taxes or an increase in the benefits age. By a narrow margin, respondents preferred increasing the benefits age.

There is historical precedent for increasing the benefits age. In 1983, Congress mandated a gradual increase that would begin to take effect twenty years later, in 2003. Under this legislation, the benefits age is scheduled to rise gradually from sixty-five in 2002 to sixty-seven in 2027.

It is interesting to consider whether this legislation would have been approved by a majority of fully informed, selfish voters. The change had no effect on the benefits age of voters born before 1937. These voters were forty-six years or older in 1983 and constituted about half of the voting population. Under our pay-as-you-go assumptions, voters born before 1937 who remain in the labor force after 2002 will be net gainers, since their benefits are unchanged and their tax burden reduced. Those voters born before 1937 who retire by 2002 will be neither gainers nor losers, since both their benefits and their taxes are unaffected.

Voters from age eighteen to forty-six in 1983 all suffer a postponement of the beginning of their own benefits. Despite this loss, they must continue to pay taxes to support full benefits from age sixty-five for all cohorts born before 1937. Calculations show that the expected present value of this change is negative for everyone from age ten to forty-six.

If voters older than forty-six favored and voters younger than forty-six opposed the change, the population would be about equally split between supporters and opponents. But a large fraction of the older group would have had no expectation of being in the labor force after 2002.[12] Voters who expect to be retired after 2002 have no selfish motive for favoring or opposing the change. If retired voters were to abstain or split their vote, the 1983 legislation would have been rejected by a majority of fully informed, selfish voters. But given the gradual and deferred nature of this proposal, the expected gains or losses for most voters are small in absolute terms. Where direct self-interest is weak, other considerations may prevail. For example, older voters who plan to be retired after 2002 might have been persuaded that increasing the retirement age for those younger than themselves will help to ensure that benefit levels will not be reduced during their retirement. Younger voters may not have vigorously opposed the change, since its negative impact is experienced twenty to fifty years in the future.

Would selfish voters today support a proposal to extend these increases gradually to age seventy, with a two-month increase each year, starting in 2027, reaching age sixty-eight in 2033, age sixty-nine in 2039, and age seventy in 2045? The age distribution of self-interest for this proposal is quite similar to the distribution of gainers and losers from the 1983 legislation. The benefits age would not change for voters who will be at least sixty-seven years old in 2027. These voters are currently age forty-five or older and constitute 51 percent of the voting-age population and 58.5 percent of those who actually vote. Members of this group who expect to be in the labor force after 2027 would gain from the proposal, while those who expect to be retired have no personal stake in the outcome.

Much as we found in the case of the 1983 legislation, this gradual increase in retirement age would adversely affect all voters currently age eighteen to forty-five. If voting is selfish, support for the change would have to come from voters who are currently older than age forty-five. For those older voters who plan to be retired by 2027, this gradual increase would have no direct financial impact. However, they might be persuaded to support such legislation if they were convinced that the alternative to increased retirement ages was a reduction in benefit levels.

Discussion

Related Research
We are not the first to use a median-voter model to investigate the political stability of the U.S. Social Security system. Galasso (1999) studied the effect of a slowdown in the U.S. population growth rate on the median voter's demand for social security benefits. He constructed a computable general equilibrium growth model of the U.S. economy. This model includes a pay-as-you-go social security system and assumes that the size and productivity of the labor force grow at constant rates. It also assumes that capital accumulation comes only from domestic saving. In the model, the level of social security benefits uniquely determines steady-state stationary equilibrium consumption paths for individuals of each age. Galasso calibrates parameters of his model so that existing social security benefits are at the level that would be preferred by a voter of median age. In his baseline economy, population grows at a constant rate of 1.2 percent (a historical average growth rate). He then examines an alternative economy in which a constant population growth rate of 0.78 percent is assumed. (This is the average annual growth rate predicted by the Social Security Administration for the U.S. population over the next fifty years.) He notes

that a reduction in the growth rate of population introduces the same two opposing forces that we have observed. The lower population growth rate implies a higher dependency ratio and hence a higher social security tax burden for workers. On this account, for a person of a given age, the preferred social security benefit level will be lower with slower population growth. However, with the slower population growth, the median voter age rises. Since a voter's preferred level of benefits (and taxes) is an increasing function of her age, this effect tends to increase the equilibrium benefit level. In Galasso's simulations, the latter effect is stronger, and the equilibrium benefit level rises by about 4 percent.

An attractive feature of Galasso's model is that it makes explicit predictions about future levels of social security, while our own model simply predicts the likely direction of such changes. To obtain these quantitative estimates, Galasso had to make several extremely strong and somewhat arbitrary assumptions about preferences, production, and the macroeconomy. For his method to work, he also must confine his attention to a comparison of two long-run steady-state growth paths, one of which has reached equilibrium with a constant higher growth rate of population growth and the other with a constant lower rate of population growth. This procedure does not seem to be well suited to the actual demographic trajectories for the United States and Europe over the next fifty years. Instead, the demographics of the first half of this century are dominated by the aging of a large baby-boom generation, which had been preceded and will be followed by much smaller age cohorts.

An earlier study by Bohn (2003) estimates support for social security benefits in the United States, using an approach that is similar to ours. Bohn's approach, like ours, is to use a partial equilibrium model with a constant discount rate. As did we, Bohn used census data for cohorts that have already been born and official projections of birth and death rates to estimate the demographic makeup of future populations. He calculated the expected present value of the current social security program for persons of each age, using a 3 percent discount rate. His qualitative conclusions are similar to ours, though by his calculations, social security is a somewhat less attractive investment than we find it to be. Bohn concludes that political support for maintaining social security benefits is strong and likely to remain so.[13]

Major European countries have experienced larger demographic shifts than the United States, with falling birthrates and an aging population. According to the *OECD Factbook* (OECD, 2005), in the United

States, the ratio of persons older than age sixty-five to those in the labor force will rise from 0.24 in 2005 to 0.34 in 2020. Over the same period in Germany, this ratio will rise form 0.37 to 0.45; in France, from 0.38 to 0.50; and in Italy, from 0.46 to 0.56.

We are aware of three interesting studies that indicate that in Europe, the aging of the population is likely to lead to increased rather than decreased political support for social security. In a paper entitled "Pensions and the Path to Gerontocracy in Germany," Sinn and Uebelmesser (2002) investigate the net present values of the Germany social security system to persons of each age. By their calculation, in the current population, a majority of selfish voters would gain from a *reduction* of benefits. Over the next three decades, as Germany's population ages, the pivotal age at which voters begin to favor social security will increase. But the median age of voters will increase more rapidly. In consequence, after about 2015, a majority of German voters would gain from increases rather than decreases in social security benefits.

Uebelmesser (2004) applies the methods of the Sinn-Uebelmesser study to France and Italy. She finds that in Italy until 2006 and in France until 2014, the population will be quite evenly divided between voters who would gain from a permanent decrease and those who would gain from a permanent increase in pay-as-you-go pensions. After 2006 in Italy and 2014 in France, a majority would favor increases.

A recent study by Galasso and Profeta (2004) applies the methods used in Galasso's (1999) earlier study[14] of U.S. social security to the same questions for France, Germany, Italy, Spain, and the United Kingdom. This paper also offers a useful description of social security benefits and taxes in these countries. For each country, the authors conclude that although the burden of social security will rise for younger taxpayers, the increased median age will result in a net increase in the level of benefits supported by the median-age voter. The predicted percentage increase in politically sustainable benefit levels is especially large for Germany (33 percent), Spain (52 percent), and the United Kingdom (42 percent) and more modest for France (10 percent), Italy (15 percent), and the United States (15 percent).

Further Issues

How Well Informed Are Voters?

Any study based on models of rational voters must confront the issue of how informed and sophisticated the voters can be assumed to be.

This chapter evaluates the self-interest of voters by comparing estimates of the expected present value of the social security taxes that they will pay with the expected present value of benefits that they will receive. These costs and benefits are calculated using actuarial probabilities of the length of life and demographic projections of the age distribution of the population.

Unlike Galasso (1999), Cooley and Soares (1999), and Galasso and Profeta (2004), we do not go so far as to assume that voters take into account the general-equilibrium consequences of their actions in a long-run equilibrium-growth model. While it might be reasonable to assume that voters pay attention to expert advice on these highly technical matters, we believe that even among economists there is little consensus about the size and direction of general-equilibrium effects of social security on such variables as interest rates, capital stocks, and real wages. We think it is more reasonable to follow the tradition of private-sector general-equilibrium analysis, where consumers are assumed to know their own preferences and to optimize subject to parametric prices.

Though our calculations do not require that voters foresee the general-equilibrium effects of changes in social security on prices and wages, they do require voters to make demographic projections that few individuals are likely to make on their own. The statistics on which we base our estimates are available to everyone and similar conclusions are likely to be reached by most analysts who study them. To the extent that voters are selfish and guided by the advice of opinion leaders who share their self-interest, the predictions of our model are likely to be reasonable approximations.

We believe that it is useful to know how well-informed selfish voters would vote on social security issues but are acutely aware that most voters are neither well informed nor thoroughly selfish. There is room for much more systematic exploration of voters who are guided by simpler and perhaps systematically incorrect heuristics for decisions.

Equilibrium and Beliefs
We have calculated expected returns for voters who believe that contemplated changes in pension benefits will be once-and-for-all. In this, we follow Browning (1975), who observed that in a once-and-for-all election, persons of median age and higher would prevail in selecting a pension plan that benefits the current elderly at the expense of all future generations. In actuality, social security policy is not set on a

once-and-for-all basis. The issue of benefit levels and methods of finance can be and is frequently revisited by Congress and by voters.[15]

Polls report that about one-fourth of all voters are "not at all confident" that current levels of benefits will be available for them when
they retire (Shaw and Mysiewicz, 2004). Voters who believe that current benefit levels will not be available for their own retirement are
likely to favor reducing benefit levels. But suppose that voters believe
that if benefits are maintained today, they will be maintained for their
entire lifetimes, and if they are cut today, they will not be restored. As
our calculations have shown, for the foreseeable future, with these
beliefs, a majority of selfish voters would support maintaining current
benefit levels. Thus the belief that current decisions about benefit levels
are once-and-for-all would not be refuted by the course of events.[16]

Is it also reasonable for voters to believe that cuts in current social security benefits are not likely to be restored? To address this question,
let us note that there are two distinct possible equilibria for the social
security system. Each is sustained by a different set of self-confirming
beliefs. In one self-confirming equilibrium, voters believe that current
benefit levels will be sustained. In the other equilibrium, people believe
that social security benefits will disappear in the future. If voters believe this, then every voter who is younger than the current benefits
age would gain from a reduction of benefit levels. Selfish voting would
result in the elimination social security benefits, thus confirming the
workers' pessimistic beliefs about the future of social security. Given
the existence of this alternative equilibrium, it is reasonable for voters
to believe that if benefit levels are reduced today, they are unlikely to
be restored in the future.

Concern for Family
Our estimates of political support for social security benefits have been
based on the assumption that people vote in their own self-interest
as measured by expected present values. While this assumption is an
interesting starting point, it not an adequate representation of voters'
incentives.

We believe that the most important effect missed by the selfish-
voting assumption is that people care strongly about the economic
welfare of their own parents and their own children. Young people
whose parents receive social security are indirect beneficiaries of these
payments. Old people who are not in the labor force may care about
the tax burdens that their children or grandchildren bear. It would be

instructive to conduct a disaggregated analysis of individuals' valuations of payments received by and taxes collected from their children and surviving parents. It would also be interesting to see the results of public opinion polls on attitudes toward social security in which respondents were asked whether they had children, grandchildren, or surviving parents. As far as we know, such survey results are not currently available.

Forced Savings, Insurance, and Charity

Social security is not simply a redistribution between age cohorts. It provides insurance against misfortune in the labor market, and it functions as a mechanism for reducing poverty among the aged. The social security system works as a form of lifetime earnings insurance by offering a higher ratio of benefits to taxes for those with low lifetime earnings.[17] Social security also reduces old-age poverty by operating as an instrument of forced saving. As Lindbeck and Weibull (1988) explain, rational voters with altruistic motives may favor a forced saving plan as an alternative to providing direct relief for the impoverished elderly. In this chapter, we have made no allowances for the value that voters put on the forced savings and social insurance functions of social security. Accounting for these would imply stronger support for benefits.

Conclusions

In an economy with falling birth rates, pay-as-you-go social security offers an extremely low rate of return on taxes paid over the course of a worker's life. Young people voting their self-interest would choose to eliminate all benefits. But in a democracy, the middle-aged and the old are also allowed to vote. While workers who are in their mid-forties would have benefited from elimination of social security when they were younger, they now find that the expected present value of future benefits exceeds that of future costs from social security. By our estimates, workers begin to be net beneficiaries from the future benefits and costs of social security while in their early forties. At present, the median age of those who vote in elections is the late forties. Accordingly, almost two-thirds of those who vote would benefit from maintaining or increasing current benefits. Over the next four decades, as the population ages, the tax cost of providing social security benefits will increase. As a result, middle-age workers will find social security less attractive, and the age at which voters begin to favor social security will rise to the mid-forties. But at the same time, the median age of voters will rise to the low fifties. Throughout this entire period, a majority of selfish voters will prefer maintaining the current level of benefits to a once-and-for-all reduction in benefits.

Public opinion polls in the United States confirm that there is strong majority support for maintaining social security benefits at current levels. An indication that this support will persist as the population ages comes from the European experience. In France, Germany, and Spain, the ratio of pensioners to workers is much higher than in the United States and similar to the ratio that expected in the United States in 2030. In these countries, despite social security tax rates that are much higher than those in the United States, public-opinion polls show clear majority support for maintaining at least the current level of benefits.

On the issue of the age at which benefits should begin, self-interest does not simply align the old against the young. Increases in the benefit age would benefit young voters and some older voters. Voters currently old enough to receive benefits and are still earning wages would gain from a small increase in the retirement age, while those who are retired will neither gain nor lose. Those who would lose from an increased benefit age are the middle-age voters who lose more in benefits than they save in reduced taxes. Through the year 2010, a majority of the voting population will belong to the middle-age group opposed to an increase. By 2020, this group will fall to slightly less than half the population. Assuming current labor-force participation rates for those older than the benefits age, about one-third of voters will gain from an increased benefits age, and about 20 percent will be indifferent.

We do not believe that voting is entirely governed by selfish motives nor do we believe that most voters are well informed about the expected costs and benefits of social security. This simple model of selfish, informed voters can at best be considered a crude approximation. Its predictions, however, seem to be broadly consistent with voting outcomes and opinion polls, both in the United States and in Europe.

Notes

1. ⟨http://www.ssa.gov/history/nestor.html⟩.

2. The Excel format makes it relatively easy to explore the effects of parameter variations reflecting alternative assumptions about the discount rate, excess burden in taxation,

voter participation rates, changes in projected mortality and birth rates, immigration rates, and retirement age.

3. This is the U.S. social security retirement age for persons born between 1943 and 1954.

4. The units on the vertical axis represent the expected net present value of a $1 increase in annual benefits paid to persons over age sixty-six.

5. Voter-participation rates in the November 2000 election are reported by age in a U.S. census document found at ⟨http://www.census.gov/population/socdemo/voting/p20-542/tab01.xls⟩.

6. The poll also reports a significant positive relationship between respondents' age and probability of support for high benefit levels.

7. The social security tax rate for 2005 is 12.4 percent of all earnings less than $90,000. Half of this tax is collected from employers, and half directly from workers.

8. Social security benefits are determined by an indexed average of lifetime annual incomes according to the following rule: annual benefits include 90 percent of the first $7,500 in earnings, plus 32 percent of the next $38,000, plus 15 percent of earnings between $45,500 and $90,000. For details, see ⟨http://www.ssa.gov/OACT/ProgData/benefits.html⟩.

9. This has been the case since the year 2000. Previously, social security benefits were reduced by $1 for each $3 in earnings.

10. See Employment Status of the Civilian Noninstitutional Population by Age, Sex, and Race at ⟨http://www.bls.gov/cps/cpsaat3.pdf⟩.

11. This statement needs minor modification if some individuals are indifferent between more than one best outcome.

12. In 1982, about 15 percent of the voting population was age sixty-five or higher. These people, if they survived until 2002, would be at least eighty-four years old. Labor-force participation rates for persons older than eighty are less than 6 percent.

13. Bohn's paper also includes an interesting analysis of Medicare and health insurance. He is somewhat less sanguine about the future of Medicare.

14. Each country is assumed to be a closed economy. All capital investment is assumed to be financed by domestic savings, and all domestic savings are invested in the home country. The realism of this assumption seems questionable for the United States and much more so for individual countries in Europe.

15. Sjoblom (1985) seems to have been the first to point this out. Sjoblom presents a simplified model of old-age benefits in which an intertemporal transfer scheme is maintained as a subgame perfect Nash equilibrium in an intergenerational game. Cooley and Soares (1999) and Boldrin and Rustichini (2000) extend Sjoblom's analysis and study the interaction between capital accumulation and social security in general-equilibrium models of a closed economy with constant population growth rates.

16. It would not have to be true that belief in the survival of social security is self-confirming. It could have been that impending demographic changes would result in a majority of self-interested voters voting to reduce benefit levels at some future time, even if they did not expect reductions to occur.

17. See note 8.

References

Boeri, Tito, Axel Börsch-Supan, and Guido Tabellini. (2001). "Would You Like to Shrink the Welfare State? A Survey of European Citizens." *Economic Policy*, 16(32), 9–41.

Bohn, Henning. (2003). "Will Social Security and Medicare Remain Viable as the U.S. Population Is Aging? An Update." Technical report, University of California, Santa Barbara.

Boldrin, Michele, and Aldo Rustichini. (2000). "Political Equilibria and Social Security." *Review of Economic Dynamics*, 3(1), 41–78.

Bowman, Karlyn. (2005). "Attitudes about Social Security Reform." Technical report, American Enterprise Institute, Washington, DC, available at ⟨http://www.aei.org/docLib/20050701_socialsecurity0701.pdf⟩.

Browning, Edgar. (1975). "Why the Social Insurance Budget Is Too Large in a Democracy." *Economic Inquiry*, 13, 373–388.

Cooley, Thomas, and Jorge Soares. (1999). "A Positive Theory of Social Security Based on Reputation." *Journal of Political Economy*, 107(1), 135–160.

Feldstein, Martin. (1997). "How Big Should Government Be?" *National Tax Journal*, 50(2), 197–213.

Feldstein, Martin. (2005). "Structural Reform of Social Security." *Journal of Economic Perspectives*, 19(2), 33–55.

Galasso, Vincenzo. (1999). "The U.S. Social Security System: What Does Political Sustainability Imply?" *Review of Economic Dynamics*, 2(3), 698–730.

Galasso, Vincenzo, and Paola Profeta. (2004). "Lessons for an Ageing Society: The Political Sustainability of Social Security Systems." *Economic Policy*, 19(38), 63–115.

Lindbeck, Assar, and Jorgen Weibull. (1988). "Altruism and Time Consistency: The Economics of Fait Accompli." *Journal of Political Economy*, 96(6), 1165–1182.

Liu, Liqun, and Andrew Rettenmaier. (2004). "The Excess Burden of the Social Security Tax." *Public Finance Review*, 32(6), 631–649.

Miron, Jeffrey, and Kevin Murphy. (2001). "The False Promise of Social Security Privatization." Technical report, Bastiat Institute, ⟨bastiat@mediaone.net⟩.

Organization for Economic Cooperation and Development (OECD). (2005). *OECD Factbook, Economic, Environmental and Social Studies*. OECD Publishing, available at ⟨http://titania.sourceoecd.org/vl=2968547/cl=89/nw=1/rpsv/factbook/01-01-02.htm⟩.

Pew Research Center. (2005). "AARP, Greenspan Most Trusted on Social Security: Bush Failing in Social Security Push." Technical report, Pew Research Center, Washington, DC, available at ⟨http://www.pewtrusts.com/pdf/PRC_Mar05_Social_Security.pdf⟩.

Shaw, Greg, and Sarah Mysiewicz. (2004). "The Polls: Trends in Social Security and Medicare." *Public Opinion Quarterly*, 68(3), 394–423.

Sinn, Hans-Werner, and Silke Uebelmesser. (2002). "Pensions and the Path to Gerontocracy in Germany." *European Journal of Political Economy*, 19, 153–158.

Sjoblom, Kriss. (1985). "Voting for Social Security." *Journal of Political Economy*, 45(3), 225–240.

Slemrod, Joel. (1998). "Methodological Issues in Measuring and Interpreting Taxable Income Elasticities." *National Tax Journal*, 51(4), 773–788.

Uebelmesser, Silke. (2004). "Political Feasibility of Pension Reforms." *Topics in Economic Analysis and Policy*, 4(1), 1–21.

Ziliak, James, and Thomas Knieser. (1999). "Estimating Life-Cycle Labor-Supply Tax Effects." *Journal of Political Economy*, 107(2), 326–359.

5 Free Choice of Unfunded Systems: A Preliminary Analysis of a European Union Challenge

Gabrielle Demange

Most European countries have set up a mandatory unfunded pension scheme, often called *first pillar*, financed through contributions levied on wages. Although this common characteristic is crucial, the systems significantly differ in two dimensions at least. First, although benefit rules have evolved, systems can still be classified as they were at their set up. Some are mostly "Bismarckian" with individuals' pensions that are earnings-related, while others are mostly "Beveridgean" with flat pensions. Second, the level of the mandatory contributions (hence, the level of the pension benefits) varies significantly across countries. For example, this level represented in 2003 roughly 9 percent of the gross domestic product in the United Kingdom, 16.5 percent in France, 19.5 percent in Germany, and 32.7 percent in Italy.[1] Thus, the *redistribution* carried out within a generation and the *level* of the contributions are two major characteristics that differentiate European systems. Currently, the minimal contributing period necessary to give pension rights is long, thereby limiting the portability of the systems. This limitation constitutes a barrier to workers' mobility, which may slow down labor integration, a major objective of the European Union (EU).

There are various ways to diminish the impact of such barriers. One is harmonization. Given the current differences in the systems and the problems of transition, agreement on a common system or even on steps toward convergence can only be slow. Another somewhat indirect but potentially powerful way to influence social security systems is free choice. By *free choice*, I mean to let any EU citizen to choose the system of any EU country *without* moving. Owing to the differences in the social security taxes and the benefit rules, free choice could trigger a drastic change in the allocation of individuals between the various systems. Would all systems survive? What would be the impact on efficiency, redistribution, and ultimately on citizens' welfare?

The purpose of this chapter is to explore these questions in as simple a model as possible while still accounting for the basic features just outlined. The analysis is limited to two countries with identical fundamentals. Economies are modeled as overlapping-generation models to discuss the tradeoff between physical investment and direct intergenerational transfers (such as those performed by unfunded systems). To account for intragenerational redistribution, workers within a generation differ in their productivity. The growth rate of population and rate of return on investment are exogenous and constant over time.

An unfunded social security system is in place in each country and is mandatory for its citizens. A system is characterized by two parameters—the contribution rate on earnings and the Bismarckian factor that determines the intragenerational redistribution operated by the system.[2] Even though the economies are identical, these parameters may differ in the two countries to account of the stylized facts referred to above. I investigate the situation in which the citizens of both countries can freely choose either system without having to move.

What effect may free choice have? Roughly speaking, the choice of an individual is determined by comparing the rates of return expected from each system (Aaron, 1966). Two factors influence this comparison. Not surprisingly, one factor is related to the efficiency of intergenerational transfers (Samuelson, 1958; Gale, 1973). If the growth rate of the population is less than the rate of return on investment, for example, efficiency considerations favor the system with the lower contribution rate. The second factor is the redistribution operated within each system. In contrast to efficiency, redistribution affects individuals in a differential way according to their earnings. Furthermore, the *effective* redistribution within a system is influenced not only by its design (Bismarckian factor and contribution rate) but also by the distribution of earnings of its contributors (even a Beveridgean system operates no redistribution if earnings are all equal). This is a crucial point for understanding free choice since the contributors to each system are no longer determined by nationality.

Under free choice, individuals' choices affect the redistribution levels within each system, which in turn determine individuals' choices. A simple example illustrates this interaction. Let contribution rates be equal in the two countries, and let one system be Beveridgean and the other be Bismarckian. Initially, in the absence of liquidity constraints, workers with wages smaller than average are better off in the Beveridgean system than in the Bismarckian. At the opening of the systems, low-income workers presumably choose the Beveridgean system, and wealthy workers choose the Bismarckian one (as is surely true if they base their choice on the initial situation). If this is the case, however, the average contributors' earnings to the Beveridgean system will diminish (and that to the Bismarckian will raise). As a result, the effective redistribution within the Beveridgean system decreases, and the initial incentives to choose it is reduced.

To assess the full impact of free choice, this chapter considers a steady-state equilibrium. The wage distribution of the contributors to each system is constant overtime, determined by the choices of individuals who correctly expect the returns of each system for them (the so-called rational expectations hypothesis). I show that a (not necessarily unique) equilibrium always exists. Furthermore, several types of equilibria may occur, depending on whether one or both systems are active and which system is chosen by the high-income workers. I investigate how the various parameters—characteristics of the systems, population growth rate, return to investment, wage dispersion—influence the equilibrium type.

If both systems cannot be active in equilibrium, one system will be selected in the long run by all citizens and the other will be de facto eliminated. How to interpret this result? To suppose, as in this chapter, that the opening of the systems would take place without any adjustment in their characteristics is not very realistic. The result nevertheless suggests that if the systems cannot both be active, then adjustments must be sufficiently fast or a system will be eliminated. Allowing for fast adjustments may be an even more unrealistic assumption owing to the current important differences between systems and the strong resistance to reforms.

The question addressed by this chapter is political. The opening of systems limits the margins of maneuvering of a country. The analysis however differs from the approach referred to as the political approach to social security. The purpose of this literature, as initiated by Browning (1975), is to explain the characteristics of a system by considering various decision-making processes, such as planner, median voter, lobbies (see, for example, the review by Galasso and Porfeta, 2002). This paper clearly differs since its goal is to analyze the interaction between different systems taking the characteristics of the systems as given, inherited from the past. On this respect, the closest analysis to ours is that of Casarico (2000). She also looks at the specific problem of integration and pension systems, with a focus that is somewhat complementary to ours. A more precise comparison is given after the analysis of the model.

Finally, the impact of national pay-as-you-go (PAYG) systems on the individuals' decisions to migrate has been examined by several authors (e.g., Hombourg and Richter, 1993; Breyer and Kolmar, 2002). Individuals must contribute to the system where they live and may differ only by a migration cost. Thus, in contrast with our analysis, redistribution is not an issue, and the driving force explaining why people move is the differences in (endogenous) population growth and interest rate across countries.

The chapter introduces the model and determines the initial situation when a mandatory system is in place within each country. It then studies equilibrium configurations when the two systems are opened to the citizens of both countries and considers some dynamics before gathering proofs in the final section.

The Model

I consider two countries, denoted by A and B, with the same economy but with a different pension system.

The Economy in a Country

The economy in each country is described by the same overlapping-generations model, with a structure close to that of Diamond (1965). Each generation lives for two periods, there is a single good that can be either consumed or invested, and population grows at a constant rate $g - 1$. An individual works only during the first period of his life, with an inelastic supply normalized to 1.

The technology of production is linear with marginal productivities of capital and labor that are constant over time. The quantity of goods available at date t results from the return on investment at the previous period and from labor of the current young generation. An amount s of capital invested in period $t - 1$ will produce rs units of goods in period t, where r is the exogenous return to investment. As for labor, workers differ in their productivity/wages w. A w-worker denotes someone who produces and earns w. Wages are distributed on $[w_{min}, w_{max}]$ with a mean denoted by $\bar{w}$. Thus the total quantity of good available at date t per head of old agents is $g\bar{w} + rs_{t-1}$ if s_{t-1} was the average quantity invested in period $t - 1$. The distribution of wages is assumed to be continuous and constant across generations.

Individuals' preferences bear on consumption levels when young and old, denoted by c^j and c^v (there is no altruism motive) and are strictly increasing in each argument. Preferences may be heterogeneous.

I assume away liquidity constraints. This assumption allows one to conduct the analysis by working with *intertemporal wealth* only without specifying preferences. Let us consider an individual who receives labor income net of contributions $(1 - \tau)w$ in the first period of his life and expects to receive a pension benefit π in the second period (dropping unnecessary time index). He faces the following successive constraints:

$$c^y + s = (1 - \tau)w \quad \text{and} \quad c^o = sr + \pi, \tag{5.1}$$

where s is an investment if positive and a loan if negative. This imply

$$c^y + c^o/r = (1 - \tau)w + \tau\frac{\pi}{r}. \tag{5.2}$$

In other words, the discounted value of consumption levels is equal to the intertemporal wealth, defined as the value of net labor income plus the discounted rights to pension. Conversely, in the absence of constraint on s, the intertemporal constraint (5.2) describes all feasible consumption plans: (5.1) and (5.2) are equivalent.[3]

Thus, *in the absence of liquidity constraints*, the welfare of an individual varies as his intertemporal wealth. As a result, the impact of a pay-as-you-go system on an individual's welfare can be analyzed through the impact on wealth. Similarly, the choice between two systems is determined by comparing the wealth values expected from contributing to either system.

Remarks

1. Growth in productivity/wages can be introduced in the usual way by interpreting $g - 1$ as the growth rate of the aggregate wage bill.

2. The assumption of a linear technology excludes endogenous variations in productivity, as would obtain with a nonlinear production function. Related to this, the absence of liquidity constraints makes sense only if aggregate savings are positive (see also note 5).

3. The ratio workers to retirees, equal to g, is exogenous. This ratio is sensitive to some policies, especially to social security. Labor participation changes over time, owing to changes in legislation affecting the

choice of retirement date or the number of working hours, for instance. Also it has been suggested that life expectancy and fertility are influenced by social security (see Philipson and Becker, 1983, and De la Croix and Doepke, 2003, for instance). These aspects are not addressed here.

Characteristics of a Pension System

In the initial situation, a pension system is in place in each country and is mandatory for its citizens. Once systems are opened, each young individual will be able to choose between the two systems. This section describes the functioning of a system without specifying who contributes to it (and dropping unnecessary country index).

A system is *unfunded* (PAYG), characterized by two parameters specifying the contribution rate τ and the redistribution Bismarckian factor α.

Contributions are levied on wages, with a constant rate τ: a young w-worker contributes τw. By construction, the system is balanced. Thus, at date t, given $\bar{w}_t$ the average wage level of the contributors to the system and g_t the number of contributors per pensioner, the *average* pension benefits per pensioner $\bar{\pi}_t$ is equal to

$$\bar{\pi}_t = \tau g_t \bar{w}_t. \tag{5.3}$$

The Bismarckian factor determines the benefit rule, which relates the pension benefits of a specific pensioner to the contributions he made in the previous period. Let us consider a pensioner at t who earned w at period $t - 1$ while the average wage over the contributors to the system was $\bar{w}_{t-1}$. He thus contributed $w/\bar{w}_{t-1}$ times the average level of contributions. If the Bismarckian factor is α, the pensioner receives benefits given by[4]

$$\pi_{w,t} = \left(\alpha \frac{w}{\bar{w}_{t-1}} + (1 - \alpha)\right)\bar{\pi}_t. \tag{5.4}$$

A pensioner whose contribution was equal to the average contribution per capita $w = \bar{w}_{t-1}$ receives benefits equal to the average benefits per pensioner $\bar{\pi}_t$, whatever value for α. Note that for $\alpha = 0$, all pensioners receive this level independently of the amount of their previous contributions: the system is Beveridgean. At the opposite, a Bismarckian system obtains for $\alpha = 1$, since pension benefits are proportional to contributions. Thus, for α between 0 and 1, the system combines a Beveridgean system and a Bismarckian one. This is a crude description of the current systems, which are much more complex (see, for example, the Whitehouse 2003 report on nine OECD countries).

Pension Systems

Initially, each young worker contributes to the mandatory pension system of his country. I consider the steady-state situation in which the system is in place and is expected to remain in place. After examining a country, I draw some brief comparisons between distinct systems.

National Systems

Let us consider a country with a system characterized by the parameters (τ, α). While in place, the average level of wages of the contributors is $\bar{w}$. Also, the numbers of contributors per pensioner is equal to g. This gives $g_t = g$, and $\bar{w}_{t-1} = \bar{w}_t = \bar{w}$ at a steady state, Therefore, from expressions (5.3) and (5.4), a w-worker will receive a pension benefit equal to $[\alpha w + (1 - \alpha)\bar{w}]\tau g$. Plugging this value into (5.2) gives the value for intertemporal wealth:

$$W(w) = \left[1 + \tau\left(\frac{g}{r} - 1\right)\right]w + \tau\frac{g}{r}(1 - \alpha)(\bar{w} - w). \tag{5.5}$$

Note that in the absence of a PAYG system, wealth would be simply equal to the wage w. Thus, the system has a positive impact on an individual if $W(w)$ is larger than w. To highlight the impact of each characteristic, it is convenient to define

$$R = 1 + \tau\left(\frac{g}{r} - 1\right) \quad \text{and} \quad D = \tau\frac{g}{r}(1 - \alpha). \tag{5.6}$$

With this notation, wealth writes as $W(w) = Rw + D(\bar{w} - w)$.

The factor R can be described as the *rate of return* of the system at the steady-state situation: whatever value for α, average wealth is equal to $R\bar{w}$, whereas without a PAYG system, it would be equal to average wage $\bar{w}$. Furthermore, in the absence of redistribution, the wealth of a w-worker is given by Rw for any wage w. Thus, each individual benefits from the system[5] if the rate R is larger than 1—that is, if the growth rate of the population is larger than the rate of return on investment, and each one is hurt by the system in the opposite case of a rate R less than 1. In other words, *at steady states, a Bismarckian PAYG system makes* *every individual better off if g > r and everyone worse off if g < r*. The distinction between the two cases is well known since Gale (1973), who referred to them respectively as the Samuelson and classical cases.

In the presence of redistribution, the analysis remains valid on average since average wealth is $R\overline{w}$. In addition to Rw, the wealth of a w-worker is affected by a term stemming from redistribution $D(\overline{w} - w)$, which is positive for wages less than the average and negative otherwise. As a result, even if $g < r$, a system can nevertheless be beneficial to some low-income workers or, at the opposite, even if $g > r$, a system can be detrimental to some high-income workers. Since the redistribution term is proportional to D, the factor D determines the *extent* of the redistribution. Note that D depends not only on the Bismarckian factor but also on the contribution rate and the ratio g/r.

Comparing Systems
Even though the two countries, denoted by A and B, have the same economy (identical population growth, return to investment, and wage distribution), their systems may differ significantly and hence have a different impact on citizens welfare. The characteristics of the system in country $I = A, B$ are denoted by (τ^I, α^I). From (5.6), the rate of return to system I and the extent of the redistribution are given by

$$R^I = 1 + \tau^I \left(\frac{g}{r} - 1\right) \quad \text{and} \quad D^I = \tau^I \frac{g}{r}(1 - \alpha^I), \tag{5.7}$$

and the wealth of a w-worker in country I is

$$W^I(w) = R^I w + D^I(\overline{w} - w). \tag{5.8}$$

In the Samuelson case $g > r$, the system that has the highest rate of return is the one with the largest contribution rate. In the classical case, it is the opposite. From now on, the system that has the highest rate of return will be referred to as the *more efficient* system. This is justified as follows.

In the absence of redistribution, the welfare of citizens in different countries but with the same wage w is easily compared through their wealth $R^I w$. Hence, at the steady state with Bismarckian systems, a w-worker is better off in the country that has the highest rate of return R^I.

In the presence of redistribution, the *average* wealth of the citizens is larger in the country with the largest return. Thus, with adequate transfers, all contributors to the less efficient system could be made better off by changing their contribution rate to that of the other country (that is, decreasing it in the classical case and increasing it in the Samuelson case). Note that there is an important difference between the two cases if one considers, instead of steady states, the transition from the less to the more efficient system. Whereas in the Samuelson case, every individual can be made better off, in the classical case $g < r$ surely some individuals have to be hurt in a transition toward the more efficient system (by similar arguments as used in the seminal paper by Gale, 1973).

Equilibrium under Free Choice

This section considers the situation in which each country opens its social security system to any citizen of the other country. More precisely, each young worker must contribute to a social security system but can freely choose between the two systems without moving. The choice is made once when young.

To choose between system A or B, a w-worker evaluates the wealth that he expects from each. Let us spell out this evaluation. The pension that is anticipated from a system depends on the wage level of its current and next contributors and on the growth rate of the number of contributors. Current wages determine the future redistributive gains or losses within a system, and next wages together with the growth rate determine the level of pension benefits. Let w_{t-1}^I and w_t^I be the anticipated average wage of the young contributors to system I at the current period $t - 1$, and let the subsequent period t, and $g_t^I - 1$ be the anticipated growth rate of the number of contributors. According to (5.3) and (5.4), a w-worker will expect pension benefits equal to

$$\left[\alpha^I \frac{w}{w_{t-1}^I} + (1 - \alpha^I) \right] \tau^I g_t^I w_t^I$$

from contributing to system I. This yields the level of intertemporal wealth

$$(1 - \tau^I)w + \tau^I \frac{g_t^I}{r} [\alpha^I w + (1 - \alpha^I)w_{t-1}^I] \frac{w_t^I}{w_{t-1}^I}. \tag{5.9}$$

We look for a *stationary equilibrium*, which requires two conditions: (1) in each system, the number of contributors grows at a constant rate equal to that of the population, and the average wage of the contributors is constant over time, and (2) individuals base their choices on these variables, which are correctly expected. Before making this definition more precise, it is convenient to analyze the choices of individuals who have (not necessarily correct) stationary expectations.

The System That Is More Favorable to High Income
The analysis of individuals' choices assuming *stationary and identical expectations* leads to a simple typology of the systems. Under stationary expectations, individuals expect the same types of workers to choose the systems at the current and next period. Thus, they expect the number of contributors to each system to grow as the population $g_t^I = g$ and the average wage of the contributors to each system to be constant overtime $w_t^I = w_{t-1}^I$ for $I = A, B$. Let us denote by w^I this constant expectation. From (5.9) and using the expressions (5.7) of R^I and D^I, the intertemporal wealth expected by a w-worker from contributing to system I is

$$W^I(w^I, w) = R^I w + D^I(w^I - w). \tag{5.10}$$

The choice of a system by a w-worker is made accordingly by comparing the wealth values obtained from A and B—namely, by the sign of

$$W^A(w^A, w) - W^B(w^B, w)$$

$$= [(R^A - D^A) - (R^B - D^B)]w + D^A w^A - D^B w^B.$$

The key point is that this expression is linear with respect to wage w and that expected levels w^A and w^B affect only the level and not the slope. Assume the slope to be positive. (In the sequel, we exclude the degenerate case in which the slope is null.) If an individual prefers A to B, then all those who earn more than him also prefer A to B. This leads to the following definition:

Definition 5.1 System A is said to be more favorable than system B to high-income workers if

$$[R^A - D^A] - [R^B - D^B] > 0,$$

which, replacing the R^I and D^I by their expressions, is equivalent to

$$\tau^A \left(1 - \frac{g}{r} \alpha^A \right) < \tau^B \left(1 - \frac{g}{r} \alpha^B \right). \tag{5.11}$$

System A is less favorable to high-income workers than B if the inequalities are reversed. Under stationary and identical expectations, the workers who choose the system that is more favorable to high-income workers are those whose wage is larger than a given threshold.

Which system is the more favorable is determined by the difference in efficiency (as measured by $R^A - R^B$) relative to the difference in the extent of redistribution (as measured by $D^A - D^B$). If both systems are Bismarckian, there is no redistribution whatsoever, and the system the more favorable than the more efficient one to high-income workers. More interesting is the case of systems that differ in their redistribution. It is worth recalling that in Europe systems with rather flat benefits tend to be associated with low contribution rates. Consider the case where the system with the smaller Bismarckian factor (say, B) has the smaller contribution rate: $\alpha^A > \alpha^B$ and $\tau^A > \tau^B$. From (5.11), the system the more favorable to high-income workers is the one with the lowest product $\tau^I(1 - \alpha^I g/r)$. Thus, under neutrality (for example, $g = r$), the more Bismarckian system A is not necessarily the more favorable to high-income workers. As the ratio g/r decreases, the more inefficient a PAYG system is, and the more likely it is that the system with the lower contribution rate is the more favorable to high-income workers.

Example

To illustrate this point, let us consider the case of France (A) and the United Kingdom (B). The tax rate in the United Kingdom is roughly half that in France, $\tau^A/\tau^B \approx 2$. Also, the U.K. system is much more redistributive than the French system.[6] According to some data, the parameters $\alpha^A = 0.8$ and $\alpha^B = 0.2$ are reasonable. The threshold value of g/r that determines whether A is more favorable to high income than B is $1/1.4 \approx 0.7$. This gives the following:

• For $g/r > 1$, A is more efficient and more favorable to high-income workers than B;

• For $1 > g/r > 0.7$, A is less efficient but more favorable to high-income workers than B; and

• For $g/r < 0.7$, A is less efficient and less favorable to high-income workers than B.

Thus, the U.K. system, although much more redistributive than the French system, can be more favorable to high-income workers thanks to its low contribution rate. This is especially true if PAYG systems are perceived as inefficient.

Not surprisingly, the ratio of growth rate to investment return plays a crucial role. Which value for this ratio is reasonable? This is a delicate question because it is not clear which return should be chosen for r. A period here represents roughly thirty years. If one takes for r the return on the stock market since the end of World War II and for g the projected growth rate of aggregate wage bill, the compounding effect will give a low value for g/r. This is, however, related to the equity premium puzzle. If, indeed, individuals are risk averse and ready to pay a high-risk premium, then one should take for r a much smaller value than the stock-market return. Also, a PAYG system provides retirees with an annuity, thereby insuring them against some of the risks of living into old age. Making insurance compulsory avoids the usual problems encountered in markets with asymmetric information. As documented by various studies, the premium associated to the longevity risk is roughly 5 percent (see Brown, Mitchell, and Poterba, 2001). To account for this premium, an extra return on a PAYG system could be introduced. Due to these difficulties and the uncertainty on future, I discuss in next section equilibria for different values of g/r.

Equilibrium

Given an anticipated average wage w^I of the contributors to each system I, let w^* be the wage level defined by $W^A(w^A, w^*) - W^B(w^B, w^*) = 0$. To fix the idea, assume system A to be more favorable to high-income workers. The individuals who choose system A are those who earn more than w^*. Note that the threshold w^* may not be in the range of wages. If $w^* \leq w_{min}$, for example, all individuals choose A, and if $w^* \geq w_{max}$, all choose B.

Individuals' anticipation on contributors' average wages determine their choices, which in turn determine the realized wages. To get an equilibrium, anticipation and realization must be consistent. This leads to the following definition:

Definition 5.2 Let system A be more favorable than B to high-income workers. An equilibrium is determined by average wages w^A and w^B and threshold w^* that satisfy $W^A(w^A, w^*) - W^B(w^B, w^*) = 0$ and the following expectations conditions:

• If w^* is in $]w_{min}, w_{max}[: w^A = E[w|w \geq w^*]$, $w^B = E[w|w \leq w^*]$, then both systems are active, and the equilibrium is called an *AB*-equilibrium;

• If $w^* \leq w_{min}: w^A = \overline{w}$, $w^B = w_{min}$, then only system *A* is active, and the equilibrium is called an *A*-equilibrium;

• If $w^* \geq w_{max}: w^A = w_{max}$, $w^B = \overline{w}$, then only system *B* is active, and the equilibrium is called a *B*-equilibrium.

For an active system, the expectation condition says that the anticipation of the average wage of the contributors to an active system is correct equal to its expectation conditional on individuals' choices.[7] For an inactive system, the condition needs a justification: since there are no contributors, the conditional expectation of their average wage is not well defined. Hence individuals' behaviors are supported by some beliefs about this wage.[8] In the above definition, the beliefs are those justified by a perfect equilibrium argument. If the set of contributors to *B* is small, for example, it is formed by the individuals whose wages are close to the minimum. Taking the limit, if only *A* is active, the belief on w^B is the minimum wage. A similar argument justifies that with only *B* active, the belief on w^A is set to the maximum wage.

Before going further, it is helpful to note that *the system the less favorable to high-income workers is eliminated whenever it is also the less efficient.* The intuition is clear. Suppose there is an *AB*-equilibrium, and consider a w^*-worker who is indifferent between *A* and *B* (a similar argument shows that a *B*-equilibrium does not exist by considering workers with wage w_{max}). By choosing *A*, the worker would benefit from the larger efficiency return provided by *A*. Furthermore, since the wage w^* is not greater than w^A, he can only benefit from redistribution in *A* instead of being penalized by it in *B*: he definitely prefers *A* to *B*, a contradiction. The analysis is more complex if, from the point of view of low-income workers, efficiency and redistribution benefits enter into conflict. The following proposition characterizes the equilibrium configurations in function of the parameters:

Proposition 5.1 Let system *A* be more favorable than *B* to high-income workers. There exists

• An *A*-equilibrium if and only if

$$W^A(\overline{w}, w_{min}) - R^B w_{min} \geq 0 \Leftrightarrow R^B - R^A \leq D^A \frac{\overline{w} - w_{min}}{w_{min}} ; \qquad (5.12)$$

- A B-equilibrium if and only if

$$W^B(\overline{w}, w_{max}) - R^A w_{max} \geq 0 \Leftrightarrow D^B \frac{w_{max} - \overline{w}}{w_{max}} \leq R^B - R^A; \tag{5.13}$$

- An AB-equilibrium if either an A- and a B-equilibrium both exist and (5.12) and (5.13) hold or no one exists and neither (5.12) nor (5.13) holds.

It follows that an equilibrium always exists. As already said, it can only be an A-equilibrium if A is more efficient: (5.12) holds but not (5.13) if $R^B \leq R^A$. Otherwise, the tradeoff between efficiency and redistribution for low-income or top-income workers determines equilibrium configurations. To see this, let us explain how the equilibrium conditions are obtained. To check whether A alone can be in equilibrium, assume that A is chosen by every worker. The average wage w^A is equal to the overall mean $\overline{w}$. To form an equilibrium, it suffices that workers whose wages are close to the minimum level w_{min} have no incentives to subscribe to B. This gives condition (5.12), which results from the following tradeoff. By subscribing to B, w_{min}-workers lose all the redistribution benefits in A without getting any in B (because wages in B are roughly identical), but they also benefit from the larger return in B (assumed to be more efficient). If the loss outweighs the efficiency gain, an A-equilibrium is obtained. Since the larger the ratio $\overline{w}/w_{min}$ is, the larger the loss in redistributive benefits, a low value for the minimum wage makes it more likely that an A-equilibrium will exist. Similarly, a large value for the extent of the redistribution in A (subject to A being more favorable to high-income workers) makes it more likely that an A-equilibrium will exist.

Similarly, a B-equilibrium is obtained if workers whose wages are close to the maximum level w_{max} have no incentives to subscribe to A, which gives condition (5.13). The condition is strong: it requires that top-income workers are better off by subscribing to system B applied to the whole population rather than by subscribing to A without redistribution loss. As the ratio $w_{max}/\overline{w}$ and the extent of the redistribution in B increase, the redistribution losses for a top-income worker subscribing to B rather than to A outweighs the efficiency gains: B alone is in equilibrium only for a small enough ratio and small value for D^B.

Note that the above arguments are valid whatever the assumption on the distribution of earnings, whether continuous or not: only the incentives of the top- or bottom-income workers matter.[9] This insight is likely to be quite robust and to extend to more general benefit rules.

According to this discussion, as the range of wages is enlarged, the redistribution effects become predominant and determine the equilibrium. Workers who most benefit from redistribution and those who are the more penalized by it are both encouraged to choose the system that is more favorable to high-income workers: for sufficiently low w_{min} and sufficiently large w_{max}, only condition (5.12) holds. This gives the following corollary:

Corollary If the range of wages is sufficiently large, then only the system that is more favorable to high-income workers is active at equilibrium.

Instead, various equilibrium configurations are possible when the dispersion of wages is not too large and the system the less favorable to high income is the more efficient. Even the three types of equilibrium can simultaneously exist. As long as redistribution or efficiency is not dominant factor, the incentives conditions, as given by (5.12) and (5.13) are to some extent independent: one bears on incomes at the bottom, and the other at the top. This is illustrated by the following example.

Example (Continued)
Consider again the illustrative case in which $\alpha^A > \alpha^B$ and $\tau^A > \tau^B$. We know that when one system is both more efficient and more favorable to high-income workers than the other, it is only active at equilibrium. It immediately follows that only the more Beveridgean system B is active if pay-as-you-go systems are sufficiently inefficient, while it is the more Bismarckian system A if they are sufficiently efficient.[10] Taking the values of the France–United Kingdom example above, this gives the following:

• For $g/r > 1$, an A-equilibrium obtains because system A is more efficient and more favorable to high income than B;

• For $g/r < 0.7$, a B-equilibrium obtains because A is less efficient and less favorable to high-income workers than B.

It remains to determine what happens when efficiency and redistribution enter into conflict, which occurs here for $1 > g/r > 0.7$: A is more favorable to high-income workers but less efficient than B. The case $g/r = 0.8$ is illustrated in figure 5.1.

In the top graph, the dashed line represents $R^B w - W^A(\overline{w}, w)$ as a function of w. According to (5.12), there is an A-equilibrium if it is negative at w_{min}—that is, if $w_{min} < a \approx 0.6$. Similarly, the normal line represents $W^B(\overline{w}, w) - R^A w$, and according to (5.13) there is a B-equilibrium if it is positive at w_{max}, which gives $w_{max} < b \approx 1.5$. The difference in wealth at the initial situation $W^A(\overline{w}, w) - W^B(\overline{w}, w)$ is also represented (the thick line). This is useful for subsequent welfare comparisons and for understanding the initial incentives to choose one system rather than another. Here the difference is increasing in w because A is more favorable than B to high-income workers. Also it is negative at the mean value $\overline{w}$ because B is more efficient than A and $W^I(\overline{w}, \overline{w}) = R^I \overline{w}$.

The bottom graph summarizes the equilibrium types as a function of the range of earnings keeping the mean constant. When the range is small ($w_{min} > 0.6$ and $w_{max} < 1.5$), there is only a B-equilibrium: efficiency effects are dominant. One checks that for these values, at the initial situation, all citizens in A would prefer system B: the difference $W^A(\overline{w}, w) - W^B(\overline{w}, w)$ is negative in the relevant range for w. This is always true, as is shown in proposition 5.2. As the range is increased, we move to the northwest and only the A-equilibrium remains: the redistribution effects become dominant.

Welfare

In light of these results, one may wonder whether introducing free choice is beneficial. To avoid considering too many cases, I discuss the situation in which an I equilibrium is obtained (I do not consider an AB-equilibrium). Then the winners or losers are easily determined. To see this, note that any w-worker gets an intertemporal wealth equal to $W^I(\overline{w}, w)$. Thus, citizens in country I are not affected by the reform, while in J the losers (respectively, winners) are those for whom the intertemporal wealth $W^J(\overline{w}, w)$ was larger (respectively, smaller) than $W^I(\overline{w}, w)$.

To fix the idea, let A be more favorable to high-income workers. Then, using that $W^I(\overline{w}, \overline{w}) = R^I \overline{w}$, the following inequalities hold:

$$(R^A - R^B)\overline{w} > W^A(\overline{w}, w) - W^B(\overline{w}, w) \quad \text{for } w < \overline{w}, \quad \text{and} \tag{5.14}$$

$$(R^A - R^B)\overline{w} < W^A(\overline{w}, w) - W^B(\overline{w}, w) \quad \text{for } w > \overline{w}. \tag{5.15}$$

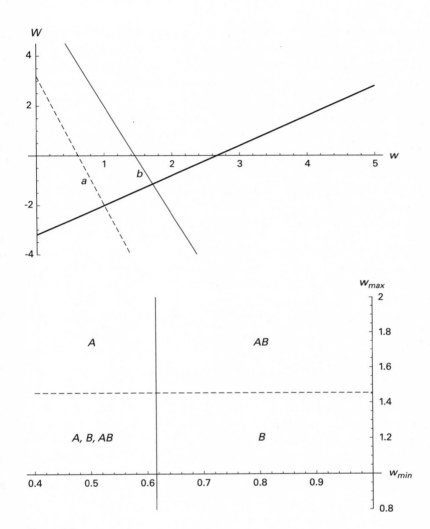

Figure 5.1

Parameters: $\tau A/\tau B = 2$, $\alpha^A = 0.8$, $\alpha^B = 0.2$, $g/r = 0.8$, $w = 1$.

Top graph: The horizontal axis represents w, the vertical one differences in wealth, multiplied by 100. The thick line represents $W^A(w, .) - W^B(w, .)$, the dashed line $R^B w - W^A(w, w)$ (there is an A-equilibrium if $w_{min} < a \approx 0.6$) and the normal line: $W^B(w, w) - R^A w$ (there is a B-equilibrium if $w_{max} < b \approx 1.5$).

Bottom graph: Equilibria as function of w_{min} and w_{max}.

If A is not less efficient than B, there is a A-equilibrium only. Also, surely in country B all citizens whose income is larger than $\bar{w}$ are made better off from (5.15) since $R^A - R^B \geq 0$. Other citizens also are better off—maybe all if efficiency gains are large enough relative to redistribution effects.

Assume now that A is less efficient than B. If a B-equilibrium obtains, the opening of the systems is beneficial without ambiguity, as stated by the following proposition:

Proposition 5.2 The system that is more favorable to high-income workers can be eliminated only if, at the initial situation, all individuals are better off with the other system. If A is more favorable to high-income workers, a B-equilibrium exists only if

$$W^B(\bar{w}, w) \geq W^A(\bar{w}, w) \quad \text{for any } w \text{ in } [w_{min}, w_{max}] \tag{5.16}$$

and thus leads to a (weak) Pareto improvement over the initial situation.

Condition (5.16) is strong, but it is not a sufficient condition for a B-equilibrium to exist. The range of wages must be small enough. Consider the example again. If $1.5 < w_{max} < 2.8$ and $w_{min} < 0.6$, only the A-equilibrium exists, but B applied to the whole population gives a larger wealth to every one than A.

Instead, if the A-equilibrium obtains, some B citizens must lose since the less efficient system is now in place in country B. In particular, from (5.14) and the fact that $R^A < R^B$, all workers who earn less than the average wage are worse off. Since the average wage is typically larger than the median value, more than a majority of workers in B are made worse off by the reform. How can this happen? The dynamics contemplated below help to explain this point. Assuming that initially all workers who prefer B choose it, system A becomes more attractive, which triggers new choices, which may eventually lead to all choosing A. It can even happen that all workers in B are hurt at a A-equilibrium. In that case, implementing B for everybody would be weakly Pareto improving. This occurs if (5.16) is met but the A-equilibrium obtains. This is surely the case if the A-equilibrium is unique ($1.5 < w_{max} < 2.8$ and $w_{min} < 0.6$ in the example).

To sum up, even though the model is very simple, the welfare impact of the opening of the systems largely depends on the situation at hand. If redistribution losses or gains are too important, there are few chances that a Pareto improvement will be obtained.

At this point, it is worth comparing our analysis with Casarico (2000). In two countries with identical economies, compulsory pension systems are in place, unfunded in one country and fully funded in the other. Redistribution plays no role (the analysis is conducted with a representative individual in each country). The chapter focuses on the impact of the differences in pension systems on capital integration when capital becomes fully mobile, labor remaining immobile. Production is carried out through a neoclassical production function. Owing to the different pension systems, investments (and hence their returns) differ in the two countries before capital integration. Capital integration has a welfare effect because the return to investment is equalized across countries. While this effect is clearly absent in our analysis, Casarico does not allow workers to choose a system. If they could, they would all choose the more efficient (since there is no redistribution).

Dynamics

By keeping the tax rate constant, the balance of a system is ensured through adjustments in pension benefits. As a result, a system can be thought of as a defined-contribution one. In a correct expectations framework, as just considered, it is also a defined-benefit one. It may no longer be true under some dynamics. Dynamics are determined by expectations and information. At the time that workers have to choose a system, they are concerned with the wage level of the current and next contributors to each system. The current ones determine the future redistributive gains or losses within a system, and the next ones give the level of pension benefits. Starting from the initial situation in which each system in place in a country is exclusively for the citizens, I consider here the evolution of the systems driven by myopic expectations.

Myopic expectations mean that workers at time t who do not know yet the choice of their contemporaries and descendants expect that they will perform the same choice as the previous generation. For example, initially, all workers assume that the average contributors' wage is identical in each system and is equal to $\bar{w}$. A threshold value w_0^* for wages is determined, according to which all workers with income larger (respectively, smaller) than the threshold choose A (respectively, B), still assuming A is more favorable than B to high-income workers. Afterwards, the evolution of the system is described as follows. Let w_{t-1}^* be the threshold value between A and B at time $t - 1$.

Workers at time t observe this value. Under myopic expectations, they expect the choice of current and next contributors to remain unchanged. Thus, they expect the average wage level of the current and next contributors to each system to be given by

$$w_{t-1}^A = E[w|w \geq w_{t-1}^*], \quad w_{t-1}^B = E[w|w \leq w_{t-1}^*]. \tag{5.17}$$

It follows that a w-worker at date t evaluates the wealth generated by system I as $W^I(w_{t-1}^I, w)$ defined by (5.10) and chooses between A and B, accordingly. A new threshold w_t^* level is determined and so on.

Proposition 5.3 Let system A be more favorable than B to high-income workers. Assume myopic expectations. Dynamics converge to (1) the (unique) A-equilibrium if A is more efficient than B, and (2) in one step to the B-equilibrium if it exists. Also dynamics surely converge to an equilibrium if $D^B E[w|w \leq x] - D^A E[w|w \geq x]$ is non-decreasing.

In the first two cases convergence always occurs. Note that the B-equilibrium Pareto dominates the A-equilibrium if both exist (by proposition 5.2). Therefore a good equilibrium is selected. In other cases, an additional assumption is needed. To understand why, consider the opening of the systems in which workers choose the systems assuming the same distribution within each one. Since those who choose B are less wealthy than those who choose A, the redistribution within the system B is diminished and within A increased: more individuals will choose A next period. The monotonicity assumption ensures that the set of workers who choose A will grow. The assumption is satisfied if D^A is sufficiently low (A Bismarckian, for instance) or if wages are uniformly distributed.[11]

Concluding Remarks
Even though the model is simple in many dimensions, it helps to highlight some features that are likely to be quite robust. First, the analysis shows that the system that is preferred by high-income workers is not necessarily the more Bismarckian one. Both the levels of the contribution rates and the efficiency or inefficiency of unfunded systems play important roles. In particular, in situations in which unfunded are perceived as very inefficient, the system with the lower contribution rate is preferred. Second, a large dispersion of wage earnings eliminates the system that is less favorable to high-income workers even if it is

the more efficient: the redistribution effects become dominant for the workers who most benefit from redistribution or for those who are the most penalized by it. Third, free choice does not necessarily lead to select the more efficient system. In some cases, the new situation may be Pareto dominated by the initial one.

The analysis has been conducted under strong simplifying assumptions. It should be extended in several directions to test the robustness of the results. Production and endogenous factor prices could be introduced. Uncertainty about production and population growth would make comparisons between the rates of return of the systems less trivial and more realistic. Liquidity constraints, which are likely to be binding on low-income workers, should be taken into account.

Finally, to incorporate political elements into the analysis would be interesting. It would require describing the adjustments of the systems confronted with the impact of free choice, even if such adjustments are slow. The analysis would then be similar in some aspects to that of fiscal competition (see, e.g., Epple and Romer, 1991; Wildasin, 2003). A basic concern is whether factor mobility, as dictated by the European construction, necessarily undermines redistributive policies. Not surprisingly, the literature on taxation between areas—regions, jurisdictions, countries—and on the limitation on redistribution due to the mobility of capital or labor is vast and growing (see the survey of Cremer and Pestieau, 2003).

Proofs

Recall that under the assumption of stationarity, the wealth of a w-worker contributing to system I with expectations w^I is given by (5.10)

$$W^I(w^I, w) = R^I w + D^I(w^I - w).$$

Proof of Proposition 5.1   Let us determine the conditions under which there is an active equilibrium with only A. In this case, $w^A = \bar{w}$ and $w^B = w_{min}$. An equilibrium is obtained if and only if an individual whose wages are minimum is not incited to choose system B. This is written as $W^A(\bar{w}, w_{min}) - W^B(w_{min}, w_{min}) \geq 0$. Using the expression of wealth (5.10), this gives the inequality (5.12).

In a similar way, a situation with only B active forms an equilibrium if an individual whose wage is maximal is not incited to choose system A. Since $w^A = w_{max}$ and $w^B = \bar{w}$, this gives $W^A(w_{max}, w_{max}) - W^B(\bar{w}, w_{max}) \leq 0$ which yields (5.13).

It remains to consider an AB-equilibrium. Let the function ϕ be defined on $[w_{min}, w_{max}]$ by

$$\phi(x) = W^A(E[w|w \geq x], x) - W^B(E[w|w \leq x], x). \tag{5.18}$$

By continuity of the distribution of wages, the function ϕ is continuous. An equilibrium with two active systems is associated with w^* in $]w_{min}, w_{max}[$ that satisfy $\phi(w^*) = 0$. Note that (5.12) is equivalent to $\phi(w_{min}) \geq 0$ and (5.13) to $\phi(w_{max}) \leq 0$. By continuity of ϕ, it follows that if no I-equilibrium exists, there is an interior w^* such that $\phi(w^*) = 0$. Similarly, if both equilibria exist and the inequalities are strict, there is also an AB-equilibrium.   ∎

Proof of Proposition 5.2 As just seen, a B-equilibrium exits iff $W^B(\overline{w}, w_{max}) - W^A(w_{max}, w_{max}) \geq 0$. Since $W^A(w_{max}, w_{max}) = R^A w_{max} \geq W^A(\overline{w}, w_{max})$ (because of the redistribution loss), this gives $W^B(\overline{w}, w_{max}) - W^A(\overline{w}, w_{max}) \geq 0$, which implies $W^B(\overline{w}, w) - W^A(\overline{w}, w) \geq 0$ for any w (because B is less favorable to high-income workers).   ∎

Proof of Proposition 5.3 To simplify notation, set $\Delta = R^A - R^B - D^A + D^B$. The assumption that system A is more favorable to high-income workers than B is written as $\Delta > 0$. The choice of a w-worker at t is made on the basis of the difference in expected wealth

$$W^A(w_{t-1}^A, w) - W^B(w_{t-1}^B, w) = \Delta w + D^A w_{t-1}^A - D^B w_{t-1}^B, \tag{5.19}$$

where the values w_{t-1}^A are w_{t-1}^B are the average wages of the contributors to each system observed at time $t - 1$. By positivity of Δ, the function is increasing in w. Thus, all workers whose wage is larger than $(D^B w_{t-1}^B - D^A w_{t-1}^A)/\Delta$ choose A, and the others choose B. If this wage value is larger than w_{max}, then everybody chooses A, and if it is smaller than w_{min}, then everybody chooses B. To define the threshold w_t^*, it is convenient to consider the projection P on the interval $[w_{min}, w_{max}]$:

$$P(x) = w_{min} \quad \text{if } x < w_{min},$$

$$= x, x \in [w_{min}, w_{max}],$$

$$= w_{max} \quad \text{if } x > w_{max}.$$

The threshold w_t^* is defined by

$$w_t^* = P((D^B w_{t-1}^B - D^A w_{t-1}^A)/\Delta). \tag{5.20}$$

The values w_{t-1}^A are w_{t-1}^B expected at t are based on observed at time $t-1$. Thus, at the opening of the systems $t = 0$, both are equal to the average wage

$$w_{-1}^B = w_{-1}^A = \overline{w} \tag{5.21}$$

and afterwards at $t > 0$, they satisfy

$$w_{t-1}^A = E[w|w \geq w_{t-1}^*] \quad \text{and} \quad w_{t-1}^B = E[w|w \leq w_{t-1}^*]. \tag{5.22}$$

Conditions (5.20), (5.21), and (5.22) define w_0^* and w_t^* as a function of w_{t-1}^*. A fixed point w^* of the sequence gives an equilibrium. This is clear if w^* is in $]w_{min}, w_{max}[$. Otherwise—say, if $w^* = w_{max}$ is a fixed point—then knowing that everybody chooses B at $t-1$, everybody makes the same choice at t: condition (5.13) is fulfilled and a B-equilibrium is obtained. Similarly, w_{min} is a fixed point iff there is an A-equilibrium.

We first prove that $w_t^* \leq w_0^*$ for any t. Note that w_0^* is the threshold value associated with expectations $w_{-1}^A = w_{-1}^B = \overline{w}$. At any subsequent step, the average wage in A can only be larger and that in B can only be smaller. This implies that the incentives to choose A are larger than at the initial step. Formally note that the inequalities $E[w|w \geq x] \geq \overline{w} \geq E[w|w \leq x]$ hold whatever x. Thus, surely $w_{t-1}^A \geq \overline{w} \geq w_{t-1}^B$. Since P is nondecreasing, (5.20) yields $w_t^* \leq w_0^*$.

Assume first A to be more efficient than B: $R^A - R^B \geq 0$. Since inequalities $E[w|w \geq x] \geq x \geq E[w|w \leq x]$ always hold, $(D^B w_{t-1}^B - D^A w_{t-1}^A) \leq (D^B - D^A) w_{t-1}^*$. Thus, if $D^B - D^A \leq 0$, the argument of P in (5.20) is negative: $w_t^* = w_{min}$ whatever t, the (unique) A-equilibrium is obtained at the opening. If $D^B - D^A > 0$, then $\Delta \geq D^B - D^A \geq 0$: the argument of P in (5.20) is less than w_{t-1}^*. Thus, the sequence w_t^* decreases as long as it is above w_{min}: it converges to the A-equilibrium.

Assume now that a B-equilibrium exists. From proposition 5.2, everybody chooses B initially: $w_0^* = w_{max}$. Afterward, (5.13) gives $w_1^* = w_{max}$: the B-equilibrium is reached. Conversely, if a B-equilibrium does not exist, surely $w_1^* < w_{max}$. Otherwise, $w_1^* = w_{max} \leq w_0^*$ implies that w_{max} is a fixed point of the sequence—namely, that there is a B-equilibrium.

Finally, assuming that B is more efficient than A, consider the situation without a B-equilibrium. Let the function $D^B E[w|w \leq x] - D^A E[w|w \geq x]$ be nondecreasing. By induction, using $w_1^* \leq w_0^*$, the sequence w_t^* decreases thus converges (since it is bounded). Furthermore, since $w_1^* < w_{max}$ (because there is no B-equilibrium), the sequence w_t^* converges to a value strictly less than w_{max}—that is, to an equilibrium of type AB or A.   ■

Notes

École des Hautes Études en Sciences Sociales at Paris-Jourdan Sciences Economiques, École Normale Supérieure, 48 Boulevard Jourdan, 75014 Paris, France, e-mail ⟨demange@pse.ens.fr⟩. This chapter benefited from the detailed comments of George Casamatta, Robert Fenge, Christian Gollier, Fabien Moizeau, and Pierre Pestieau. I also thank the seminar participants of the November 2004 CESifo conference "Strategies for Reforming Pension Schemes" for their remarks.

1. Cross-country comparisons are hazardous and vary according to the definition of *social security*. In line with the objectives of the chapter, I have tried to consider only the first pillars the systems. Data for France, Germany, and Italy are taken from ⟨http://www.ssa.gov/policy/docs/progdesc/ssptw/2004-2005/europe/guide.html⟩. The same document gives 23.8 percent for the United Kingdom, but it includes the second pillar, which is also mandatory but funded. For a description of the U.K. system, see the European Union Commission and the Council Joint Report *Adequate and Sustainable Pensions* (2003).

2. I use here the modeling of Casamatta, Cremer, and Pestieau (2000).

3. The pension may not be correctly anticipated (even though we require it to be at equilibrium). The only assumption that is needed is that the anticipation is single-valued: the young individual makes decisions as if he will receive π.

4. The benefit rule can also be written as

$$\frac{\pi_{w,t}}{w} = \left(\alpha + (1 - \alpha)\frac{\overline{w}_{t-1}}{w} \right) \frac{\bar{\pi}_t}{\overline{w}_{t-1}},$$

which shows how replacement rates vary with income.

5. The argument cannot be extended too much. It cannot be deduced from expression (5.6) that if $g > r$, then increasing the rate of contribution always leads to a Pareto improvement. Beyond a certain contribution rate, no young individual saves, which invalidates the approach by intertemporal wealth. To treat this question correctly, the return on capital must be endogenous, determined by a production function. Then the rate of return becomes larger than population growth if saving/investment is sufficiently low.

6. This remark does not account for the reform that has just been decided in France. The minimum level for pension benefits has been increased up to 85 percent of the minimal wage. For a large fraction of low-income earners, this constraint may become binding, which would make the French system more Beveridgean than previously. I thank Thomas Piketty for mentioning this point to me.

7. Note that because the wage distribution is identical in the two countries, the wage distribution in the union of the two countries is identical to that of a single country. Thus, if only I is active, then $w^I = \overline{w}$.

8. A referee objects that a young individual can choose a system that has no retirees (say, B) and get pension benefits when old for free. It is true only if in next period a young person will agree to contribute to B. Looking at intertemporal wealth, which amounts to considering stationary behavior, accounts for this requirement.

9. With a discrete distribution, conditions are for an I-equilibrium to exist. The AB-equilibria may be a little bit different: some may be semipooling, meaning that individuals with the same wage choose distinct systems (they must be indifferent between both).

10. The first case holds if both inequalities $g < r$ and $\tau^B(1 - \alpha^B g/r) < \tau^A(1 - \alpha^A g/r)$ hold, and the second holds if both inequalities are reversed.

11. Since A is less efficient and more favorable to high income than B, both inequalities $0 > R^A - R^B > D^A - D^B$ hold. Thus, the monotonicity condition is met if the slope of $E[w|w \geq x]$ is not larger than that of $E[w|w \leq x]$. This is true for a uniform distribution since the conditional expectations are, respectively, equal to $(w_{max} + x)/2$ and $(x + w_{min})/2$.

References

Aaron, H. (1966). "The Social Security Paradox." *Canadian Journal of Economics and Political Sciences*, 32, 371–376.

Breyer, F., and M. Kolmar. (2002). "Are National Pension Systems Efficient If Labor Is (Im)perfectly Mobile?" *Journal of Public Economics*, 83, 347–374.

Brown, J. R., O. Mitchell, and J. M. Poterba. (2001). "The Role of Real Annuities and Indexed Bonds in an Individual Accounts Retirement Program." In J. Campbell and M. Feldstein, eds., *Risk Aspects of Investment-Based Social Security Reform*. Chicago: University of Chicago Press for NBER.

Browning, E. (1975). "Why the Social Insurance Budget Is Too Large in a Democracy." *Economic Inquiry*, 13, 373–388.

Casamatta, G., H. Cremer, and P. Pestieau. (2000). "The Political Economy of Social Security." *Scandinavian Journal of Economics*, 102, 502–522.

Casarico, A. (2000). "Pension Systems in Integrated Capital Markers." *Topics in Economic Analysis and Policy*, 1, 1–17.

Cremer, H., and P. Pestieau. (2003). "Factor Mobility and Redistribution: A Survey." Mimeo.

De la Croix, D., and M. Doepke. (2003). "Inequality and Growth: Why Differential Fertility Matters." *American Economic Review*, 93, 1091–1113.

Diamond, P. (1965). "National Debt in a Neoclassical Growth Model." *American Economic Review*, 55, 1126–1150.

Epple, D., and T. Romer. (1991). "Mobility and Redistribution." *Journal of Political Economy*, 99(4), 828–858.

European Union Commission and Council. (2003, March). *Adequate and Sustainable Pensions*. Brussels.

Galasso, V., and P. Profeta. (2002). "The Political Economy of Social Security: A Survey." *European Journal of Political Economy*, 18, 1–29.

Gale, David. (1973). "Pure Exchange Equilibrium of Dynamic Economic Models." *Journal of Economic Theory*, 6(1), 12–36.

Homburg, S., and W. Richter. (1993). "Debt and Public Pension Schemes in the European Community." *Journal of Economics*, suppl. 7, 51–63.

Philipson, T., and G. Becker. (1998). "Old-Age Longevity and Mortality Contingent Claims." *Journal of Political Economy*, 106(3), 550–574.

Samuelson, P. (1958). "An Exact Consumption-Loan Model of Interest with or without the Social Contrivance of Money." *Journal of Political Economy*, 66, 467–482.

Whitehouse, E. (2003). "The Value of Pension Entitlements: A Model of Nine OECD Countries." OECD Social, Employment, and Migration Working Paper 9.

Wildasin, D. (2003). "Fiscal Competition in Space and Time." *Journal of Public Economics*, 87, 2571–2588.

III

Funded Pension Systems

6 Public Policy and Retirement Saving Incentives in the United Kingdom

Woojen Chung, Richard Disney, Carl Emmerson, and Matthew Wakefield

How can governments encourage households to save for retirement? In the United Kingdom, many households rely on private pensions rather than social security for much of their retirement income (see Johnson, Stears, and Webb, 1998; Banks, Blundell, Disney, and Emmerson, 2002; Banks, Emmerson, Oldfield, and Tetlow, 2005). Given the importance of retirement saving in the United Kingdom, there has recently been well-publicized concern as to the extent of a savings gap between how much working-age individuals should save for retirement and what they actually save (Pensions Commission, 2004). There is not much agreement in the literature, however, about which policies work in enhancing retirement saving and which policies do not. The prolonged debate around this question in the United States (see Bernheim and Scholz, 1993; Poterba, 1994; "Government Incentives for Saving," 1996; Attanasio and DeLeire, 2002) has led to no general conclusions. There is very little evidence for the United Kingdom on the issue despite the plethora of recent U.K. reforms of both the pension and the tax regimes covering retirement saving.

Economists point to the difficulties that households face in making the consistent, cognitive choices that are required to engage in what Diamond (2004) terms "adequate preparation" for retirement (rather than more narrowly "adequate saving"). Recent evidence for the United Kingdom suggests that individuals have relatively low levels of basic financial numeracy, that these levels decline with age, and that lower financial numeracy is associated with lower levels of pension coverage even when we control for other measures of cognitive ability, wealth, and education (Banks and Oldfield, 2006). Leaving aside the broader question of whether such deficiencies provide a rationale for greater public provision of social security (as opposed to policies aimed at improving individuals' abilities to plan their own finances), there is the narrow question of whether individuals understand and therefore respond to changes in retirement saving incentives. This is an important issue for policy makers. Indeed, much of the debate in the United States around the interpretation of evidence on household responses to changes in retirement-saving incentives has implicitly reflected the contrasting views of researchers about whether households are broadly making lifetime-consistent choices or whether limited cognitive functioning leads to the use of rules of thumb or other potentially time-inconsistent saving strategies.

Limited cognitive abilities of would-be savers have been adduced as a reason for greater prescription of household saving behavior by the government—underpinning, for example, the case for defaulting individuals into a private pension plan rather than relying on individuals making active decisions to save for retiement, as proposed in the United Kingdom in the government's recent White Paper (Department of Work and Pensions, 2006) in the light of the recommendations of the Pensions Commission (2005). Some proponents of government intervention to regulate retirement saving levels have a tendency to see the government as the benevolent nonmyopic agent that is able to formulate rational policies to provide adequate retirement incomes in the face of the time inconsistency, myopia, or other cognitive failures of households. Indeed, in an extreme version of this hypothesis, households may actively vote for a government with retirement policies (such as design of a social security program or tax regime) that reflect the intertemporally consistent preferences of the median voter when that voter knows that he or she will be temporally inconsistent in their own saving behavior (Cremer, De Donder, Maldonado, and Pestieau, 2006).

But this is an implausible argument. As Diamond (2004, p. 5) states: "the political process is not equivalent to a consistent approach to policy over time (which, it seems to me, is an essential property of democracy given divergent preferences and views)." If public retirement policies are themselves temporally *in*consistent (and this fits in well with the central strand of macroeconomic theory, which starts from the premise that governments have strong incentives to behave in an inconsistent manner), then the difficulties facing households that are attempting to adopt time-consistent retirement strategies are heightened. To put the point a different way, a retrospective analysis of household behavior that suggests that households have failed to prepare adequately for retirement may simply reflect past public-policy failures rather than cognitive failures by households.

The United Kingdom offers an interesting case study of this issue. Various policies in recent years have been designed to broaden the fraction of households actively saving for retirement and also to raise the amount of retirement saving per household. Some of these policies are summarized in the next section of the chapter. This U.K. retirement-policy trajectory has not always been consistent over time, and it is thereby hardly surprising that saving outcomes also appear, to the retrospective observer, to be time inconsistent or to lack any sense of rational behavior. But this may primarily reflect the inevitably inconsistent approach to policy over time described by Diamond rather than cognitive failure.

To investigate these issues further (and having described the main changes to the policy regime in the next section), we focus on two policy experiments that occurred in U.K. retirement-saving policy in the last two decades. The first is the introduction of Personal Pensions in April 1988, and the second is the introduction of Stakeholder Pensions in April 2001.

The case of Personal Pensions is discussed below. Personal Pensions are individual retirement accounts with insurance companies that, when introduced, provided generous incentives to individuals differentiated by age group. Standard actuarial calculations suggest that to offset the effects of compound interest and make the incentive to save in a defined-contribution pension approximately equal for all individuals, incentives should be skewed toward older individuals. However, the incentive structure that was implemented effectively geared incentives toward younger individuals, perhaps reflecting the view that younger households had short time horizons and therefore did not prioritize retirement saving. The outcome in terms of enrollment (and also after the government changed its policy in the mid-1990s) is described in the section on Personal Pensions.

When the Stakeholder Pensions were introduced in April 2001, these were no-frills individual retirement accounts and employers with more than five employees who do not offer other private pension provision were obliged to nominate a stakeholder pension for their workers. They were designed to overcome some of the difficulties arising from the charging structure of Personal Pensions, which were believed to lead to excessively high charges and were again intended to increase the proportion of households actively saving for retirement. The policy was explicitly targeted for middle earners, although a concurrent and less publicized change in the structure of incentives had a different incentive effect across the household income distribution. We describe these changes and show how the responses of households in terms of increased enrollment in private pensions reflected these various changes in incentives.

Finally, the chapter draws together the evidence from these case studies. It is impossible to say whether the evidence supports the proposition that households have fully understood and temporally consistent retirement saving plans. Indeed, without a benchmark of optimality derived from a sophisticated structural calibration exercise drawing on parameter values from empirical studies of retirement saving in the United Kingdom, it is hard to know what optimal household saving would be like in the United Kingdom (for analysis of this kind for the United States, see Scholz, Seshadri, and Khitatrakun, 2006). What *is* clear from these case studies, however, is that a significant number of households appeared to understand the true incentives arising from these policy experiments, possibly rather better than the policy makers themselves as in both the cases of Personal Pensions and Stakeholder Pensions, the outcomes appeared at odds with the professed aims or targets of the policies themselves. At the very least, these results suggest that we should err on the side of caution in asserting that policy makers in government have superior knowledge to households about what should be the optimal behavior of the latter in the context of retirement saving.

Retirement Saving Policy in the United Kingdom: A Brief Survey

The Structure of Pension Arrangements

Historically, U.K. retirement pensions have derived from two sources—(1) publicly provided social security, which is composed of a flat contributory or means-tested benefit supplemented by an earnings-related component introduced in the late 1970s, and (2) company-provided, defined-benefit (DB) (where the benefit is defined as a function of earnings, often final salary) occupational pensions. The introduction of the earnings-related component to social security from April 1978, known as the State Earnings-Related Pension Scheme (SERPS), provides one test of the impact of the changing policy regime on retirement saving behavior since accrual rates in this new pension regime were cohort-specific. Attanasio and Rohwedder (2003) exploit this cross-cohort experiment to measure a significant offset between public pension provision and private retirement saving.

In the early 1980s, the Thatcher administration became increasingly concerned with the future costs of the social security program and initiated a program of cutbacks in the generosity of both the flat and earnings-related components of the public program. At the same time, the government was anxious to encourage greater retirement saving and sought to broaden the range of private retirement saving vehicles that attracted favorable tax treatment. From April 1988, it extended the facility for contracting out (see the next subsection) to allow defined-contribution (DC) plans, whether provided by the employer or purchased as an individual retirement account from an insurer (a Personal Pension), to replace the earnings-related state benefit, SERPS. There were also changes in tax reliefs and other arrangements that are described in the next subsection.

Personal Pensions generated a good deal of controversy, primarily because they were perceived as having excessive administrative charges and because misselling led some individuals to leave their high-quality private DB plans and purchase more risky DC plans instead. They also (as is shown in the section on Personal Pensions) proved extremely financially costly to the government, which reversed its policy of generous tax reliefs on Personal Pensions in the mid-1990s. This immediately dampened demand for Personal Pensions.

The incoming New Labour administration, having promised a fundamental welfare reform in 1998, then decided to introduce a new category of personal pension, the Stakeholder Pension, from April 2001 (the differences from standard Personal Pensions are described in the section on Stakeholder Pensions) along with a host of changes to the social security regime. However, even these changes were deemed inadequate, and a series of critical reports led to new proposals for both social security and private pensions in 2005. Fundamental changes to the tax treatment of pensions have also occurred between 2001 and 2006 that are described below where appropriate.

Tax Reliefs and Contracting Out
In the U.K. program, there are two forms of implicit subsidy to retirement saving—the tax treatment of contributions to private pension schemes and the system by which private pensions may contract out of part of the social security program. Each needs a brief explanation

to motivate the ensuing discussion of changes to retirement saving vehicles and tax changes.

The U.K. tax treatment of retirement saving has historically been broadly EET. That is, contributions to pension schemes are tax-exempt (E) up to a ceiling, accrued returns to funds were partially tax-exempt (E) (although this has been curtailed by the removal of tax credits on equity dividends in 1997), and pensions are taxable (T) in payment other than a tax-free lump sum (although this too was capped in the late 1980s). Relative to other forms of investment, pensions have historically been somewhat less favorably treated than owner-occupied housing and more favorably treated than investment in financial assets. However, these differentials have eroded over time (for further details, see Dilnot, Disney, Johnson, and Whitehouse, 1994; Emmerson and Tanner, 2000; Booth and Cooper, 2002; and Leicester and Oldfield, 2004).

For employer-provided defined-benefit plans, the cap on tax relief effectively took the form of a cap on the final value of the pension that could be provided by an approved plan, since contribution rates must be actuarially adjusted to achieve the target benefit given the return on the pension fund. In defined-contribution schemes, in contrast, the tax-relief ceilings have taken the form of age-specific limits on the value of contributions that are eligible for tax relief. We discuss changes to these limits in greater detail in the context of the introduction of Stakeholder Pensions in April 2001. In April 2006, a major attempt was made to simplify this complex system of reliefs such that individuals can contribute up to the value of their gross earnings (up to an extremely high annual cap set at £215,000 in 2006 to 2007) to a pension each year as long as the total value of their pension fund or funds (whether a defined-benefit or defined-contribution plan) does not exceed a lifetime limit set at £1.5 million in 2006 to 2007, set to rise annually reaching £1.8 million in 2010 to 2011.

A second important feature of the U.K. pension program is that private pension schemes can contract out of the earnings-related tier of the public program. Originally, when only defined-benefit company pension plans were approved for contracting out, the private plan would take over responsibility from the state for paying an earnings-related pension to its retired members (this was known as the guaranteed minimum pension), and in exchange the employer and employee would pay lower social security contributions to the government. The government would wish approximately to balance the present value of forgone contributions against its gain in lower social security benefit payments in the future, although since individual pension funds were not risk-rated (by, for example, the ratio of prospective contributors to pensioners), this contracting-out arrangement subsidized the typical company's pension plan (Dilnot et al., 1994).

As mentioned earlier, in the late 1980s the government decided to encourage private provision of retirement saving vehicles by also permitting defined-contribution plans to contract out of the earnings-related tier of the social security program. These defined-contribution plans could be employer-provided or provided as individual retirement accounts by insurers. The latter, which initially dominated the defined-contribution provision, are known as Personal Pensions. The key feature of the contracted-out Personal Pension is that the value of the rebate of social security contributions is paid directly through the Department of Work and Pensions (previously Department of Social Security) to the pension provider on behalf of the individual. This minimizes the administrative cost of the contracting-out arrangement, although providers may (and did) exact a charge for managing the whole account. A typical retirement contract might include additional saving by the individual and possibly his or her employer. Such additional saving might in the future be affected by recent proposals (see Department of Work and Pensions, 2006) that would mean that individuals and their employers would make contributions to a private pension unless the employee actively chooses to opt out. We do not assess this proposal in the current chapter, but the implications of the combination of rebate structure and tax reliefs that existed when Personal Pensions were introduced in our analysis in the next section have relevance to this proposal.

Policy Experiments?
It is apparent from this all-too-brief run-through of U.K. pension policy that there have been numerous policy experiments implemented. The informational requirements for the rational saver of any one regime are daunting, without even considering whether households could anticipate the trajectory of reform that actually unfolded. Unfortunately for the researcher into household behavioral responses, the sheer frequency of these changes and the paucity of microdata make it difficult to track the effects of any one change. Hence, as described in the introduction, we look at two episodes in some detail to examine individual behavioral responses to changes in tax and retirement saving regimes.

It should also be noted (and this turns out to be important for our analysis of Stakeholder Pensions) that the basis of the personal tax system in the United Kingdom is the individual, so that household optimization will take account of individual tax-relief entitlements and incomes. However, both tax credits and means-tested benefits (which are important in the United Kingdom but are less central to the analysis here) are assessed on a family basis. We do not consider in detail the interaction between individual retirement saving and household-assessed entitlements to means-tested benefits here, although the issue is mentioned again in the section on Stakeholder Pensions.

Personal Pensions

The Introduction of Personal Pensions
In April 1988, individuals in the United Kingdom were offered the possibility of contracting out of the State Earnings-Related Pension Scheme (SERPS) into an Approved Personal Pension (APP) (and this could be backdated to April 1987). An APP is an individual retirement account offered by an approved insurer, in which an individual accumulates his or her pension contributions into a fund, the proceeds from which then had to be used to buy an annuity from an insurance company on retirement. The pension could be drawn at any age between fifty and seventy-five, and this flexible date of annuitization as well as the portability of APPs between employers suggested that such schemes would be particularly attractive to mobile workers inadequately covered by a company pension plan. In this section, we describe the incentives to contract out of SERPS and to purchase an APP and illustrate the effects of these incentives on behavior.

The then Conservative government saw greater choice of private pension arrangements as an essential ingredient in the desire to free up the labor market by encouraging greater flexibility and portability of pension arrangements. In 1985, it argued that "A major factor in the demand for personal pensions has always been that they should be fully portable. People must be able to take their own pensions with them without any loss when they change jobs. The Government are committed to ensuring that barriers in pensions do not affect job mobility" (Department of Social Security, 1985, 15). The introduction of Approved Personal Pensions was seen as a central component to this strategy of greater labor-market flexibility.

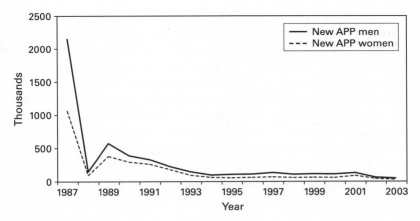

Figure 6.1
Approved Personal Pensions: New contracts.

The Department of Social Security had used as a working assumption that half a million people would choose to contract out of SERPS and opt to put their contracted-out rebate of social security contributions into a Personal Pension, although a contingency plan allowed for up to one and three-quarter million optants (Disney and Whitehouse, 1992a, 1992b). In the event, roughly 6 million new APP contracts had been approved by 1992, the bulk of them in the first year (see figure 6.1).

In terms of the reduction in public pension contributions arising from the transfer of contracted-out rebates to APP optants over the period 1988 to 1993, the cost to the government of this mass exodus from the public pension program was estimated to be £9.3 billions in 1991 values. It was simultaneously estimated by the government's spending watchdog, the National Audit Office, that this would lead to a prospective reduction in future spending on public pensions (SERPS) of £3.4 billion (National Audit Office, 1991). Overall, this policy therefore represented a net cost to the government of almost £6 billion, labelled by the *Financial Times* on January 4, 1991, as "The Pensions Débâcle."

Why did this discrepancy between predicted enrollment and actual enrollment, which was so expensive to the government's finances, occur? Was it a cognitive failure by individuals (perhaps arising from a temporary fad, illustrated by the rapid decline in new contracts after 1992), or was it a forecasting failure by government? To understand this, it is useful to look at the incentives to individuals to purchase an APP and the ways that these incentives varied across age groups. As described above, the key incentive to encourage Personal Pensions was that the government offered to transfer a proportion of the individual's social security contribution, known as the National Insurance (NI) contribution, into their *personal pension fund* in return for the individual forgoing entitlement to the social security benefit (SERPS) on reaching pensionable age. The individual would forgo the entitlements that would have accrued from the years in which they were contracted out of SERPS, but it was always open for the individual to contract back in to SERPS at a later stage in their working life, thus retaining their Personal Pension fund while accruing SERPS entitlements for the part of their working life for which they paid full NI contributions.

To make this contracting-out attractive, the government set the rebate of NI contributions for people who opted into a Personal Pension at 5.8 percent of earnings between a contribution ceiling and floor. In addition, as an extra incentive to attract workers to opt out of SERPS, for individuals who were not already opted out into a company pension plan, an extra 2 percent reduction in the NI contribution rate would apply from the starting date (1988) until April 1993. For anyone contracting out before April 1989, this extra incentive was paid for the previous two tax years as a lump sum into his or her personal pension account. Taking account of tax relief on individual pension contributions, this payment by the government of 5.8 percent plus 2 percent in NI contributions plus tax relief was worth 8.46 percent of eligible earnings (Disney and Whitehouse, 1992b) and even more in the first year for those who chose to take advantage of the retrospective provision.

It is worth repeating that this 8.46 percent contribution by the government into any individual's APP involved no additional contributions by the individual (although any such contributions would also be tax relieved, as described in the next section) and the only cost to the individual was that by opting to receive this contribution rebate, they would forgo accruing any entitlements to the earnings-related social security benefit (SERPS) for the period during which they were opted out of SERPS. So to understand the incentives involved for individuals to make this decision, it is necessary to value the prospective accrued value of their Personal Pension fund, relative to what those individuals would have obtained from the government investing those contributions in SERPS.

Using data from successive Family Expenditure Surveys to derive lifetime earnings profiles and given the rules underlying SERPS accruals and alternative assumptions as to the return accrued by the Personal Pension account, Disney and Whitehouse (1992a, 1992b) modeled the incentives for an individual to choose between opting to buy a personal pension or opting to remain in SERPS. A key issue is that a funded individual retirement account such as an APP is broadly front loaded in the sense that contributions made early in the working life compound in the fund over a longer period. In contrast, contributions to the unfunded public program, SERPS, do not exhibit this feature. Indeed, normally one might expect defined-benefit pension accruals to be backloaded in the sense that earnings rise over the life cycle and thus years of service at later, higher, earnings levels will increase pension accruals disproportionately. However, as in the United States, social security calculations in the United Kingdom revalue earnings earlier in life in relation to an average earnings index. This serves to somewhat flatten the effective age-earnings profile in calculating incremental social security entitlements. Finally, in judging an appropriate rate of return for contributions to a funded APP, it should be noted that the Government Actuary's Department (2000) estimated that real yields on bonds for the period 1985 to 1997 averaged 3.5 percent (average real returns on equities averaged 7.6 percent from 1963 to 1999) and that commission charges on APPs averaged the equivalent of a one percentage point reduction in returns over the period after April 1988.

For each individual with heterogeneous age-wage profiles, the optimal strategy of choosing between an APP and SERPS varied given the incentives existent in 1988. Disney and Whitehouse (1992b) illustrate the incentives with several illustrative examples. Figure 6.2 provides the illustration for a man on the average lifetime earnings trajectory of a skilled worker. Applying the accrual rules for SERPS, the applicable rebate of National Insurance contributions and various assumptions about the real rate of return on the APP fund *net of charges*, the year-by-year increment to the final value of the pension from each additional year's tenure in an APP paying different returns, and to SERPS, given the man's projected age-earnings profile, are plotted in the figure.

The age-earnings profile of pension increments in SERPS reflects the flattening of the age-earnings profile arising from the revaluation of

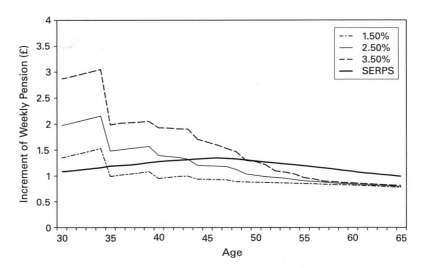

Figure 6.2
Annual increments to final pension age from the purchase of a personal pension (at three rates of return) versus SERPS.

earnings in calculating SERPS accruals by an average earnings index. The different incremental profiles for the APP reflect different assumptions as to the net-of-charges real return on the fund. The discontinuities reflect future changes in the projected contracted-out rebate made by the Government Actuary's Department in the early 1990s. (In fact, as is shown below, the whole system of rebates was subsequently radically revised.) Figure 6.2 shows that the differential between returns from APP and SERPS is age-varying and that there is an enormous discrepancy between the returns to opting for an APP relative to remaining in SERPS at all but the lowest assumed rate of return for younger individuals in the workforce. The cross-over points between the SERPS profile and the various APP profiles under different assumed rates of return show that at the very conservative real return of 1.5 percent this particular individual should opt for an APP, contract back in to SERPS at around age thirty-five, at 2.5 percent at around age forty-three, and at 3.5 percent (the average return over the relevant two decades) at age forty-eight or forty-nine. It is fair to say that these types of calculations were fairly well understood by financial advisers in this period although few individuals were able to make these actuarial calculations from first principles.

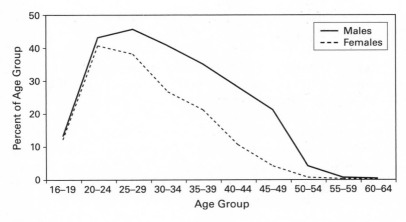

Figure 6.3
Age distribution of Personal Pension optants.

To understand how these incentives affected behavior, no particularly sophisticated econometric strategy is required. We can simply look at the disparity in the age-related incentives to contract-out in figure 6.2 and see whether these were mirrored in actual behavior. Keeping in mind that younger workers had the greatest incentive to opt out of SERPS into an APP as demonstrated in figure 6.2, figure 6.3 illustrates the actual pattern of opting out of SERPS into an APP by age group, by measuring the age structure of the stock of Personal Pension optants as at 1992 from official statistics (the year before the contracted-out rebate was to be significantly reduced). It can be clearly seen that the age structure of APP optants clearly matches the pattern of differences in returns by age group between an APP and SERPS. Moreover, the fact that optants extended into their late forties suggests that individuals envisaged real rates of return of at least 2.5 percent per year on their funds. By way of a benchmark, over 40 percent of individuals in the younger age groups opted to switch in that short time interval between 1988 and 1992—a dramatic change that confounds the often asserted view that younger workers are unresponsive to pension incentives. It is striking that even a large number of sixteen- to nineteen-year-olds opted into Personal Pensions—a group that even a standard life-cycle model would suggest to have heavily discounted its future retirement income. It is likely that these were predominantly "rebate only" optants who took the opportunity to invest the public rebate to their personal pension fund without making any additional contributions of their own.

The Reform of Personal Pension Incentives in the Mid-1990s

It is now apparent from combining figures 6.2 and 6.3 why the introduction of Personal Pensions generated such a large net cost to the government. The overall incentives, especially to young people, to contract out of SERPS into Approved Personal Pensions (APPs) far exceeded the amount required to achieve the goal of increased private pension coverage, and a large number of individuals, particularly young people, responded to these incentives. Indeed, one reason why high commission charges (an oft-cited rationale for the failure of Personal Pensions) failed to deter young people from buying Personal Pensions was that the excessively generous rebates to young people had effectively provided a rent that could be shared between purchaser and provider. This excess incentive stemmed from a forecasting error that rested on the apparent presumption that young people, in particular, were unresponsive to pension incentives unless these incentives were demonstrably large. This policy experiment shows that consumers (perhaps via financial advisers) were sufficiently financially adept to understand these differential incentives, as indicated by the age structure of optants in figure 6.3.

In the mid-1990s, therefore, the government set about rectifying the distorted incentive structure in the APP rebate regime. To understand this second policy experiment, it is necessary to refer to figure 6.2. This showed that the key problem with the APP rebate structure, given the frontloading of returns to defined-contribution pension plans, is that a flat rebate structure gave large windfall gains to younger APP purchasers. Even though the additional 2 percent rebate would end in 1993, a constant rebate rate by age gave an excessive incentive to young APP purchasers, while encouraging older APP purchasers to switch back into the public program, SERPS. Thus an incentive structure based on the presumption that individuals broadly understood and responded to incentives rather than being intrinsically myopic or irrational would structure the contracting-out rebate to give an incentive to a sufficient proportion of every age group to contract out at some reasonable rate of return while avoiding the intramarginal gains arising from the existing rebate structure. This clearly implied that the contracted-out rebate for APP optants should *rise* with age so that for each age there would be a neutral contracted-out rebate that would

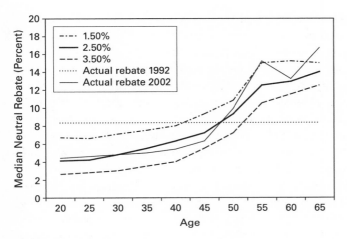

Figure 6.4
Median neutral contracted-out rebate by age and real rate of return.

give the worker on median earnings (or any other earnings level, depending on the target rate of opting out by the government) an incentive to contract out for any given expected rate of return on the Personal Pension fund.

Such a structure was calculated in Disney and Whitehouse (1992a) (and further analyzed in a more general framework by Palacios and Whitehouse, 1998). The neutral rebate structure is illustrated for a man on median earnings in 1992 at various ages and by various prospective rates of return and is depicted in figure 6.4. To illustrate, compared with the actual effective rebate rate of 8.46 percent (see previous discussion)—the horizontal line in figure 6.4—the rebate rate required to persuade a twenty-year-old man on median earnings to contract out of SERPS into an APP would be under 7 percent at a return of 1.5 percent per annum falling to less than 3 percent at a rate of return of 3.5 percent. This would rise to, respectively, 11 percent and 7 percent by age fifty. By structuring incentives in this manner, the government could in principle obtain a target rate of contracting out at much less cost to the public finances, changing the level of the average rebate to be higher when prospective real returns were lower (and vice versa) and also adjusting the rebate level to ensure a target rate of opting out.

In 1997, the government switched policy and introduced age-related rebates. The actual rebate structure as it operated in 2002 is illustrated, and this age-related rebate structure appears to be consistent with the government assuming that real returns would continue to exceed 2.5 percent per annum (for further discussion of the assumptions, see the Government Actuary's Department, 2000). At one level, one can applaud this policy as an evidence-based reversion to policy making based on the presumption that individuals responded to retirement saving incentives. At another level, it also provides a further test of individual responses to changing retirement saving incentives since, if the new rebate structure eliminated any age-specific differences in the incentive to opt out, the discrepancy in opting-out rates by age illustrated in figure 6.3 should be eliminated.

This last hypothesis is illustrated in figure 6.5 using data on APP *commencements* (that is, new APP contracts) from 1987 to 1988 to 2003 to 2004 using data from the Department of Work and Pensions (2005). Both men and women are included, since they faced the same structure of rebates. The incentives are slightly different insofar as women could draw their state pension somewhat earlier. However, differential longevity is not pertinent since the rebate component of the annuity is required to be gender-neutral (not priced to reflect differential expected longevity by gender). Subject to any change arising from the introduction of Stakeholder Pensions (which is discussed in next section), we might expect to see a gradual leveling out over time in the proportions of different age groups opting for APPs as the age-related rebates eliminated the differential incentive for young people to opt out (and indeed for older people to revert to or remain in SERPs), although one might think that new optants might primarily come from new labor-market entrants over time.

As figure 6.5 illustrates, the early years saw APP optants being drawn primarily from young age groups (as also depicted in the stock estimate in figure 6.3), but by the end of the period, optants were drawn almost equiproportionately from all age groups, for both men and women, as the restructuring of incentives would suggest. In fact, after 1997, when the rebate structure changed, there is some visual evidence that the proportion of older new optants jumped, exactly as the change in relative incentives would predict, although the difference in total numbers is relatively small. Again, no formal econometric technique is required clearly to illustrate the impact of this regime change on behavior.

This introduction of age-related contracted-out rebates set the incentive structure on an appropriate economic basis. However, as real returns on equity funds and long-term bond rates declined in the late

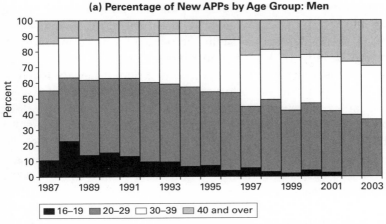

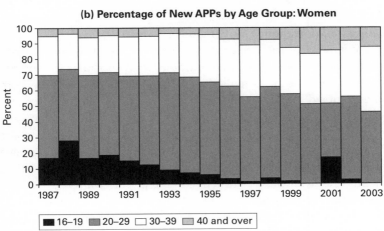

Figure 6.5
Approved Personal Pension contract commencements 1987–1988 to 2003–2004 by age
and sex (includes Stakeholder Pensions after 2001).

1990s, Approved Personal Pensions became less popular. New saving instruments not specifically targeted at retirement, such as personal equity plans, tax-exempt special saving accounts (TESSAs), and individual saving accounts (ISAs), were increasing in popularity. Moreover, and not surprisingly given the large effective public subsidy given to Personal Pensions, the net addition to aggregate retirement saving over and above government subsidies arising from Personal Pensions was probably rather small throughout the 1990s (for evidence, see Disney, Emmerson, and Wakefield, 2001; Disney, Emmerson, and Smith, 2004). This led the government into another rethink of retirement saving, leading to the introduction of Stakeholder Pensions in April 2001, the analysis of which forms the basis of the next section.

Stakeholder Pensions

The Rationale for Stakeholder Pensions
One of the lessons of the Personal Pension experiment is that across-the-board tax incentives give large, intramarginal subsidies to particular groups. Indeed, as far as net saving is concerned, the wealth effects from these subsidies might outweigh any marginal incentive effects arising from the tax change. An alternative strategy is to develop saving instruments targeted specifically at groups in the population with inadequate retirement saving. The rationale for introducing new instruments is presumably that, for one reason or another, existing instruments are insufficiently attractive to the target group.

In this section, we consider a reform that embodied both these policy strategies of tax relief and targeting at a particular group—the introduction of Stakeholder Pensions in the United Kingdom in 2001. The Green Paper (Department of Social Security, 1998) that proposed Stakeholder Pensions argued that existing provision of private pensions was inadequate in significant respects. Employer-provided pension plans covered predominantly only high earners and public-sector workers, while Personal Pensions, given their high upfront administrative charges, were also seen as most suitable for persistent and higher-income savers. It argued that "People on middle incomes want to save more for retirement but current pension arrangements are often unsuitable or expensive. Our new secure, flexible and value-for-money stakeholder pension schemes will help many middle earners to save for a comfortable retirement" (Department of Social Security, 1998, p. 48).

The Green Paper defined *middle earners* as those individuals earning between £9,000 and £18,500 per annum. Although Stakeholder Pension schemes were open to everyone, it was assumed that this target group was most likely to take up the new retirement saving instrument. Many high earners, as mentioned, had access to other retirement saving instruments, whereas low earners were assumed to be better off contracted with the public second-tier pension (the State Earnings-Related Pension Scheme, SERPS, superseded in April 2002 by the more redistributive State Second Pension, S2P), rather than opting for a private pension arrangement.

The Green Paper also proposed a number of other changes to the pension regime, including a reform to the structure of tax reliefs that was also subsequently implemented. As mentioned above, employee contributions to retirement saving accounts in the United Kingdom obtain tax relief against income tax up to a ceiling of earnings (the U.K. direct tax system is individual-based). Until the advent of Stakeholder Pensions, the ceiling was proportional to earnings and more generous for older individuals. An important difference between the post–Stakeholder Pension tax regime and the previous tax regime is that *all* individuals, irrespective of any earnings, are able to make gross contributions of up to £3,600 a year to their private pension (whether it is a Stakeholder Pension or another form of private pension). This change in tax reliefs, as we illustrate in the next section, disproportionately affects low and zero earners. Those with very low earnings would need a source of resources to save in a pension, and the Green Paper noted one possibility: "The changes will also make it easier for partners to contribute to each other's pensions, again within the overall contribution limits, should they choose to do so" (Department of Social Security, 1998, p. 63).

The introduction of Stakeholder Pensions therefore provided both a visible targeting of a new retirement saving instrument on a specified group and a change in the tax regime for pensions. The latter was less publicized at the time but had a potential impact on retirement saving incentives for certain groups.

Unlike Personal Pensions, which had an immediate albeit controversial impact, the general perception in the U.K. finance industry is that the introduction of Stakeholder Pensions has been a disappointment, with low initial sales of this product and a decline in overall take-up of private pensions since 2001. In fact, evidence from the Department

of Work and Pensions (2003) itself suggests little evidence of enrollment or interest in the new product among the target group of middle
earners who did not have an existing private pension. Although
the number of holders of Stakeholder Pensions exceeded 1 million by
late 2002 (compare this with the 4 million new optants for Personal
Pensions in the first year illustrated in figure 6.1), many of these new
pension arrangements seem to have arisen from individuals switching
from other schemes (notably Personal Pensions) and from existing
Group Personal Pensions being reconstituted as Stakeholder Pensions.
This perception led to lobbying for further changes to the private pension regime (e.g., Association of British Insurers, 2003) and to a well
publicized officially sponsored report suggesting the need for an alternative approach that defaulted individuals into a private pension plan
to encourage retirement saving (Pensions Commission, 2005).

Aggregate statistics may suggest that the reform had little effect on
coverage, but overall trends may conceal differential effects across sub-
populations. Of particular interest are the impact on coverage among
the targeted group of middle earners and the impact, if any, of the
change in the structure of tax reliefs. Adverse common trends in overall private pension coverage may have dominated any Stakeholder
Pension effect, and we might not rule out the possibility that any aggregate downward trend in pension coverage might have been even
greater had Stakeholder Pensions not been introduced. However, to
uncover any differential effect across groups requires a rather more
sophisticated empirical strategy than that utilized above in the section
on Personal Pensions.

Therefore, this section estimates the impact of the introduction of
Stakeholder Pensions on the proportion of households that have a
private pension. We do not consider the impact of Stakeholder Pensions on the *volume* of retirement saving in this chapter because of limitations in both household and aggregate data on the magnitude of
retirement saving. We show that there was a take-up response to
Stakeholder Pension, although this is concealed in the aggregate data.
Differential changes in coverage across income groups emerge, exactly
as an analysis of a targeted policy might suggest. But we show that
these differential effects are not along the lines predicted by the 1998
Green Paper—namely, an increase in take-up among middle earners.
Our results suggest that it is low earners rather than middle earners
who have responded to the introduction of Stakeholder Pensions, offsetting an overall declining trend in the probability of retirement sav-

ing among the rest of the population, including middle earners. These conflicting trends are concealed by the "no change" (in fact, slight decline) in the aggregate.

Why is it that increased private pension coverage among *low* earners offsets the aggregate change, rather than changes in coverage among the middle-income group targeted in the Green Paper? We show why by modeling the effect of spouse's earnings on the probability of an individual's take-up of a private pension in this section. We suggest that the changes in tax limits allowed households to reorganize their saving strategy to take advantage of the new structure of tax reliefs that had an impact. In contrast, the simultaneous highlighting of targeting on middle earners in the Green Paper had no significant effect on the probability of enrollment in private pensions.

Stakeholder Pensions: Brief Description

Stakeholder Pensions were proposed in the Green Paper *Partnership in Pensions* (Department of Social Security, 1998), and after some revisions in the light of consultation, they were introduced in April 2001. Rhetorically targeted at people earning between £9,000 and £18,500 a year who did not already have a private pension, Stakeholder Pensions were intended primarily to increase the level of private pension provision among that group. Like all personal pensions and some occupational pension schemes, Stakeholder Pensions are defined-contribution schemes, in that pension benefits depend on the accumulated value of the fund. They differ from Personal Pensions, however, in having compulsory minimum standards, a different governance structure, guaranteed workplace access for those working for moderate or large employers, and a simpler and more uniform charging structure.

Since 2001, companies employing at least five people that do not offer occupational pensions are required to nominate a Stakeholder Pension provider after consultation with employees; provide employees with information on Stakeholder Pensions; and channel employees' contributions to the nominated pension provider. Neither employees nor employers are compelled to contribute to a Stakeholder Pension, and indeed firms employing fewer than five people were completely exempted from the requirement to nominate a provider. Stakeholder Pensions have a simple charging structure: an initial annual cap on charges was set at 1 percent of the fund, with no charges either upfront or on withdrawals from the fund.[1] Moreover, contributors can start and stop contributing at any time, and schemes have to accept all contributions of £20 or more. Compulsory minimum standards are intended to provide a greater degree of uniformity between Stakeholder Pensions offered by different pension providers than previous pension arrangements. By making pension providers offer a relatively uniform product, it was hoped that there would be less need for individuals to seek independent financial advice before taking out a Stakeholder Pension.

Evidence from the financial industry suggests that *new* take-up of Stakeholder Pensions, even among the target group of middle earners, has been rather limited. British Household Panel Survey (BHPS) data also show that, even before the introduction of Stakeholder Pensions, enrollment in private pensions among the target group was substantial, with around 80 percent having some form of private pension in 2000 (see Disney, Emmerson, and Tanner, 1999, for similar evidence from the early 1990s, well before the reform was announced). The BHPS also suggests that, among middle earners in 2000, those who *did not* have a private pension were more likely to have experienced a period out of employment over the previous nine years and when in work, on average, had lower earnings than those with a private pension. Median liquid financial assets in 1995 were just £300 among those without a private pension in 2000 compared to £1,400 among those with a private pension. Not only was the Stakeholder Pension target group relatively small, but the characteristics of those middle earners might well suggest that, if they could afford to save more, they would be better advised to save in a more liquid form for precautionary purposes rather than saving in a private pension.

Contribution Ceilings
A feature of the Stakeholder Pensions reform that was less discussed at the time but that turns out to be rather important lies in the change to contribution ceilings relative to those that applied to defined-contribution retirement saving instruments such as Personal Pensions before April 2001. Employee contributions to Stakeholder Pensions are made net of tax, with the government then contributing the equivalent basic rate tax to the individual's scheme. Higher-rate taxpayers can go on to claim more relief in line with their higher marginal income tax rate. Returns are broadly tax-exempt, and pensions are then taxed at withdrawal except for up to 25 percent of the fund, which can be withdrawn tax-free. These aspects of the tax regime broadly followed the existing regime for Personal Pensions, which also allowed tax-relieved

Table 6.1
Maximum contributions as a percentage of earnings by age: Pre-2001 regime

Age at Start of Tax Year	Maximum Contributions as Percentage of Earnings
35 or under	17.5%
36–45	20.0
46–50	25.0
51–55	30.0
56–60	35.0
61–75	40.0

Notes: Contributions are subject to an overall earnings cap. In 2004 to 2005, this was set at £102,000. Maximum contributions include contributions by both the employer and employee.

contributions up to a maximum of earnings differentiated by age, as depicted in table 6.1.

However, an important change in the tax regime associated with the introduction of Stakeholder Pensions, applying also thereafter to Personal Pensions, is that *all* individuals, irrespective of any earnings, are able to make gross contributions of up to £3,600 a year (which for a basic-rate taxpayer would require a net contribution of £2,808). Individuals are then allowed higher contributions in line with their earnings as in the previous regime in table 6.1. The effect of this change is to raise contributions limits significantly for low-earning individuals, especially for younger age groups (since maximum contributions as a proportion of earnings were lower). Figure 6.6 depicts the effect of the change post-2001 on the maximum gross contribution limits by gross relevant earnings for the various age groups in table 6.1. Note that individuals with zero income can also contribute up to the £3,600 maximum and that the United Kingdom's tax system is individual-based so that each individual in a couple can contribute up to this maximum.[2]

Empirical Analysis

This section investigates the determinants of the household decision to save for retirement using information from the Family Resources Survey (FRS). The FRS is a large-scale repeated cross-section of households designed to elicit information on household characteristics, income, and other economic circumstances. The FRS asks individual respondents who are in work or who have ever worked (below age

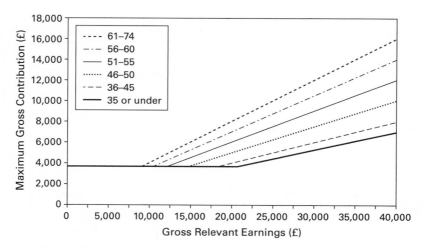

Figure 6.6
Maximum annual gross contribution limit to the Stakeholder Pension tax regime, by annual gross relevant earnings and age.

sixty-five) whether they or their employer contributes to a pension scheme. The pension arrangements are delineated as a personal/private pension, a company-run pension scheme, a stakeholder pension, or some other arrangement. Panel A in table 6.2 provides data from the Family Resources Survey for the four (tax) years 1999–2000 to 2002–2003 on pension holdings by type. According to the table, overall coverage by private pensions has declined slightly over the period. Coverage by employer-provided plans has been constant, and a decline in coverage by Personal Pensions has been not quite offset by the introduction of Stakeholder Pensions and by a slight rise in the number of people with multiple plans.

Panel B reveals the striking finding that coverage has fallen among the high- and medium-earnings groups over the period (these are the bands delineated by the Green Paper, of £18,500+ and £9,000 to £18,500 respectively).[3] Coverage has *risen* among low earners and even (marginally) among those reporting zero earnings who are below state pension age. At first sight, these combined findings from table 6.2 are paradoxical given the intentions stated in the Green Paper. They suggest that the introduction of Stakeholder Pensions has had no effect on overall coverage and indeed coverage by any kind of pension has fallen among the target group of middle earners. Nor can these

Table 6.2
Pension coverage by type of pension and earnings band, 1999–2000 to 2002–2003

	Year				
	1999 (percent)	2000 (percent)	2001 (percent)	2002 (percent)	Δ1999–2002 (percent point)
Panel A: Employees only					
Type of pension:					
Personal pension	11.3%	10.3%	9.8%	8.4%	−2.9
Stakeholder pension	0.0	0.0	0.8	1.2	+1.2
Occupational pension	47.9	47.9	48.0	48.1	+0.2
Combined	1.9	2.0	2.2	2.4	+0.4
Aggregate coverage	61.2%	60.2%	60.7%	60.2%	−1.0
Sample size	20,829	20,010	21,655	22,939	85,433
Panel B: All people of working age					
Coverage by earnings band:					
Zero	3.4%	3.6%	3.5%	3.6%	+0.1
Low	35.0	35.5	36.9	36.6	+1.6
Medium	69.7	68.7	68.8	67.3	−2.4
High	86.9	86.3	85.7	84.6	−2.4
Aggregate coverage	44.4%	44.1%	44.7%	44.4%	0.0
Sample size	29,351	27,927	30,071	31,813	119,162

Source: Own calculations, Family Resources Survey 1999–2000 to 2002–2003.
Note: The sample includes individuals between school-leaving age and state-pension age, although a few individuals have to be excluded due to missing data. The sample in panel B is used for the regressions reported in later sections. Rounding explains why figures in the right-hand column may be slightly different from the difference between the 1999 and 2002 columns.

declines be explained by a decline in employer-provided occupational pension provision, since this remains constant. Finally, despite the Green Paper suggesting that low earners might be better off in the second-pillar state scheme, this is the only group to see a substantial increase in private pension coverage.

To permit a more formal analysis, we write a model of retirement saving that accounts for the targeting of the reform:

$$Y_{it}^* = \theta' Z_{it} + \pi' d_t + \gamma' X_{it} + \varepsilon_{it}. \tag{6.1}$$

The dependent variable Y_{it}^* is the outcome of the retirement saving decision of individual i at time t and is a latent variable that may be regarded as measuring whether an individual gains positive utility benefit from saving in a private pension. Z_{it} is a vector delineating the earnings group (high, medium, low, or zero, as described previously) in which the individual i is located at time t; d_t is a vector of time dummies; X_{it} is a vector of covariates; and θ, π, and γ are vectors of parameters.

The *observed* outcome variable is whether an individual saves in a private pension at a particular point in time. Define this dichotomous outcome as Y_{it} in contrast to Y_{it}^*. With a normally distributed error term, this set-up describes a probit model (the form that we use below). This modeling strategy allows for the discrete nature of our outcome variable and avoids a possible outcome in a linear probability specification of predictions outside the logically permissible range for probabilities, in particular of a negative probability of saving in a pension for some in the zero-earnings group.

The hypothesis that we test in our differences-in-differences exercise is whether the introduction of Stakeholder Pensions had effects on the probability of purchasing a private pension that varied across earnings groups (the effect on the target group of middle earners is especially interesting), with the counterfactual being that in the absence of the reform the purchase probabilities for the different groups would have determined by common trends. If we could estimate the linear relationship (6.1), then the extent of any differences across groups would be measured by the coefficient on the interaction between earnings group and an indicator variable (I_t) for the period during which Stakeholder Pensions were available (from 2001 onward). This is the coefficient α in equation (6.1'):

$$Y_{it}^* = \theta' Z_{it} + \pi' d_t + \gamma' X_{it} + \alpha' Z_{it} I_t + \varepsilon_{it}. \tag{6.1'}$$

However, in a nonlinear model such as the probit, calculated marginal effects on interaction terms cannot be thought of as giving a difference-in-difference measure analogous to the coefficients from a linear model.[4] As Blundell, Costa Dias, Meghir, and Van Reenen (2004) point out, within the set-up for a discrete outcome, the common trends assumption may not hold for the expectations of Y_{it} (the saving probabilities) but for a transformation of the distribution of the outcome variable and specifically for the inverse probability function.[5] In other words, the assumption of common trends is made for the index rather than for the probability itself.

Blundell et al. (2004) explain how this common trends assumption can be formalized and used to construct a differences-in-differences estimator.[6] The technique as it applies to the current problem is explained in detail in Chung, Disney, Emmerson, and Wakefield (2005) and used to estimate the treatment effects reported in the next sections. These estimated treatment effects are averages across all treated individuals that can be thought of as measuring the average impact of treatment on the treated.

Econometric Results: Model in Differences

Before moving to the treatment framework, table 6.3 provides a simple model (in differences) of the probabilities of respondents purchasing

Table 6.3
Probability of having a private pension: Model in differences

Variable	Coefficient	DF/dx	Standard Error
Age 25–29	0.493**	0.193	0.020
Age 30–34	0.800**	0.311	0.020
Age 35–39	0.904**	0.349	0.019
Age 40–44	0.949**	0.365	0.020
Age 45–49	1.025**	0.391	0.021
Age 50–54	1.011**	0.386	0.021
Age 55–59	0.926**	0.356	0.022
Age ≥60	0.743**	0.290	0.030
Male	−0.047**	−0.017	0.010
Couple	0.155**	0.058	0.011
GSCE or below	−0.300**	−0.114	0.012
A level or below	−0.083**	−0.031	0.013
Year = 2000	−0.017	−0.006	0.013
Year = 2001	−0.012	−0.005	0.013
Year = 2002	−0.045**	−0.017	0.012
Zero earnings	−2.740**	−0.664	0.019
Low earnings	−1.240**	−0.390	0.016
Midearnings	−0.412**	−0.153	0.015
Partner's earnings	0.003**	0.001	0.0003
Log likelihood	−52,619.4		
Number of observations	119,162		

Source: Family Resources Survey.
Note: Defaults are graduate age under 25, female, single, year 1999–2000 with high earnings. ** = 1 percent significance, * = 5 percent significance. Coefficient on constant omitted. *dF/dx* coefficients can be interpreted as marginal (policy) effects (see text).

any private pension (whether provided by the individual's employer or by an insurer), using data from the Family Resources Survey 1999–2000 to 2002–2003. We exclude the self-employed from the sample to reduce the number of interactions, although the results are not thereby altered. The mean probability of purchasing a private pension is 44.4 percent. The model simply relates this probability of purchase to underlying characteristics and a time trend. A key issue is how this probability varies across the earnings groups (zero, low >£0 to <£9,000, medium £9,000 to <£18,500, and high £18,500+). The marginal effects can be directly interpreted as relating to changing characteristics, given that the model is in differences.

The model shows a rising probability of having a private pension with age up to age fifty-four. Relative to the default group (age less than twenty-five), twenty-five to twenty-nine-year-olds have a 19.3 percentage point (ppt) increased probability of contributing to a private pension, and thirty- to thirty-four-year-olds a 31.1 ppt increased probability. Thereafter, with rising age, the probabilities remain roughly constant. Men are just under 5 ppt less likely to buy pensions, other things being equal (a crucial *caveat*) (this may reflect the longer lifetime expectancy of women), and a member of a couple is more likely to buy a pension (perhaps again reflecting the possibility of receiving an inherited pension on the death of a spouse or else of self-selection by martial status). As expected, higher educational attainment is associated with greater probability of purchasing a private pension.

The next set of coefficients is of particular interest. First, the year dummies are negative (relative to 1999–2000) and significant for 2002–2003 suggesting, on average, a 1.7 ppt lower probability of contributing to a private pension in 2002–2003 relative to 1999–2000. This reflects the downward trend noted in table 6.2, although only the fall in the last year is statistically significant at conventional levels. Second, table 6.3 shows, as might be expected, that the level of earnings is an important predictor of purchase of a private pension. Relative to the high-earnings group, a middle earner is 15 ppt less likely, a low earner 39 ppt less likely, and a zero earner 67 ppt likely to purchase a private pension. Again, these marginal effects can be compared with the comparisons of averages in table 6.2. Finally, the higher the partner's earnings, the more likely that the individual will purchase a private pension.

Econometric Results: Model in Quasi-Difference-in-Differences

We now move to the treatment model, the results of which are reported in table 6.4. The results are labeled Quasi-difference-in-differences because they use the introduction of Stakeholder Pensions as the treatment, as summarized in text equation (6.1′). Estimating (6.1′) allows us to compare coefficients with those from the model in differences in table 6.3 and also gives a fuller impression of whether there are important differences across earnings groups.

Column (1) provides the coefficients from the model described in text equation (6.1′). Coefficients on characteristics in the difference-in-differences specification are broadly the same as before, although those attached to earnings level are slightly larger in magnitude. It is also interesting to notice that the year effects become more strongly negative for 2001 and 2002, and both are now highly significant, whereas this was only true for the later year in the model in differences in table 6.3. This reflects the fact that with the interaction terms included these coefficients are driven by the decline in coverage among high earners (the omitted earnings group), and we have seen that this group had a relatively large decline in coverage (see table 6.2).

Inspection of the treatment coefficients—the interaction of earnings level with the dummy variable identifying the years after Stakeholder Pensions were introduced—would suggest that the policy had no significant impact on coverage among middle earners. In contrast, the coefficients for the analogous interaction terms for low earners and zero earners are significant (at 1 percent and 5 percent levels, respectively) and suggestive of effects offsetting the negative time trend.

As suggested above, the true treatment effects of the introduction of Stakeholder Pensions cannot be read off from the marginal effects that would be associated with these reported coefficients. Using the Blundell et al. (2004) procedure described above, these effects can be calculated as follows:

Zero earnings group	0.3 ppt (0.4 ppt)
Low earnings group	3.6 ppt (1.7 ppt)*
Middle earnings group	1.6 ppt (1.1 ppt)

Standard errors are in parentheses, estimated by bootstrapping with 1,000 repetitions, and * indicates significance at the 5 percent level.

These results indicate that the largest and most significant impact of Stakeholder Pensions relative to trend (of around 3.6 percentage

Table 6.4
Probability of having a private pension: Quasi-difference-in-differences

Variable	(1) Own Earnings Band		(2) Own plus Spouse's Band	
	Coefficient	Standard Error	Coefficient	Standard Error
Age 25–29	0.493**	0.020	0.486**	0.020
Age 30–34	0.799**	0.020	0.797**	0.020
Age 35–39	0.904**	0.019	0.906**	0.020
Age 40–44	0.949**	0.020	0.951**	0.020
Age 45–49	1.025**	0.021	1.029**	0.021
Age 50–54	1.011**	0.021	1.022**	0.021
Age 55–59	0.926**	0.022	0.945**	0.022
Age ≥60	0.742**	0.030	0.767**	0.030
Male	−0.048**	0.010	−0.015	0.010
Couple	0.155**	0.011	0.091**	0.012
GSCE or below	−0.300**	0.012	−0.295**	0.012
A level or below	−0.083**	0.013	−0.083**	0.014
Year = 2000	−0.017	0.013	−0.016	0.013
Year = 2001	−0.079**	0.026	−0.071*	0.032
Year = 2002	−0.111**	0.026	−0.105**	0.031
Zero earnings	−2.783**	0.027	−2.780**	0.032
Low earnings	−1.303**	0.023	−1.313**	0.028
Midearnings	−0.440**	0.021	−0.474**	0.025
Partner's earnings M/H	0.003**	0.0003	0.098**	0.039
Zero E*StakePen	0.080*	0.036	0.051	0.044
Low E*StakePen	0.120**	0.029	0.081*	0.036
Mid E*StakePen	0.040	0.028	0.031	0.034
Zero E*Partner's earnings M/H	—	—	0.088	0.057
Low E*Partner's earnings M/H	—	—	0.030	0.045
Mid E*Partner's earnings M/H	—	—	0.102*	0.044
StakePen*Partner's earnings M/H	—	—	−0.015	0.052
Zero E*StakePen*Partner's earnings M/H	—	—	0.077	0.079
Low E*StakePen*Partner's earnings M/H	—	—	0.093	0.061
Mid E*StakePen*Partner's earnings M/H	—	—	0.020	0.060
Log likelihood	−52,607.6		−52,503.7	
Number of observations	119,162		119,162	

Source: Family Resources Survey.
Note: Defaults are graduate age twenty to twenty-four, female, single, year 1999–2000 with high earnings, partner has zero or low earnings. Coefficient on constant omitted. **1 percent significance, *5 percent significance. *Zero E*StakePen* = individuals with zero earnings interacted with a dummy for the stakeholder pension regime (post–April 2001). *Zero E*Partner's earnings M/H* = individuals with zero earnings interacted with dummy for whether spouse had medium or high earnings. Other interactions have similar interpretations.

points) has been on low earners. The impact of the reform on those with zero earnings was overstated by the standard errors in table 6.4, and we also find no significant effect on middle earners. Thus, the results effectively confirm the descriptive patterns in the second panel of table 6.2.

Further Analysis: The Role of Spouse's Earnings

The results so far are inconsistent with the targets in the Green Paper. The aggregate comparisons in table 6.2 and the results in tables 6.3 and 6.4 column (1) suggest that low and even zero earners may have increased the enrollment in private pensions after the reform, although overall coverage remains very low for this last group, and the calculations of the true difference-in-differences estimator using the Blundell et al. (2004) calculation and formulation of common trends also casts some doubt on the zero earner finding. Nevertheless, *any* finding, however tentative, that suggests that people with zero or low earnings increasingly took out private pensions is somewhat surprising (unless they have substantial unearned income).

The result becomes less surprising when we consider the fact that *each* individual in a household can invest up to the ceiling in a Stakeholder Pension, irrespective of the individual's own income. The results are consistent with the idea that some low earners in the household have taken out Stakeholder Pensions because the household was previously constrained by the effective limit on the value of retirement saving arising from the contribution ceiling (see figure 6.6). Thus the replacement of the cap as a proportion of earnings by the single figure (£3,600) may lie behind this change. For example, a spouse with low or even zero earnings can invest up to the limit in a Stakeholder or Personal Pension if there are sufficient resources in the household as a whole. If pensions are simply used by the household as a device for engaging in relatively tax-favored saving, this might be seen as an undesirable by-product of the reform. On the other hand, it could be argued that a policy that, for example, redistributed pension resources from a rich partner to a spouse with low lifetime individual income was socially desirable (a point recognized in the quote from the Green Paper above). This also generates a specific testable prediction: if we include spouse's earnings among the explanatory variables, the probability of a low (or zero) earner contributing to a pension in the Stakeholder Pension regime should be *positively* related to the spouse's earnings.

The model where we allow for spouses' earnings is written as follows:

$$Y_{it}^* = \theta'Z_{it} + \tau'S_{it} + \pi'd_t + \gamma'X_{it} + \alpha'Z_{it}I_t + \beta S_{it}I_t$$

$$+ \lambda Z_{it}S_{it} + \varphi Z_{it}S_{it}I_t + \varepsilon_{it}, \tag{6.2}$$

where all variables are defined as before except S, which is an indicator variable of the income band of the spouse of individual i at time t. We are now interested not just in the coefficient vector α but also in the coefficients ϕ, which measure the impact of the spouse's income band on the retirement saving probability of an individual in a given income band. Again, we use the Blundell et al. method to calculate the treatment effects for this more complex specification. However, because we now have many more interactions, we simplify the modeling of partner's earnings so that these are either zero/low (below £9,000) or medium/high (£9,000 and above). This coarser grouping seems reasonable as it differentiates inactive or low-paid spouses (part-time workers) from full-time or better-paid working spouses. However, we maintain the four-way distinction for individual earnings.

Table 6.4 column (2) presents the results. Most of the coefficients on characteristics are similar to the estimates in column (1). The coefficient on sex is no longer significant now that we have allowed for interactions of partner's earnings and each individual's own earnings band. The year dummies have slightly lower coefficients but still suggest a significant downward trend in the aggregate probability of purchasing a private pension over time.

The coefficients on the interactions are of most interest, although few are now individually significant. For example, only the low-earnings treatment (interaction with the dummy identifying the poststakeholder period) is significant, confirming that the effect on nonearners is not very robust, at least without consideration of partner's earnings. To interpret the coefficients on the interactions, we carry out joint tests of significance for each of the (Z_i) earnings groups in turn. For each group, we test the joint significance of the pair of coefficients:

$(Z_i = X) *$ After stakeholder and

$(Z_i = X) *$ After * Partner mid/high earnings

The null hypothesis is that the pair of coefficients is jointly zero. Our results are as follows:

For Z_i = zero earnings, rejects null at 10 percent level, p-stat 0.0725.

For Z_i = low earnings, rejects null at all conventional levels, p-stat 0.0001.

For Z_i = midearnings, *cannot* reject null at conventional levels, p-stat 0.4004.

The results suggest that low earners with partners with middle or high earnings and, rather less robustly, zero earners with similar partners were affected by the reform. Middle earners were unaffected. We can identify whether there are significant treatment effects using the Blundell et al. (2004) procedure described previously.

These additional treatment effects for being in the poststakeholder period and including spouse's earnings brackets are as follows:

Zero-earning group with zero/low earning partner	0.1 ppt (0.3 ptt)
Zero-earning group with medium/high-earning partner	1.1 ppt (0.8 ppt)
Low-earning group with zero/low-earning partner	2.6 ppt (1.6 ppt)
Low-earning group with medium/high-earning partner	5.2 ppt (2.3 ppt)*
Medium-earning group with zero/low-earning partner	1.7 ppt (1.3 ppt)
Medium-earning group with medium/high-earning partner	1.4 ppt (1.4 ppt)

Standard errors in parentheses, estimated by bootstrapping with 1,000 repetitions, and * indicates significance at the 5 percent level.

This result confirms that the impact of the introduction of stakeholder pensions is strongest among low earners who have a high- or medium-earning partner, suggesting that the change to the contribution limits has allowed families with higher joint earnings to utilize the new arrangements to increase the tax-relieved component of their retirement saving. This is most likely to explain the increase in coverage among this group of earners. Without this impact, the analysis suggests, coverage by private pensions would have declined even more after 2001.[7] In fact, when we formally test the model explicitly on whether pension coverage is affected by whether the household's contribution limits have changed as a result of the 2001 change in tax reliefs, this is exactly the result that we obtained (Chung et al., 2005).

Alternative Explanations and Interpretation
The key assumption in a differences-in-differences approach is the common-trend assumption—here, that in the absence of the policy reform, the trends among the earnings groups' coverage would have been identical. First, we can ask whether there is any reason to believe that the behavior of high earners (who we assumed to be the control given their existing high coverage by private pensions) would have been different from other earnings groups. There is no other significant policy reform that is pertinent here, such as a change in the structure of marginal tax rates. Perhaps of more pertinence in explaining falling overall pension coverage by pension schemes (table 6.2) is the change in the financial climate from the beginning of 1998 to the end of 2002, during which the FTSE 100 fell by 31 percent, whereas house prices rose by almost exactly 50 percent (using the Halifax plc index). This might have induced savers to switch away from pension funds (which were at this stage largely equity-dominated) to investment in housing stocks. So if high earners exhibited greater substitutability in their asset portfolios, either from economies of scale or greater financial acumen, this might explain the disparate trends. However such a story finds it hard to explain similar trends in pension coverage among high and middle earners, especially with the results when we include the spouse interactions.

Alternatively, we can focus not on the control group but on the group for which the treatment effect is most marked—low earners. Here there *is* an important change in the tax and benefit regime that coincides with the introduction of Stakeholder Pensions in April 2001. As described briefly above, the period saw the replacement of SERPS, the second-tier pension, by the State Second Pension (S2P) (which was introduced in April 2002 but announced in the 1998 Green Paper). S2P is more explicitly redistributive toward low lifetime earners in its design. In addition, the means-tested benefit for pensioners, known as the minimum income guarantee (MIG), was consistently indexed to earnings rather than prices throughout the late 1990s and early 2000s (unlike the rest of the pension program), so increasing its real value for low earners and reinforcing the disincentive to save for retirement. In a final important development (albeit one that came in effect *after* the data used in the analysis above, which was from the four financial years from 1999–2000 to 2002–2003), the MIG was renamed the Pension Credit Guarantee (PCG) in October 2003, and a new Pension Credit Savings Credit introduced for families containing an individual age sixty-five or over. This last reform essentially reduced the withdrawal rate from 100 p to 40 p in the pound for families with an individual age sixty-five or over who was in receipt of a full basic state pension but thereby increased dramatically the coverage of means-tested benefits among the pensioner population. Analysis of all these trends suggests that whereas replacement rates cohort by cohort for the public pension program have already peaked for average earners, low earners are likely to see increasingly generous replacement rates from the public program for several decades yet (Disney and Emmerson, 2005).

This analysis suggests that, if anything, we might expect coverage among low earners (at least, for those who understood the implications of all these reforms) to fall *faster* than that for high and middle earners. In fact, we have found the reverse, suggesting that our estimate of the treatment effect may if anything be a lower bound on the effect. Moreover, this interpretation does not explain the result for low earners who have a high- or middle-earning partner, who might not be eligible for income-tested benefits (levied on a household basis rather than an individual basis). Overall, we believe that the story adduced in this chapter for the treatment effect is the most plausible one.

To summarize that story, our differences-in-differences estimates suggest that a no-change result for the aggregate pension coverage conceals differences across households that, given the nature of the reform package, are consistent with the standard economic model. A general decline in pension coverage has been offset by an increase in coverage among lower earners. That this increase has not been among middle earners—the heralded target group for the stakeholder pension reform—is not surprising given evidence on pension coverage and other characteristics in this group prior to the reform. That lower earners seem to have responded also should not be a surprise once one realizes that the reforms to tax reliefs that accompanied the introduction of stakeholder pensions mainly affected those with low and zero earnings and given that we know (not least from experience of the personal pensions episode) that individuals do respond to such incentives.

Conclusions

Our starting point was the policy debate concerning the best ways of encouraging people to save for their retirement. Personal Pensions were introduced in April 1988 as a means of encouraging workers to opt out of the social security program and to encourage labor-market flexibility. Stakeholder Pensions, introduced in April 2001, were targeted by the government for middle earners as a means of filling a perceived gap in retirement saving products. The introduction of Stakeholder Pensions was also associated with a less publicized change in the contribution limits that allowed lower earners to make larger contributions to retirement saving schemes. Our analysis represents the first systematic attempt, to our knowledge, to examine the whole trajectory of these recent policy developments on the probability of households engaging in retirement saving.

Aggregate data suggest that the introduction of Personal Pensions had a massive effect on the extent of private pension take-up, whereas Stakeholder Pensions had little impact on the overall propensity to save for retirement. Dissatisfaction with the outcomes from both reforms, for different reasons, have led policy makers and analysts to question whether these behavioral responses were consistent with rational lifecycle saving behavior. Accompanied by qualitative evidence that cast doubt on individual's cognitive abilities, this provided a rationale for the move toward greater compulsion of retirement saving in the policy proposals of the mid-2000s.

Our analysis of these two major reforms, exploiting the evidence on household behavior and the differential incentives that applied to various household types, suggests a rather different story. The Personal Pension contracting-out regime initially offered an enormous incentive to young people to purchase Approved Personal Pensions, and this is exactly mirrored in the distributions of optants for APPs by age. Once the contracting-out regime was changed more fully to reflect the differential incentives between groups, this disproportionate response disappeared. The extent of the response was not forecast, perhaps because the relevant authorities had a view of the world that perceived young people as unresponsive to pension incentives. Net (public and private) saving in Personal Pensions was minimal in these early years, but this is not surprising given that the government was effectively giving new optants around 8 percent of their earnings to put in these accounts. Once the government tightened up the contracting-out regime, the demand for Personal Pensions lessened, but it does appear that saving rates among remaining optants increased (Disney, Emmerson and Wakefield, 001). All of this is consistent with standard economic theory.

Coming t Stakeholder Pensions, the story is different. The headline target of the policy was middle earners, but we can find no evidence that the refo n affected pension take-up rates among this group. Arguably, this no surprising since Stakeholder Pensions offered no specific new incenti to this group. It was the associated change in contribution tax lim that offered differential incentives. It appears from our analysis that as with the Personal Pension reform, individuals (or their financial ad sers) did indeed perceive the incentives implicit in the reform of ta reliefs and responded accordingly—with greater take-up of pension a ounts in households exploiting the raising of the relief threshold fo zero and low earners, including those with higher-earning spou es. Again, the pattern of responses to incentives is consistent with the tandard economic model.

Our overa conclusion is that changes in the availability of saving instruments nd tax incentives *do* affect saving behavior—a result incidentally nfirming much of the U.S. literature on the impact of contribution mits on saving in individual retirement accounts (see "Government Incentives for Saving," 1996, and the literature cited therein; see a o Attanasio and DeLeire, 2002). However, the episodes we have cons lered also show that it is important to look at the details (in these case the consequences of rebate structures and tax reliefs) when attemp ng to understand how a policy might work in practice or when evalu ting it after the event.

The fact tha the saving behavior of individuals is responsive to policy changes al suggests erring on the side of caution when designing reforms to the pension saving regime. This is not only because dramatic reforms with implications that are not fully understood may lead to large r sponses beyond the scope of the aims of the policy (one interpretation f the initial rebates associated with the personal pension reform) b also because repeated large reforms are hardly conducive to the ins tutional stability that must help individuals who, we have seen, are rward looking when they plan their retirement saving. An assessment f whether the latest two major sets of pension reforms in the United ingdom—one enacted in April 2006 and the next proposed in May 006 (see Department of Work and Pensions, 2006)— are consistent ith this advice or further examples that "the political process is not equivalent to a consistent approach to policy over time" (Diamond, 2004) lies outside the scope of this chapter.

Notes

Corresponding author: Richard Disney, School of Economics, Sir Clive Granger Building, University of Nottingham, Nottingham, NG8 2NA, e-mail ⟨richard.disney @nottingham.ac.uk⟩. Financial support from the Economic and Social Research Council's Centre for the Microeconomic Analysis of Public Policy at Institute for Fiscal Studies (grant number M535255111) is gratefully acknowledged. The ESRC Data Archive at Essex made available the data used here, and the data are copyright of the Archive. The authors thank Erich Battistin, Tim Besley, Richard Blundell, Monica Costa Dias, Sarah Smith, and seminar participants at the Centre for Applied Micro-econometrics at the University of Copenhagen, the Financial Markets Group Research Centre at the London School of Economics, HM Treasury, the Institute for Fiscal Studies, the Royal Economic Society Conference 2005, and the Economics of Ageing Research Training Network meeting in Paris for useful assistance and comments on material contained in this chapter. Any errors and all opinions expressed are those of the authors.

1. In 2004, after lobbying from the finance industry, the Treasury increased this charge cap from 1 percent to $1\frac{1}{2}$ percent for the first ten years that a product is held. For more details, see HM Treasury (2004).

2. Clark and Emmerson (2003) discuss other features of the tax treatment of Stakeholder Pensions, in particular in relation to individual saving accounts. A subsequent, more sweeping reform to the ceilings on pension contributions introduced in April 2006 is discussed in the section on tax relief and contracting out.

3. We gross up weekly earnings data to provide these annual earnings bands. This inevitably produces measurement error. For example, some people will wrongly be attributed zero earnings for the year based on current zero earnings. In addition, the Green Paper sometimes refers to £20,000 and sometimes to £18,500 as the highest income of middle earners. In general, we work with the latter definition in the Family Resources Survey data, revalued over time in line with earnings growth.

4. In addition to the points raised here about the common trends assumption, it is also the case that the marginal effects on interaction terms in nonlinear models that are automatically generated by software packages (in our case, by STATA version 8) often do not give a true measure of interaction effects. For more details, see Ai and Norton (2003).

5. Which is assumed to be known and for the probit is $\Phi^{-1}(\cdot)$.

6. Although the method is similar to the linear case in its use of a control group to predict an unobserved counterfactual, the nonlinearity does require two additional restrictions on the nature of the error terms. Only group effects are allowed for, and the groups being compared are assumed to have the same residual variance. See Blundell et al. (2004, 580).

7. When we split our control (high-earning) group into those with partners with medium/high versus low/zero earnings, this general result holds in terms of coefficient values, although the additional regressors raise the overall standard errors of the estimates.

References

Ai, C., and E. C. Norton. (2003). "Interaction Terms in Logit and Probit Models." *Economic Letters*, 123–129.

Association of British Insurers. (2003). *Stakeholder Pensions: Time for Change*. London.

Attanasio, O., and T. DeLeire. (2002). "The Effect of Individual Retirement Accounts on Household Consumption and National Saving." *Economic Journal*, 112, 504–538.

Attanasio, O., and S. Rohwedder. (2003). "Pension Wealth and Household Saving: Evidence from Pension Reforms in the U.K." *American Economic Review*, 93(5), 1499–1521.

Banks, J., R. Blundell, R. Disney, and C. Emmerson. (2002). *Retirement, Pensions and the Adequacy of Saving*. IFS Briefing Note No. 29. Retrieved from ⟨http://www.ifs.org.uk/pensions/bn29.pdf⟩.

Banks, J., C. Emmerson, Z. Oldfield, and G. Tetlow. (2005). *Prepared for Retirement? The Adequacy and Distribution of Retirement Resources in Britain*. IFS Report No. 67.

Banks, J., and Z. Oldfield. (2006). "Understanding Pensions: Cognitive Ability, Numerical Ability and Retirement Saving." Institute for Fiscal Studies Working Paper W06/05.

Bernheim, B. D., and J. K. Scholz. (1993). "Private Saving and Public Policy." In J. Poterba, ed., *Tax Policy and the Economy* (Vol. 7). Cambridge, MA: MIT Press and NBER.

Blundell, R., M. Costa Dias, C. Meghir, and J. Van Reenen. (2004). "Evaluating the Employment Impact of a Mandatory Job Search Program." *Journal of the European Economic Association*, 2, 569–606.

Booth, P., and D. Cooper. (2002). "The Tax Treatment of UK Defined Contribution Pension Schemes." *Fiscal Studies*, 23, 77–104.

Chung, W., R. Disney, C. Emmerson, and M. Wakefield. (2005). "Public Policy and Saving for Retirement: Evidence from the Introduction of Stakeholder Pensions in the UK." Mimeo, Institute for Fiscal Studies, London.

Clark, T., and C. Emmerson. (2003). "The Tax and Benefit System and the Decision to Invest in a Stakeholder Pension." Institute for Fiscal Studies Briefing Note No. 28, London.

Cremer, H., P. De Donder, D. Maldonado, and P. Pestieau. (2006). "Voting over Type and Size of a Pension System When Some Individuals Are Myopic." Paper presented at the Eighth Economics of Ageing RTN Workshop, Paris. Retrieved from ⟨http://www.pse.ens.fr/rtn/program.html⟩.

Department of Social Security. (1985). *Reform of Social Security: A Programme for Action*. Cm. 9691. London: HMSO.

Department of Social Security. (1998). *A New Contract for Welfare: Partnership in Pensions*. Cm 4179. London: Department of Social Security.

Department of Work and Pensions. (2003). *Pensions 2002: Public Attitudes to Pensions and Saving for Retirement*. DWP Research Report 193. London, July.

Department of Work and Pensions. (2005). *Statistics on People with Second-Tier Pension Provision (STPP) by Principal Type of Cover and Tax Year*. London.

Department of Work and Pensions. (2006). *Security in Retirement: Towards a New Pensions System*. Cm 6841. London: Stationery Office. Retrieved from ⟨http://www.dwp.gov.uk/pensionsreform/whitepaper.asp⟩.

Diamond, P. (2004). "Social Security." *American Economic Review*, 94, 1–24.

Dilnot, A., R. Disney, P. Johnson, and E. Whitehouse. (1994). *Pensions Policy in the UK: An Economic Analysis*. London: Institute for Fiscal Studies.

Disney, R., and C. Emmerson. (2005). "Public Pension Reform in the United Kingdom: What Effect on the Financial Well Being of Current and Future Pensioners?" *Fiscal Studies*, 26, 55–82.

Disney, R., C. Emmerson, and S. Smith. (2004). "Pension Reform and Economic Performance in the UK." In R. Blundell, D. Card, and F. Freeman, eds., *Seeking a Premier Economy: The Economic Effects of British Economic Reforms, 1980–2000*. Chicago: Chicago University Press for National Bureau of Economic Research.

Disney, R., C. Emmerson, and S. Tanner. (1999). *Partnership in Pensions: A Commentary*. Commentary No. 78, Institute for Fiscal Studies, London.

Disney, R., C. Emmerson, and M. Wakefield. (2001). "Pension Reform and Saving in Britain." *Oxford Review of Economic Policy*, 17, 70–94.

Disney, R., and E. Whitehouse. (1992a). "Personal Pensions and the Review of the Contracting-Out Terms." *Fiscal Studies*, 13, 38–53.

Disney, R., and E. Whitehouse. (1992b). *The Personal Pension Stampede*. London: Institute for Fiscal Studies.

Emmerson, C., and S. Tanner. (2000). "A Note on the Tax Treatment of Private Pensions and Individual Savings Accounts." *Fiscal Studies*, 21, 65–74.

Government Actuary's Department. (2000). *Consultative Note: Pension Schemes Act 1993, Rebates and Reduced Rates of National Insurance Contributions for Members of Contracted-out Schemes*. London.

"Government Incentives for Saving." (1996). *Journal of Economic Perspectives*, 10, 73–138.

HM Treasury. (2004). *Charge Caps for New Stakeholder Products*. Press Release, 17 June 2004, London: HM Treasury. Retrieved from ⟨http://www.hm-treasury.gov.uk/newsroom_and_speeches/press/2004/press_57_04.cfm⟩.

Johnson, P., G. Stears, and S. Webb. (1998). "The Dynamics of Incomes and Occupational Pensions after Retirement." *Fiscal Studies*, 19, 197–215.

Leicester, A., and Z. Oldfield. (2004). "The Taxation of Housing." In *The IFS Green Budget, January 2004* (Chap. 58–74). London: IFS. Retrieved from ⟨http://www.ifs.org.uk/budgets/gb2004/04chap5.pdf⟩.

National Audit Office. (1991). *The Elderly: Informational Requirements for Supporting the Elderly and Implications of Personal Pensions for the National Insurance Fund*. London: HMSO.

Palacios, R., and E. Whitehouse. (1998). "The Role of Choice in the Transition to a Funded Pension System." Discussion Paper 9812. Washington, DC: World Bank.

Pensions Commission. (2004). *Pensions: Challenges and Choices, The First Report of the Pensions Commission*. London. Retrieved from ⟨http://www.pensionscommission.org.uk⟩.

Pensions Commission. (2005). *A New Pension Settlement for the Twenty-First Century: The Second Report of the Pensions Commission.* London. Retrieved from ⟨http://www.pensionscommission.org.uk⟩.

Poterba, J., ed. (1994). *Public Policies and Household Saving.* Chicago: Chicago University Press for National Bureau of Economic Research.

Scholz, J. K., A. Seshadri, and S. Khitatrakun. (2006). "Are Americans Saving 'Optimally' for Retirement?" *Journal of Political Economy*, 114, 607–643.

Personal Security Accounts and Mandatory Annuitization in a Dynastic Framework

Luisa Fuster, Ayşe İmrohoroğlu, and Selahattin İmrohoroğlu

The aging of the populations in the countries in the Organization for Economic Cooperation and Development (OECD) has prompted renewed academic research and political discussions of existing social insurance programs. Old-age, disability, health, and unemployment insurance programs have become the most expensive items in government budgets, and demographic projections suggest a significant increase in the old-age and health portions of social insurance in the next few decades.

Several European Union (EU) countries are already implementing reforms to minimize the fiscal burden of the demographic shock on individuals. Similar reform proposals are also being discussed for the United States' economy. In February 2005, the George W. Bush administration announced a reform proposal entitled "Strengthening Social Security for the 21st Century." Emphasizing the actuarial imbalance of the current unfunded system and the further stresses due to the projected aging of the U.S. population, this proposal called for a gradual privatization in which workers would deposit 4 percent of their income into private retirement accounts. Participation into this program was to be voluntary, and personal retirement account options and management were to be similar to that of the current federal employee retirement program, known as the Thrift Savings Plan (TSP). In other words, the most recent Bush proposal was intended to complement a down-sized public retirement system with a privatized system similar to that already in place for U.S. federal government employees. The February 2005 reform proposal failed to gain support, in part because of the excessive levels of current explicit debt and implicit social security debt. The September 11, 2001, attacks, the wars that followed the attacks, and the disastrous aftermath of hurricane Katrina also dominated the public debate and crowded out retirement issues. However,

the underlying problems that prompted reform proposals remain unre-
solved and will eventually have to be faced.

"Strengthening Social Security for the 21st Century" was based on
two previous attempts to draft a reform proposal following extensive
academic, public, and political discussions. In 2001, a President's Commission to Strengthen Social Security was appointed to formulate proposals that would help maintain the current pay-as-you-go (PAYG)
system's benefits for current retirees while improving the future pensions of current workers through personal security accounts. The
Commission proposed three plans. The first plan recommended that
workers make a voluntary contribution out of their social security payroll taxes into a personal security account (PSA), which would be
owned and managed by the worker and invested in a well-diversified
portfolio. The second plan extended this idea further and recommended diverting four percentage points of the social security payroll
tax to PSAs while reducing the indexation of current pensions by following price increases as opposed to wage increases. The third plan
introduced a mix of add-on and carve-out approaches such that a
worker who chooses to voluntarily invest an additional 1 percent of
earned income may divert 2.5 percent of social security payroll taxes,
up to $1,000 annually, to PSAs. Although all three plans are clearly
partial privatization plans, plans 2 and 3 also guarantee thirty-year
minimum-wage workers a retirement income above the poverty line.
All three plans allow for individual ownership of the accounts that can
be bequeathed to heirs. In its key features, the 2001 Commission's proposals were similar to those made by the 1997 Advisory Council on Social Security. One of the recommendations for correcting the long-term
imbalance of the program was to convert the current system to a basic,
flat-benefit program, and redirect five percentage points of the existing
payroll tax to private retirement accounts. This chapter examines, in a
generic manner, the quantitative impact of proposals of this nature
and the role played in this impact by mandatory annuitization of accumulated retirement wealth.

From Yaari (1965), we know that individuals facing mortality risk in
a pure life-cycle model find it optimal to annuitize their wealth. More
recently, Mitchell, Poterba, Warshawsky, and Brown (1999) estimate
that individuals facing mortality risk in an overlapping-generations
model without bequests are willing to give up more than 20 to 25 percent of their wealth to purchase actuarially fair annuities rather than
follow the optimal consumption plan without annuities, even in the

presence of significant preretirement social security wealth.[1] However, private annuity markets are very small. Diamond (1977) suggests that one possible reason may be the presence of asymmetric information and adverse selection and the accompanying failure in the market for annuities. Friedman and Warshawsky (1990) and Mitchell et al. (1999) document how unattractively private annuity contracts are priced in the United States and argue that adverse selection might lead to this outcome. Indeed, Feldstein (2005) emphasizes that the problem of asymmetric information and adverse selection could "weaken the functioning of private insurance markets."[2]

The large literature that attempts to quantify the overall welfare effects of unfunded social security using applied general-equilibrium models can be summarized as follows. The welfare costs of social security arise because the public provision of retirement insurance leads to a reduction in saving, a distortion in labor supply, and a distortion in the retirement decision (early retirement).[3]

Social security potentially raises individual welfare by improving risk sharing in the population.[4] In particular, social security provides partial insurance against mortality risk, individual income risk, and investment income risk.

Using an overlapping-generations setting without bequests, previous research has largely found that social security imposes an overall welfare cost on the society. As Auerbach and Kotlikoff (1987) argue, the main reason for this negative finding is the large decrease in the capital stock, which in turn leads to a significant reduction in lifetime consumption. Hubbard and Judd (1987) allow social security to provide longevity insurance, but its partial insurance aspect is not sufficient to overturn the negative lifetime consumption effect of social security. İmrohoroğlu, İmrohoroğlu, and Joines (1995, 1999) and Storesletten, Telmer, and Yaron (1999) introduce individual income risk as an additional benefit of social security but obtain a similarly negative outcome for social security.

These findings suggest that we might expect to observe widespread privatizations in the United States, EU countries, and elsewhere. There are at least three explanations for the persistence of pay-as-you-go systems, in spite of the steady-state burdens associated with them.

First, the transitional costs from a pay-as-you-go social security system to a fully privatized retirement system may be large. Huang, İmrohoroğlu, and Sargent (1997) and Kotlikoff, Smetters, and Walliser (1999) consider several alternative policy transitions from the current

U.S. system to a privatized one. De Nardi, İmrohoroğlu, and Sargent (1999) examine various alternative transitional policy responses to the aging of the U.S. population.[5] These studies and Conesa and Krueger (1999) find large transitional costs, with a majority of the currently alive population suffering welfare losses and thus blocking any reform proposal. Second, there may be political-equilibrium considerations that allow the introduction and maintenance of an unfunded social security system, as Cooley and Soares (1999) and Boldrin and Rustichini (2000) argue. Finally, it is possible that not all potential benefits of social security have been carefully modeled.[6] The insurance role of social security in shielding the participants from investment income risk is only recently being carefully analyzed. In a recent paper, Krueger and Kubler (2002) use an overlapping-generations model with a stochastic production technology and incomplete markets to evaluate the welfare consequences of introducing a small unfunded social security system. Their main quantitative finding is that the "capital crowding-out" effect mentioned above outweighs the insurance role of social security against realistic investment income risk.

The studies summarized above make the extreme assumption that consumers have little or no altruism. However, there is a substantial literature that suggests that at least a fraction of individuals behave in a way consistent with an operative bequest motive. Laitner and Juster (1996) and Wilhelm (1996) are recent examples of empirical papers that provide some evidence on the strength of altruism. This chapter assumes that individuals have two-sided altruism: they care both about their parents and their children.

Fuster (1999) and Fuster, İmrohoroğlu, and İmrohoroğlu (2003, 2007) explore the role of social security in a dynastic setting with incomplete markets and distorting taxes and show that there are qualitative and quantitative differences between the pure life cycle and the dynastic environments. They find that the "capital crowding-out" effect of unfunded social security is quantitatively much smaller in the dynastic model due to the strong additional motive to save and that "family insurance" largely makes up for the loss of publicly provided insurance in privatization experiments. Furthermore, they highlight the importance of a "flexible" labor market as one of the key conditions for a successful social security reform. When the pay-as-you-go system is eliminated, there is a sizable reduction in the labor-income tax rate, which raises labor supply and generates large welfare gains from privatization. This is especially true in an economy in which the link between contributions and benefits in the pay-as-you-go system is small.

There are three features of an economy that enhance the success of social security reform: operative bequest motives, flexible labor markets, and weak linkage between contributions and benefits.

In this chapter, we quantitatively evaluate the welfare effects of reforming social security by introducing a PSA with and without mandatory annuitization in an economic environment with uninsurable individual income shocks, two-sided bequests, borrowing constraints, and missing annuity markets. Our setup allows us to assess whether mandatory saving or mandatory annuitization of accumulated PSA wealth at retirement is welfare enhancing and, if so, for what type of households.

In our model, family insurance takes the form of intervivos transfers and bequests. There are three general types of households, depending on the number of surviving household members. In type 1 households, the parents have died, and only the children survive. In type 2 households, the children have died, and only the parents survive. Type 3 households constitute the majority and have both the parents and the children in the household. In this type, we have further heterogeneity. Since the parents and the children receive the realization of generationally persistent "ability" shocks, type 3 households are further divided into four ability combinations depending on the high- or low-ability realizations of the parents and the children.[7]

This framework is well suited to consider the annuity role of social security for single individuals versus for households where families also provide annuity insurance to their members. Our goal is to evaluate quantitatively PSA reforms with or without mandatory annuitization of PSA wealth at retirement. We do this in a setup where some households have a higher desire to annuitize wealth than others do.

We calibrate our economy to the U.S. economy, use numerical, discrete state-space methods to solve the households' recursive decision problem, and restrict attention to steady states under various pension systems.

The chapter presents the model in detail, contains calibration, gives numerical results, and presents concluding remarks.

The Model

The economic environment in this chapter follows Fuster, İmrohoroğlu, and İmrohoroğlu (2003). It is an applied general-equilibrium model with overlapping generations facing lifespan and ability uncertainty and borrowing constraints and exhibiting two-sided altruism. The cost of the model's richness in demographic and productivity dynamics is that we simplify the macroeconomic context. There is no uncertainty to the return to capital in this model. For this chapter to be self-contained, we describe the model, although some of the details can be obtained in Fuster, İmrohoroğlu, and İmrohoroğlu (2003).

Demographics and Endowments

Our setup is a stationary overlapping-generations model where in every period t a generation of individuals is born. Individuals face random lives, and some live through the maximum possible age $2T$. If the individual survives, then his lifetime support overlaps during the first T periods with the lifetime support of his father and during the last T periods with the lifetime support of his children. The total population in the economy consists of $2T$ overlapping generations of individuals with total measure one.

At birth, individuals make a draw from a distribution of abilities. An individual's ability can be high or low, and it determines both the individual's lifetime labor productivity and his life expectancy. If the ability is high, $z = H$, the individual enjoys a permanently higher labor productivity throughout his lifespan than an individual with low ability, $z = L$. The labor productivity of an individual of ability z and age j is denoted by $\varepsilon_j(z)$. We assume that from age R to age $2T$ the labor productivity is zero, so R represents the exogenous retirement age. At any other age, the individual supplies inelastically labor to firms.

An individual with high ability also enjoys a permanently higher conditional survival probabilities throughout his lifespan than an individual with low ability. With this assumption, we want to capture the fact that in the U.S. economy survival rates are higher among individuals with relatively high education levels. We will use $\psi_j(z)$ to denote the probability of surviving to age $j + 1$ conditional on having survived to age j for an individual with ability z for age $j = 1, 2, \ldots, 2T$, where $\psi_{2T}(z) = 0$ and $z \in \{H, L\}$.

We assume that abilities are correlated across generations of the same family line. In particular, ability z is a two-state, first-order Markov process with the transition probability matrix

$$\Pi(z', z) = [\pi_{ij}], \quad i, j \in \{H, L\},$$

where $\pi_{ij} = \Pr\{z' = j \mid z = i\}$, z is the labor ability of the father, and z' is the labor ability of the new born in the dynasty. To develop economic intuition about how the model works, it is important to note that there are no private insurance markets in the economy to diversify the risk of being born as a low-ability-type individual. However, the informal family structure and some partial annuities, public or privately administered if they exist, do provide some partial insurance against this type of shock.

Cohort shares are time invariant due to our assumptions of constant conditional survival probabilities and population growth rate n. Using $\mu_1(z) = \lambda(z)(1 + n)^T$ to indicate the size of cohort 1 (newborns) with ability z, relative to that of cohort $(T + 1)$ (parents), where $(1 + n)^T$ is the number of children per parent and $\lambda(z)$ is the measure of newborn individuals with ability z, we can obtain the relative sizes of the other generations recursively:

$$\mu_{j+1}(z) = \frac{\psi_j(z)\mu_j(z)}{(1 + n)}, \quad j = 1, \dots, 2T - 1.$$

Technology

There is a continuum of identical firms that produce a final good using capital and labor. The technology is represented by a constant returns Cobb-Douglas production function $Y_t = K_t^\alpha (A_t N_t)^{1-\alpha}$, where $\alpha \in (0, 1)$ is the output share of capital, Y_t is output at time t, K_t is aggregate capital input at time t, N_t is aggregate labor input at time t, and A_t is an exogenous labor-augmenting technological progress growing at a constant rate γ. Capital depreciates at a constant rate $\delta \in (0, 1)$. Since all markets are competitive, the profit-maximizing conditions imply that factor prices are set equal to marginal products—that is,

$$\tilde{r}_t = \alpha K_t^{\alpha-1}(A_t N_t)^{1-\alpha}, \tag{7.1}$$

$$\omega_t = (1 - \alpha)K_t^\alpha(A_t N_t)^{-\alpha}, \tag{7.2}$$

where $\tilde{r}_t$ is the rental price of capital, and ω_t is the wage per effective labor.[8]

Social Security and Fiscal Policy

The Benchmark Social Security System: Pay-as-You-Go In the benchmark economy, we assume that the social security system finances current pensions with the contributions of current workers.

That is, the systems transfers income from workers to retirees. In the U.S. economy, retirement benefits depend on individuals' average lifetime earnings via a concave, piecewise linear function. The marginal replacement rate decreases with average lifetime earnings indexed to productivity growth. It is equal to 0.9 for earnings lower than 20 percent of the economy's average earnings. Above this limit and below 125 percent of the economy's average earnings, the marginal replacement rate decreases to 0.33. For income within 125 percent and 246 percent of the economy's average earnings, the marginal replacement rate is 0.15. Additional income above 246 percent of the economy's average earnings does not provide any additional pension payment.

In our benchmark economy, the function that relates the pension $B_j(z)$, with the individual's ability z mimics the progressivity of the U.S. social security benefits.[9] In particular, at retirement the pension payment for each ability group is calculated as follows:

$$B_R(z) = \begin{cases} 0.9 \cdot (0.2\overline{M}) + 0.33 \cdot (M(z) - 0.2\overline{M}), & \text{for } z = L, \\ 0.9 \cdot (0.2\overline{M}) + 0.33 \cdot (1.25\overline{M} - 0.2\overline{M}) \\ \quad + 0.15 \cdot (M(z) - 1.25\overline{M}), & \text{for } z = H, \end{cases}$$

where $M(z)$ denotes the average lifetime earnings of an individual of ability z and $\overline{M}$ denotes the economy's average earnings.

Note that an individual's pension remains constant during retirement while technology grows at the rate γ. Thus, the pension per effective labor decreases during retirement at rate γ—that is, $B_j(z) = B_R(z)/(1+\gamma)^{j-R}$. Pensions are financed by taxing earnings at a rate τ, and the budget of the social security system is balanced at every period—that is,

$$\sum_z \sum_{j=R}^{2T} \mu_j(z)B_j(z) = \tau \omega N. \tag{7.3}$$

Reform 1: Personal Security Accounts without Annuitization Under a personal security account system, retirement benefits come from two distinct sources. The first tier is a flat pension benefit equal to 18 percent of per capita gross domestic product (a monthly payment of $410 in 1996). This portion of the total benefit is financed in a pay-as-you-go fashion by taxing current labor income. Hence, the social security tax rate that finances the first-tier system is set such that its aggregate revenue equals the aggregate first-tier benefits:

$$\sum_{z}\sum_{j=R}^{2T}\mu_j(z)b = \tau_s\omega N, \tag{7.4}$$

where b denotes the flat benefit, and τ_s is the social security payroll tax to finance the first-tier benefits. We can obtain the following close-form solution for the equilibrium tax rate by substituting $b = 0.18y$ and $y = \omega N/(1 - \alpha)$ in the above equation:

$$\tau_s = \frac{0.18}{1 - \alpha}\sum_{z}\sum_{j=R}^{2T}\mu_j(z).$$

The second tier of retirement benefits is financed by forced saving. Every period, the individual deposits 5 percent of earnings in PSAs. These funds are owned and managed by the individuals and are invested in the capital market, where they earn the rate of return on capital and cannot be withdrawn until the individual retires. The capital income accumulated in the PSA is not taxed during the individual's working life. The amount of second-tier benefits is determined by the wealth accumulated in these tax-favored personal security accounts.[10] These assumptions define the following law of motion of the PSA (for an individual of ability z):

$$(1 + \gamma)s_{j+1}(z) = (1 + \tilde{r})s_j(z) + \kappa\omega\varepsilon_j(z), \tag{7.5}$$

where $\kappa = 0.05$ is the social security tax that finances the second-tier benefits, $s_{j+1}(z)$ denotes the PSA funds of an age-$j + 1$ individual with ability z, and $s_1(z) = 0$. At retirement, the individual gets a lump-sum transfer of the wealth accumulated in his account, which amounts to $(1 + \tilde{r})s_R(z)$. If the individual does not survive to his retirement, his PSA funds are transferred to his estate. Note that this reform is essentially a partial privatization achieved by a mandatory saving program.

Summarizing, the pension benefits under PSA (reform 1) are described as follows:

$$B_j(z) = \begin{cases} b + (1 + \tilde{r})s_R(z) & \text{for } j = R \\ b/(1 + \gamma)^{j-R} & \text{otherwise,} \end{cases}$$

and the tax rate on earnings used to finance pensions τ is the sum of κ and τ_s.

Reform 2: Personal Security Accounts with Mandatory Annuitization In a modified version of the above reform, we consider the case of partial privatization in which the funds accumulated in the personal security account are annuitized by the institution managing the PSAs. At retirement, individuals are entitled to an annuity payment $b(z)$, which we assume to be proportional to the wealth accumulated in the PSA at retirement—that is, $b(z) = p(1 + \tilde{r})s_R(z)$, where the proportion p is determined endogenously as we explain below. The annuity payment remains constant during retirement, just like the first-tier flat pay-as-you-go benefit, and thus the annuity payment per effective units of labor decreases at the rate γ.[11]

To compute the annuity payment of each individual, the social security system has to determine the proportion p of accumulated wealth that the individual receives during retirement. This variable p is set such that the expected present value of the aggregate annuity payments of the generation that retires today equals the aggregate wealth held in PSA (the funds of individuals that are alive at retirement plus the funds of individuals that die before reaching retirement).[12] The expected present value of the aggregate annuity payments of the generation that retires today is given by

$$\sum_z p(1 + \tilde{r})s_R(z)\lambda(z) \sum_{j=R}^{2T}(1 + \tilde{r})^{R-j} \prod_{i=1}^{j-1} \psi_i(z).$$

The aggregate wealth accumulated in PSA by individuals in this cohort who survived to retirement is given by $\sum_z(1 + \tilde{r})s_R(z)\lambda(z) \prod_{i=1}^{R-1} \psi_i(z)$, and the aggregate wealth accumulated by individuals in this cohort who died before retirement is

$$\sum_z(1 + \tilde{r}) \sum_{j=2}^{R} \left(\frac{1 + \tilde{r}}{1 + \gamma}\right)^{R-j} s_j(z)\lambda(z)(1 - \psi_{j-1}(z)) \prod_{i=1}^{j-2} \psi_i(z).$$

As a result, the proportion p must satisfy the following condition:

$$p = \frac{\sum_z s_R(z)\lambda(z) \prod_{i=1}^{R-1} \psi_i(z) + \sum_z \sum_{j=2}^{R} \left(\frac{1+\tilde{r}}{1+\gamma}\right)^{R-j} s_j(z)\lambda(z)(1 - \psi_{j-1}(z)) \prod_{i=1}^{j-2} \psi_i(z)}{\sum_z s_R(z)\lambda(z) \sum_{j=R}^{2T}(1 + \tilde{r})^{R-j} \prod_{i=1}^{j-1} \psi_i(z)}.$$

The above condition implies that the return of annuities is linked to the average mortality rate across individuals with differential mortality (high- and low-ability individuals), and as a result, the return of annuities is not fair. This return could not be offered by private annuities since it would not be accepted by individuals with a high mortality rate (low ability). In contrast, the government can provide this return because annuities are mandatory. In other words, the government can overcome an adverse-selection problem (private information on differential mortality) in the annuity market because PSAs are mandatorily annuitized.

The law of motion of the aggregate wealth held in PSAs by the social security system is

$$(1+n)(1+\gamma)W_{t+1} = (1+\tilde{r})W_t + \kappa \omega N - \bar{B},$$

where $\kappa = 0.05$ and $\bar{B} = \sum_z \sum_{j=R}^{2T} b(z)(1+\gamma)^{R-j}\mu_j(z)$ denotes the aggregate annuity payments at period t. At each period t, the aggregate funds in PSA W_t are invested in the capital market.

Summarizing, the pension benefits under reform 2 are described as follows:

$$B_j(z) = \begin{cases} b + b(z) & \text{for } j = R \\ (b+b(z))/(1+\gamma)^{j-R} & \text{for } j > R, \end{cases}$$

and the tax rate on earnings used to finance pensions τ is the sum of κ and τ_s.

Government Budget   In addition to the administration of the pension system, the government taxes labor income, capital income, and consumption to finance exogenously given government purchases. We assume that the government's budget is balanced each period. Since tax rates and government expenditures are exogenous, the budget is balanced by an endogenous lump-sum transfer to the individuals. The government also collects the asset holdings and capital income of individuals who die without descendants. These resources are transferred in a lump-sum fashion to all survivors.[13]

Preferences
The preference structure in our setup follows Laitner's (1992) two-sided altruistic specification in which individuals derive utility from their own lifetime consumption and from the felicity of their predecessors and descendants. An important feature of Laitner's (1992) model is that parents and children have the same objective function during the periods when their lifetimes overlap. Due to this commonality of

interest, strategic behavior between the father and the children does not arise, and thus father and children constitute a single decision unit by pooling their resources. We call this decision unit a *household*, which is constituted by an adult male, the father, of generation j and age $T + 1$, and his $m = (1 + n)^T$ adult children of generation $j + T$ and age 1.

We model altruism as in Laitner (1992) but in a model with uncertain lifetimes. This framework allows us to evaluate the annuity role of various social security institutions when families can also provide annuity insurance to their members. Because we assume uncertain lifetimes, the composition of the household evolves stochastically in our framework. At each period, there are three types of households.[14] Type 1 households are those where the father has died. Type 2 households consist only of the father since the m children have died. Households of type 3 are those where both the father and the children are still alive. Moreover, households are heterogeneous with respect to their asset holdings, age, and abilities.[15]

The budget constraint facing an age-j household, where $j = 1, 2, \ldots, T - 1$ is the age of the youngest member(s), is given by

$$[\phi_s(h) + \phi_f(h)](1 + \tau_c)c_j + (1 + \gamma)a_j$$

$$= [1 + r(1 - \tau_k)]a_{j-1} + e_j(h, z, z') + [\phi_s(h) + \phi_f(h)](\xi_1 + \xi_2), \qquad (7.6)$$

where ϕ_s is an indicator function that takes the value m if the children are alive and 0 otherwise, ϕ_f is an indicator function that takes the value unity if the father is alive and 0 otherwise, $h \in \{1, 2, 3\}$ is an indicator of household composition, $r = \tilde{r} - \delta$, $e_j(h, z, z')$ are the after-tax earnings, c_j is the consumption of each household member, a_j denotes the asset holdings to be carried over to age $j + 1$, ξ_1 is the lump-sum redistribution of unintended bequests left behind by fathers without sons and confiscated by the government, ξ_2 is a lump-sum transfer to balance the government's budget, and τ_c and τ_k denote the consumption and capital income tax rates, respectively. All per capita aggregate quantities reported in the chapter are divided by the level of the technology A_t and therefore represented in efficiency units. As we restrict attention to steady states, consumption, asset holdings, lump-sum transfers, and earnings are in efficiency units and constant over time.

We represent the net of tax earnings of an age-j household with the function $e_j(h, z, z')$:

$e_j(h, z, z')$

$$= \begin{cases} \phi_s(h)\omega(1 - \tau - \tau_\ell)\varepsilon_j(z') + \phi_f(h)B_{j+T}(z) & \text{if } j \geq R - T, \\ \phi_s(h)\omega(1 - \tau - \tau_\ell)\varepsilon_j(z') + \phi_f(h)\omega(1 - \tau - \tau_\ell)\varepsilon_{j+T}(z), & \text{if not,} \end{cases}$$
$$(7.7)$$

where τ is the social security tax, τ_ℓ is the personal tax rate on labor income, and $B_{j+T}(z)$ denotes the pension at age $j + T$.

For $j = T$, the budget constraint of the household is given by

$$[\phi_s(h) + \phi_f(h)](1 + \tau_c)c_T + (1 + n)^T(1 + \gamma)a_T$$

$$= [1 + r(1 - \tau_k)]a_{T-1} + e_T(h, z, z') + [\phi_s(h) + \phi_f(h)](\xi_1 + \xi_2). \quad (7.8)$$

If the children survive to age T, $(1 + n)^T$ new households are constituted in the dynasty, and each of them will hold a_T assets. If the children do not survive to age T, the family line breaks.

It is assumed that households face borrowing constraints and cannot hold negative assets at any age:

$$a_j \geq 0, \quad \forall j. \qquad (7.9)$$

Individuals obtain utility from their consumption and from their predecessors' and descendants' consumption. We restrict the utility function to the constant relative risk aversion (CRRA) class because we assume a balanced growth path for our economy. We will use the language of recursive economic theory to describe the household's decision problem.

Let $V_j(a, h, z, z')$ denote the maximized value of expected, discounted lifetime utility of an age-j household with the state vector (a, h, z, z'). For a household of age $j \leq T$,

$$V_j(a, h, z, z') = \max_{\{c, a'\}} \left\{ [\phi_s(h) + \phi_f(h)] \frac{c^{1-\sigma}}{1 - \sigma} + \beta(1 + \gamma)^{1-\sigma}\tilde{V}_{j+1}(a', h', z, z') \right\}$$

subject to (7.6)–(7.9), $\qquad (7.10)$

where σ is the coefficient of relative risk aversion,

$\tilde{V}_{j+1}(a', h', z, z')$

$$= \begin{cases} \sum_{h'=1}^{3} \chi_j(h, h'; z, z')V_{j+1}(a', h', z, z') & \text{for } j = 1, 2, \ldots, T - 1, \\ \psi_T(z')(1 + n)^T \sum_{z'' \in \{H, L\}} \pi_{z'z''}V_1(a', 3, z', z'') & \text{for } j = T, \end{cases}$$

$\chi_j(h, h'; z, z')$ is the probability that a household of age j, and type h becomes type h' the next period given that the father is of ability z and the children of ability z'.[16]

Steady-State Equilibrium

A fiscal policy is a set $\{G, B, \tau_\ell, \tau_k, \tau_c, \tau_s, \kappa, \tau\}$. Given fiscal policy, a *stationary recursive competitive equilibrium* is a set of value functions $\{V_j(a, h, z, z')\}_{j=1}^T$, households' decision rules $\{c_j(\cdot), a_j(\cdot)\}_{j=1}^T$, time-invariant measures of households $\{X_j(a, h, z, z')\}_{j=1}^T$, relative prices of labor and capital $\{\omega, r\}$, a lump-sum distribution of unintended bequests ξ_1, and a lump-sum government transfer ξ_2 such that the following conditions are satisfied:

1. Given fiscal policy, prices, and lump-sum transfers, households' decision rules solve households' decision problem (7.10).

2. Firms maximize profits—that is, (7.1) and (7.2) hold.

3. Aggregation holds:

$$\tilde{K} = \sum_{j,a,h,z,z'} a_{j-1}(a, h, z, z') X_j(a, h, z, z')(1+n)^{1-j} + W,$$

$$\tilde{N} = \sum_{j=1}^{R-1} \sum_{z \in \{H,L\}} \varepsilon_j(z) \mu_j(z),$$

$$C = \sum_{j,a,h,z,z'} [\phi_s(h) + \phi_f(h)] c_j(a, h, z, z') X_j(a, h, z, z')(1+n)^{1-j},$$

where $W = \sum_z \sum_{j=1}^R s_j(z) \mu_j(z)$ is the aggregate PSA wealth in the economy, adjusted for growth.

4. The set of age-dependent measures of households satisfies

$$X_{j+1}(a', h', z, z') = \sum_{\{a,h: a'=a_j(a,h,z,z')\}} X_j(a, h, z, z') \chi_j(h, h'; z, z'),$$

$$\text{for } j = 1, \ldots, T-1; \tag{7.11}$$

the invariant distribution of age-1 households is given by conditions

$$X_1(a', 3, z', z'')$$

$$= \pi_{z'z''} \sum_{\{a,h,z: a'=a_T(a,h,z,z')\}} X_T(a, h, z, z') \chi_T(h, 3; z, z'); \tag{7.12}$$

and

$$X_1(0, 1, z', z'') = \lambda(z')\pi_{z'z''} - \sum_{a'} X_1(a', 3, z', z'') \tag{7.13}$$

—that is, new dynasties, holding zero assets, substitute for the family lines broken during any given period.

5. The lump-sum redistribution of unintended bequests satisfies

$$\xi_1 = (1+r) \sum_{j=1}^{T} a_j(a, h, z, z') X_j(a, h, z, z') \left[1 - \sum_{h'=1}^{3} \chi_j(h, h'; z, z') \right] (1+n)^{1-j}.$$

6. The government's budget is balanced:

$$\xi_2 = \tau_k r \left[\tilde{K} - \frac{\xi_1}{1+r} \right] + \tau_\ell \omega \tilde{N} + \tau_c C - G.$$

7. The budget of the social security system is balanced—that is, (7.3) or (7.4) hold, depending on the social security system in place.

8. The goods market clears

$$C + [(1+n)(1+\gamma)\tilde{K} - (1-\delta)\tilde{K}] + G = \tilde{K}^\alpha \tilde{N}^{1-\alpha}.$$

Calibration and Solution

We are going to calibrate our model economy to the long-run quantities in the U.S. economy to conduct our counterfactual experiments for reforming social security. Our main calibration target is the average capital-to-output ratio in the U.S. economy over the last fifty years—2.5. Table 7.1 shows the major modeling and calibration choices made.

A newborn in our setup is a twenty-one-year-old individual; a model period is five years. Retirement is mandatory at age sixty-five, and maximum lifespan is ninety years. The population growth rate is 1.2 percent per year, and the productivity growth rate is 1.65 percent annually. Again, these are the averages from the U.S. economy over the last fifty years. The depreciation rate is taken as 4.4 percent, and capital's share of gross national product is 31 percent.

Fiscal policy is captured by a constant annual government-to-GNP ratio of 18 percent, and taxes on labor income, capital income, and consumption, at 20 percent, 40 percent, and 5 percent, respectively.

Table 7.1
List of parameters

Demographics	
$2T = 14$	Maximum lifetime (70 years)
$R = 10$	Retirement age (45 years)
$n = 0.012$	Population growth rate (annual)
Preferences	
$\sigma = 2$	Coefficient of relative risk aversion
$\beta = 0.988$	Annual discount factor
Technology	
$\gamma = 0.0165$	Annual rate of growth of technology
$\alpha = 0.31$	Capital share of GNP
$\delta = 0.044$	Annual depreciation rate
$\lambda(H) = 0.28$	Measure of individuals with high ability
$\pi_{LL} = 0.83\ \pi_{HH} = 0.57$	Transition probability matrix of abilities
Fiscal Policy	
$\tau_l = 0.2$	Labor-income tax rate
$\tau_k = 0.4$	Capital-income tax rate
$\tau_c = 0.05$	Consumption tax rate
$G/Y = 18\%$	Government expenditure to GDP ratio

Table 7.2
Aggregate effects of reforms

	τ_s (percent)	κ (percent)	K	Y	$r(1 - \tau_k)$ (percent)	C
Benchmark	9.44%	0%	100.0	100.0	4.62%	100.0
PSA+Annuity	4.38	5	109.5	102.8	4.24	101.8
PSA	4.38	5	108.9	102.7	4.26	101.7
Elimination	0	0	106.1	101.8	4.37	101.2

The coefficient of relative risk aversion σ is set equal to 2, and the subjective discount factor β is taken as 0.988 to obtain a capital-to-output ratio of 2.5.[17]

Numerical Findings

Aggregate Long-Run Effects
We summarize the long-run effects of various types of reform in table 7.2. The benchmark steady-state describes the current U.S. economy, where pensions are provided by a pay-as-you-go system with a re-

placement rate of 44 percent and a payroll tax rate of 9.44 percent. We set the values of aggregate variables in this steady-state equilibrium equal to 100 for easy comparison with other steady-state equilibria under alternative reform proposals.

The steady state labeled *Elimination* is an equilibrium where there is no unfunded system at all and all individuals are left free to save the optimal amounts desired to support old-age consumption. The steady states labeled *PSA + Annuity* and *PSA* enforce mandatory saving at the rate of 5 percent of individuals' gross wage income in each of the years during their working life. Not surprisingly, all three alternative steady states exhibit higher capital stock than the benchmark economy since the distortion on saving is reduced with the decline of the payroll tax from 9.44 percent to 4.38 percent.

According to table 7.2, *PSA* and *PSA + Annuity* induce a higher capital stock than the elimination of social security. This is because individuals cannot borrow against the mandatory savings induced by personal security accounts. Also, the *PSA + Annuity* reform generates a (slightly) higher capital stock than the *PSA*-only reform because the funds of the deceased are invested in the capital market in the former reform, while they are transferred to the estates in the latter reform. As a consequences, aggregate mandatory savings are larger in the case of annuitized personal security accounts.

Welfare Effects

We compare the utility of a newborn household across alternative steady states for different composition and ability types using a consumption equivalent variation measure. We compute the change in consumption in each future period and state of nature, $(1 + c(h, z, z'))$, relative to the benchmark consumption level that is necessary to make the household indifferent between being born in the benchmark economy or in the alternative steady state—that is,

$$(1 + c(h, z, z'))^{1-\sigma} U_B(h, z, z') = U_R(h, z, z'),$$

where $U_B(h, z, z')$ is the average utility of a newborn household type (h, z, z') at the benchmark economy, and $U_R(h, z, z')$ is the average utility of such household at the alternative steady state. The average utility of a newborn household type (h, z, z') is computed by aggregating the utility across asset levels using the stationary distribution of assets. For instance,

Table 7.3
Welfare of newborns

	Type 3				Type 1		
	HH	HL	LH	LL	H	L	Mean
Benchmark	1.0	1.0	1.0	1.0	1.0	1.0	1.0
PSA+Annuity	1.008	0.98	1.037	1.022	1.019	0.980	1.013
PSA	0.980	0.97	1.025	1.018	1.020	1.005	1.006
Elimination	0.990	0.98	1.017	1.003	1.056	1.060	1.005
Measure of types	0.147	0.110	0.107	0.530	0.025	0.080	

$$U_B(h, z, z') = \frac{\sum_a X_{1,B}(a, h, z, z') V_{1,B}(a, h, z, z')}{\sum_a X_{1,B}(a, h, z, z')},$$

where $X_{1,B}(a, h, z, z')$ denotes the invariant distribution of states (a, h, z, z') across age-1 households, and $V_{1,B}(a, h, z, z')$ denotes the utility of an age-1 household with state (a, h, z, z') at the benchmark economy.

Table 7.3 shows the consumption equivalent variation measure for newborn households for different composition and ability types. The second and third rows show the welfare measure under the partial privatization proposals, and the last row depicts the welfare measure of households under full privatization. Notice that a welfare measure higher that 1 means that the household would prefer to be born in the alternative steady state relative to the benchmark economy. The last column of the table shows the aggregate welfare measure across all newborn household types.[18]

Type 1 households prefer the elimination of the pay-as-you-go system entirely. They prefer elimination over partial privatization, with or without mandatory annuitization. There are at least two reasons for their preference. First, these households have no fathers who would generate the demand for annuity insurance, and since these households are very young, they would rather not be subject to forced saving. Second, they might be facing binding liquidity constraints, and mandatory saving would then reduce their welfare. Another way to get the same intuition is to compare their lifetime welfare under the two PSA reforms. They prefer the one without annuitization for the same reasons listed above. In addition, type 1 households prefer the personal savings account reform to the pay-as-you-go benchmark.

Table 7.4
Return of social security for type 1 households (percentage)

	H	L
Benchmark	2.70%	2.90%
PSA+Annuity	5.51	5.49
PSA	5.10	5.41

For type 3 households, the proposed PSA reform benefits those with low preference for annuity insurance. In particular, the households with low-life-expectancy fathers (LL and LH households) are better off, whereas households with long-life-expectancy fathers (HH and HL households) are worse off, relative to the benchmark pay-as-you-go social security system.

A great majority of type 3 households finds it best of all to be born into the steady-state labeled *PSA + Annuity*, where there is mandatory saving at the 5 percent rate and wealth generated by this partial privatization program is annuitized at retirement.[19] This finding might seem surprising since our households care about leaving bequests to their relatives. However, since fathers are alive in these households, they like to hold annuities, and therefore mandatory annuitization does not lower their welfare. Moreover, the fathers are very close to retirement age, and the timing of annuitization is also in line with the households' desire to hold annuities to insure the soon-to-be retirees. The HL households prefer the pay-as-you-go system. These households benefit from the progressivity of the pay-as-you-go system because of the low-ability son, and they also receive a generous pension for the high-ability father.

The *PSA*-only reform benefits LH and LL households and hurts HH and HL households, relative to the benchmark equilibrium. This may be due to the fact that PSA does not provide annuity insurance against lifespan uncertainty, while PAYG social security does so in the benchmark equilibrium. In fact, under PSA and mandatory annuitization, all ability types but HL enjoy higher lifetime welfare than in the benchmark economy.

To see how type 1 households fare under the proposed reforms, table 7.4 calculates the expected rate of return to social security for H and L types.[20]

In both steady states with PSAs, the expected return on social security at birth is higher than the after-tax return on capital. In the case of

PSA without annuitization, there is some progressivity in the benefits since there is a first tier that is a flat benefit for every retiree. Indeed, the expected return of social security is higher for individuals with low ability (5.41 percent) than for the H types (5.10 percent). This difference between the returns for low- and high-ability households disappears when part of the retirement wealth is annuitized. In this case, high-ability households enjoy a higher rate of return (5.51 percent) than low-ability households (5.49 percent) because H types have a longer life expectancy than L types. Therefore, when the part of wealth generated by mandatory saving is annuitized at retirement, a rationale for introducing a flat first-tier pension is to compensate low-ability individuals for the fact that their expected life is shorter.

General-Equilibrium Effects The welfare effects of the different reforms of social security are partially due to general-equilibrium effects on factor prices and on the lump-sum transfers used to balance the government's budget and to redistribute accidental bequests. The increase of the capital stock due to the elimination of the pay-as-you-go system induces a decrease in the interest rate and an increase in the wage rate that favor relatively poor households. The two reforms with personal security accounts reduce the government revenue from capital income taxes (reducing the lump-sum transfer ξ_2), which favors relatively rich households. Moreover, the reform with annuitized personal security accounts reduces the redistribution of accidental bequests (ξ_1), which hurts relatively poor (and borrowing constrained) households.

In this subsection, we evaluate the importance of these general-equilibrium effects. To this end, we fix the values of the factor prices and lump-sum transfers to the levels at the benchmark economy and compute the welfare effects of the alternative reforms. We find that, for all households types, the preference ordering for social security arrangements is as follows: (1) *PSA + annuity*, (2) *PSA*, (3) *Elimination*, and (4) *Benchmark*. In this partial-equilibrium experiment, we conclude that the preference ordering of social security systems is consistent with the differential in social security returns across these economies.

Table 7.5 shows that all households would prefer to be born in the economy with personal security accounts and mandatory annuitization at retirement because the return of social security is the highest (about 6 percent) in this economy. Households of type 1 and type 3 of abilities HL, which are relatively poor and likely to be borrowing con-

Table 7.5
Welfare of newborns (fixed prices and transfers).

	Type 3				Type 1		
	HH	HL	LH	LL	H	L	Mean
Benchmark	1.0	1.0	1.0	1.0	1.0	1.0	1.0
PSA+Annuity	1.159	1.163	1.163	1.172	1.103	1.084	1.158
PSA	1.102	1.108	1.111	1.122	1.067	1.060	1.108
Elimination	1.041	1.036	1.042	1.034	1.049	1.043	1.036
Measure of types	0.147	0.110	0.107	0.530	0.025	0.080	

strained, benefit from the reform *PSA + annuity* because lump-sum transfers do not decrease due to this partial-equilibrium reform. Households of types HL and HH, which are relatively rich, prefer the reform with PSA or the elimination of social security to the benchmark system because the interest rate does not decrease with the partial-equilibrium reforms.

Table 7.5 also reveals that the loss in welfare from nonannuitization is about 5 percent; the average welfare gains for *PSA + Annuity* and *PSA only* are 15.8 percent and 10.8 percent, respectively. This value for annuities is much smaller than the Mitchell et al. (1999) estimates of about 20 to 25 percent. Our welfare benefits are not directly comparable with theirs because they compute the welfare effects of having access to an annuity market while we compute the welfare effects of reforming the pay-as-you-go social security system. Still, there are several reasons why their welfare benefits from annuitization are much higher than our estimates. First, Mitchell et al. (1999) consider the value of annuities for individuals at retirement (sixty-five years old). The closer an individual is to retirement, the higher is the benefit of having an annuity. Our welfare calculations reflect the value of annuitization for a twenty-one-year-old individual, taking into account longevity risk and individual income risk. Second, they consider selfish individuals for whom it is optimal to allocate all wealth at retirement in actuarially fair annuities. This is not the case for altruistic individuals who populate our model.

Conclusions

Public pension programs have come under renewed scrutiny with the projected increase in the share of the elderly in the population.

Economists have argued that existing pay-as-you-go social security systems lead to a reduction in national saving and discourage labor supply. The insurance role of social security against longevity risk, individual income risk, and macroeconomic risks have been mentioned as benefits of pay-as-you-go systems. Despite extensive research that evaluates the costs and benefits of unfunded social security systems, a consensus on their overall value has not emerged.

Most of the research has assumed that individuals have no bequest motives. In this chapter, we examine some of the benefits and costs of social security in a model with two-sided altruism, borrowing costs, and longevity and individual income risk. The households in our setup typically have parents and children coexisting, and their lifetime utility functions include both parents' and their children's lifetime utilities, yielding a dynastic structure. Credit markets and private annuity markets are assumed to be closed. We calibrate the model to the U.S. data and numerically solve steady-states. The welfare gains from three social security reforms are calculated, relative to steady-state, which represents the current pay-as-you-go system in the United States. One reform is a complete privatization. A second reform is a partial privatization where 5 percent of the payroll taxes are redirected to personal security accounts that earn the rate of return to economywide capital. The third reform combines this PSA with mandatory annuitization of accumulated PSA wealth at retirement.

Our main findings can be summarized as follows:

• A majority of households prefer a personal savings account reform (with or without mandatory annuitization) over the current pay-as-you-go pension system. Aggregate capital, output, and consumption, as well as individuals' lifetime welfare, are higher in the reformed pension system.

• Mandatory annuitization benefits most households.

• When we abstract from general-equilibrium effects, all household types prefer PSA with mandatory annuitization.

These results suggest the importance of annuities at retirement, especially in small. open economies whose wage rate and interest rate closely follow the world factor prices. Although the welfare benefits of annuitization are smaller in our altruistic framework, the combination of higher returns to personal security accounts and mandatory annuitization raises individuals' welfare.

Appendix 7A

Transition Probability Matrix

This transition probability matrix is a function of the age of the household and of the abilities of the father and the son and is given by

$$[\chi_j(h, h'; z, z')]_{h, h' \in \{1, 2, 3\}}$$

$$= \begin{bmatrix} \psi_j(z') & 0 & 0 \\ 0 & \psi_{j+T}(z) & 0 \\ \psi_j(z')(1 - \psi_{j+T}(z)) & (1 - \psi_j(z'))\psi_{j+T}(z) & \psi_j(z')\psi_{j+T}(z) \end{bmatrix}.$$

Computation of the Expected Rate of Return of Social Security

In this chapter, we report the expected rate of return of social security for a newborn individual. The expected return of social security is implicitly defined as the rate of return that equates the present value (at age 1) of expected tax payments to the present value (at age 1) of expected pension benefits. For a newborn individual of ability z, the present value of expected tax payments is given by

$$\sum_{j=1}^{R-1} \frac{\tau\omega(1 + \gamma)^{j-1}\varepsilon_j(z)}{(1 + r_{ss})^{j-1}} \prod_{i=1}^{j-1} \psi_i,$$

where r_{ss} denotes the expected rate of return of social security, and $\prod_{i=1}^{j-1} \psi_i$ indicates the probability that the individual is alive at any age $j > 1$. The present value of expected pension benefits is given by

$$\sum_{j=R}^{2T} \frac{(1 + \gamma)^{R-1} B_R(z)}{(1 + r_{ss})^{j-1}} \prod_{i=1}^{j-1} \psi_i,$$

where the term $(1 + \gamma)^{R-1}$ in the numerator accounts for the growth of pension benefits in the next $R - 1$ periods.[21] Thus, the expected rate of return of social security is defined as the value of r_{ss}, for which the following equation holds:

$$\sum_{j=1}^{R-1} \frac{\tau\omega(1 + \gamma)^{j-1}\varepsilon_j(z)}{(1 + r_{ss})^{j-1}} \prod_{i=1}^{j-1} \psi_i = \sum_{j=R}^{2T} \frac{(1 + \gamma)^{R-1} B_R(z)}{(1 + r_{ss})^{j-1}} \prod_{i=1}^{j-1} \psi_i.$$

Notes

We would like to thank the participants at the Conference on Social Insurance in Munich, November 5–6, 2004, two anonymous referees, Andres Erosa, and Georges de Ménil for their comments. Luisa Fuster would like to acknowledge the financial support of the Social Sciences and Humanities Research Council of Canada and the Connaught Fund. E-mail: ⟨selo@marshall.usc.edu⟩.

1. This estimate is probably an upper bound on the welfare benefit of annuities for several reasons. First, the utility calculations that yield these estimates take into account only consumption and annuities after retirement, taking as given wealth at retirement. If individuals were to make their decisions at the beginning of their working life, which is what is assumed in almost all life-cycle models, then they could plan better for mortality risk, whereas in the above calculations they are surprised with mortality at retirement. Second, these calculations abstract from general-equilibrium effects. Mortality risk tends to raise aggregate saving, which in turn lowers the return to capital. Finally, they assume that individuals have no bequest motives.

2. Starting with Hubbard and Judd (1987), quantitative models have been used to evaluate the role of social security in providing insurance against mortality risk.

3. Social security has become the last stop in the transition from unemployment insurance to disability and finally to social security for many individuals in EU countries. Although at a relatively smaller scale, the United States has also started to experience a similar transition from one public insurance program to another.

4. Following Kehoe and Levine (1993, 2001), Attanasio and Rios-Rull (2000) use a model with limited enforceability of private contracts to study the effectiveness of social insurance programs in distributing risk across individuals. They find that public insurance, designed to yield more risk sharing (such as more redistributive taxes), hinders the ability of individuals for insuring against the idiosyncratic shock so that overall it leads to a decline in risk sharing and ex-ante welfare.

5. For studies on EU countries and the United States that explore the impact of aging on social security, see Pestieau and Stijns (1999) for Belgium, Gruber (1999) for Canada, Blanchet and Pele (1999) for France, Börsch-Supan and Schnabel (1999) for Germany, Brugiavini (1999) for Italy, Yashiro and Oshio (1999) for Japan, Kapteyn and de Vos (1999) for the Netherlands, Boldrin, Jimenez-Martin, and Peracchi (1999) for Italy, Palme and Svensson (1999) for Sweden, Blundell and Johnson (1999) for the United Kingdom, and Diamond and Gruber (1999) for the United States.

6. Another justification for social insurance programs is the possibility that a fraction of the population might lack the foresight to accumulate sufficient assets for their old-age consumption. For example, Diamond (1977) and Feldstein (1985) argue that many individuals will simply not follow an optimal saving program on their own. Following the time-inconsistent preferences approach suggested by Strotz (1956), Akerloff (1998) argues that the quasi-hyperbolic model might justify the existence of social security as it acts as a commitment device in an economy populated with individuals who potentially value such an institution. However, İmrohoroğlu, İmrohoroğlu, and Joines (2003) examine the welfare effects of social security on individuals with time-inconsistent preferences and find that social security is a poor substitute for a perfect commitment technology in maintaining old-age consumption and that unfunded social security generally does not raise welfare for short-term discount rates of up to 15 percent.

7. Type 1 and type 2 households are of two ability and longevity types—high and low.

8. In what follows, we express all variables per effective units of labor.

9. This function captures the differential in pension across the average college and non-college worker observed in the U.S. economy. Individuals without college education have average lifetime earnings between 20 percent and 125 percent of the economy's average earnings. The average lifetime earnings of individuals with college education is between 125 percent and 246 percent the economy's average earnings.

10. We do not analyze whether these tax-favored accounts produce new saving. See İmrohoroğlu, İmrohoroğlu, and Joines (1998) for the impact of tax-favored individual retirement accounts on saving in the United States.

11. At any age j, the annuity payment per effective units of labor equals $b(z)(1+\gamma)^{R-j}$.

12. Notice that p is computed for the generation that retires in a given period and that we do not index p by time because we are assuming a stationary equilibrium.

13. In previous work, we have experimented with other distribution schemes for unintended bequests. Since the flow of these is only a small fraction of per-person income, our quantitative results are robust to other schemes.

14. We are assuming that in a given household all children are born at the same period and all of them die at the same period. Furthermore, we take all children in a given household to be identical regarding their labor abilities and vector of conditional survival probabilities.

15. A household survives T periods or until the father and the children have died. If the children survive to age $T+1$, each of them becomes a father in the next-generation household of the same dynasty. Otherwise, the family line is broken, and this dynasty is over. Since the population experiences broken dynasties every period, we assume that these dynasties are replaced by new dynasties to maintain our assumption of a stationary demographic structure. Since mortality rates are higher for low-ability individuals, the number of new dynasties of low ability is higher than the number of dynasties of high ability. A new dynasty begins with an individual of age 1 that holds zero assets.

16. We describe the computation of the measures of households in detail in the appendix to this chapter. For a description of the solution method, see Fuster (1999).

17. For details of the calibration choices, see Fuster, İmrohoroğlu, and İmrohoroğlu (2003).

18. Since we are comparing the welfare effects on newborn households, we do not have any type 2 households in this category.

19. Storesletten, Telmer, and Yaron (1999) also find annuitization welfare enhancing in their study of various social security reforms in a pure life-cycle setting.

20. With *social security*, we mean the sum of the pay-as-you-go payroll tax and the mandatory saving rate. See the appendix to this chapter for the computation of the overall rate of return on social security.

21. We define $B_R(z)$ for each of the social security systems in the section on social security and fiscal policy.

References

Advisory Council on Social Security. (1996). *Report of the 1994–1996 Advisory Council on Social Security*. Retrieved from ⟨http://www.ssa.gov/policy/adcouncil/report/toc.htm⟩.

Akerlof, George. (1998). "Comment." *Brookings Papers on Economic Activity*, 185–189.

Attanasio, Orazio, and Jose-Victor Rios-Rull. (2000). "Consumption Smoothing in Island Economies: Can Public Insurance Reduce Welfare?" *European Economic Review*, 44, 1225–1258.

Auerbach, Alan J., and Laurence J. Kotlikoff. (1987). *Dynamic Fiscal Policy*. Cambridge: Cambridge University Press.

Blanchet, Didier, and Louis-Paul Pele. (1999). "Social Security and Retirement in France." In J. Gruber and D. Wise, eds., *Social Security and Retirement around the World* (pp. 101–134). Chicago: University of Chicago Press.

Blundell, Richard, and Paul Johnson. (1999). "Social Security and Retirement in the United Kingdom." In J. Gruber and D. Wise, eds., *Social Security and Retirement around the World* (pp. 403–436). Chicago: University of Chicago Press.

Boldrin, Michele, Sergi Jimenez-Martin, and Franco Peracchi. (1999). "Social Security and Retirement in Spain." In J. Gruber and D. Wise, eds., *Social Security and Retirement around the World* (pp. 305–354). Chicago: University of Chicago Press.

Boldrin, Michele, and Aldo Rustichini. (2000). "Political Equilibria with Social Security." *Review of Economic Dynamics*, 3, 41–78.

Börsch-Supan, Axel, and Reinhold Schnabel. (1999). "Social Security and Retirement in Germany." In J. Gruber and D. Wise, eds., *Social Security and Retirement around the World* (pp. 135–180). Chicago: University of Chicago Press.

Boskin, Michael. (1986). *Too Many Promises: The Uncertain Future of Social Security*. New York: Dow-Jones-Irwin.

Brugiavini, Agar. (1999). "Social Security and Retirement in Italy." In J. Gruber and D. Wise, eds., *Social Security and Retirement around the World* (pp. 181–238). Chicago: University of Chicago Press.

Conesa, Juan-Carlos, and Dirk Krueger. (1999). "Social Security Reform with Heterogeneous Agents." *Review of Economic Dynamics*, 2(4), 757–795.

Cooley, Thomas, and Jorge Soares. (1999). "A Positive Theory of Social Security Based on Reputation." *Journal of Political Economy*, 107(1), 135–160.

De Nardi, Mariacristina, Selahattin İmrohoroğlu, and Thomas J. Sargent. (1999). "Projected U.S. Demographics and Social Security." *Review of Economic Dynamics*, 2(3), 575–615.

Diamond, Peter. (1977). "A Framework for Social Security Analysis." *Journal of Public Economics*, 8, 275–298.

Diamond, Peter. (1998). "The Economics of Social Security Reform." NBER Working Paper No. 6719.

Diamond, Peter, and Jonathan Gruber. (1999). "Social Security and Retirement in the U.S." In J. Gruber and D. Wise, eds., *Social Security and Retirement around the World* (pp. 437–474). Chicago: University of Chicago Press.

Feldstein, Martin. (1985). "The Optimal Level of Social Security Benefits." *Quarterly Journal of Economics*, 100, 303–320.

Feldstein, Martin. (2005). "Rethinking Social Insurance." *American Economic Review*, 95(1), 1–24.

Friedman, B., and M. Warshawsky. (1990). "The Cost of Annuities: Implications for Saving Behavior and Bequests." *Quarterly Journal of Economics*, 105(1), 135–154.

Fuster, Luisa. (1999). "Is Altruism Important for Understanding the Long-Run Effects of Social Security?" *Review of Economic Dynamics*, 2(3), 616–637.

Fuster, Luisa, Ayşe İmrohoroğlu, and Selahattin İmrohoroğlu. (2003). "A Welfare Analysis of Social Security in a Dynastic Framework." *International Economic Review*, 1247–1274.

Fuster, Luisa, Ayşe İmrohoroğlu, and Selahattin İmrohoroğlu. (2007). "Elimination of Social Security in a Dynastic Framework." *Review of Economic Studies*, 74(1), 113–145.

Gruber, Jonathan. (1999). "Social Security and Retirement in Canada." In J. Gruber and D. Wise, eds., *Social Security and Retirement around the World* (pp. 73–100). Chicago: University of Chicago Press.

Huang, He, Selahattin İmrohoroğlu, and Thomas J. Sargent. (1997). "Two Experiments to Fund Social Security." *Macroeconomic Dynamics*, 1(1), 7–44.

Hubbard, Glenn, and Kenneth Judd. (1987). "Social Security and Individual Welfare." *American Economic Review*, 77, 630–646.

İmrohoroğlu, Ayşe, Selahattin İmrohoroğlu, and Douglas Joines. (1995). "A Life Cycle Analysis of Social Security." *Economic Theory*, 6, 83–114.

İmrohoroğlu, Ayşe, Selahattin İmrohoroğlu, and Douglas Joines. (1998). "The Effect of Tax-Favored Retirement Accounts on Capital Accumulation." *American Economic Review*, 88(4), 749–768.

İmrohoroğlu, Ayşe, Selahattin İmrohoroğlu, and Douglas Joines. (1999). "Social Security in an Overlapping-Generations Economy with Land." *Review of Economic Dynamics*, 2, 638–665.

İmrohoroğlu, Ayşe, Selahattin İmrohoroğlu, and Douglas Joines. (2003). "Time-Inconsistent Preferences and Social Security." *Quarterly Journal of Economics*, 118(2), 745–784.

Kapteyn, Arie, and Klaas de Vos. (1999). "Social Security and Retirement in the Netherlands." In J. Gruber and D. Wise, eds., *Social Security and Retirement around the World* (pp. 269–304). Chicago: University of Chicago Press.

Kehoe, Tim, and David Levine. (1993). "Debt Constrained Asset Markets." *Review of Economic Studies*, 60, 865–888.

Kehoe, Tim, and David Levine. (2001). "Incomplete Markets versus Debt-Constrained Markets." *Econometrica*, 69, 575–598.

Kotlikoff, Larry, Kent Smetters, and Jan Walliser. (1999). "Privatizing Social Security in the U.S.: Comparing the Options." *Review of Economic Dynamics*, 2(3), 532–574.

Kotlikoff, Laurence, Avia Spivak, and Lawrence Summers. (1982). "The Adequacy of Savings." *American Economic Review*, 72, 1056–1069.

Krueger, Dirk, and Felix Kubler. (2002). "Pareto-Improving Social Security Reform When Financial Markets Are Incomplete!?" NBER Working Paper 9410.

Krueger, Dirk, and Fabrizio Perri. (2001). "Risk Sharing: Private Insurance Markets or Redistributive Taxes?" Working Paper, University of Frankfurt.

Laitner, John. (1992). "Random Earnings Differences, Lifetime Liquidity Constraints, and Altruistic Intergenerational Transfers." *Journal of Economic Theory*, 58, 135–170.

Laitner, John, and Thomas Juster. (1996). "New Evidence on Altruism: A Study of TIAA-CREF Retirees." *American Economic Review*, 86(4), 893–908.

Mitchell, O., J. M. Poterba, M. J. Warshawsky, and J. R. Brown. (1999). "New Evidence on the Money's Worth of Individual Annuities." *American Economic Review*, 89(5), 1299–1318.

Palme, Marten, and Ingemar Svensson. (1999). "Social Security and Retirement in Sweden." In J. Gruber and D. Wise, eds., *Social Security and Retirement around the World* (pp. 355–402). Chicago: University of Chicago Press.

Pestieau, Pierre, and Jean-Philippe Stijns. (1999). "Social Security and Retirement in Belgium." In J. Gruber and D. Wise, eds., *Social Security and Retirement around the World* (pp. 37–72). Chicago: University of Chicago Press.

Storesletten, Kjetil, Chris Telmer, and Amir Yaron. (1999). "The Risk-Sharing Implications of Alternative Social Security Arrangements." *Carnegie-Rochester Conference Series on Public Policy*, 50, 213–260.

Strotz, Robert. (1956). "Myopia and Inconsistency in Dynamic Utility Maximization." *Review of Economic Studies*, 23, 165–180.

Wilhelm, Mark. (1996). "Bequest Behavior and the Effect of Heirs' Earnings: Testing the Altruistic Model of Bequests." *American Economic Review*, 86(4), 874–892.

Yaari, M. (1965). "Uncertain Lifetime, Life Insurance, and the Theory of the Consumer." *Review of Economic Studies*, 32, 137–150.

Yashiro, Naohiro, and Takashi Oshio. (1999). "Social Security and Retirement in Japan." In J. Gruber and D. Wise, eds., *Social Security and Retirement around the World* (pp. 239–268). Chicago: University of Chicago Press.

8   Aging, Funded Pensions, and the Dutch Economy

A. Lans Bovenberg and Thijs Knaap

The pension system in the Netherlands consists of three pillars—a government-run pay-as-you-go (PAYG) system, funded compulsory occupational pension schemes, and voluntary private savings. The size of the second pillar, funded pensions, is considerable: in the year 2000, the funds had accumulated around 100 percent of gross domestic product (GDP) in assets. For many people, the accumulated rights in these funds constitute an important part of their retirement provision. Most occupational pension schemes are of a defined-benefit (DB) nature, tying the level of pension payouts to that of wages.

As in most of the Western world, the Dutch population will age during the coming decades due to the combined effects of a lower birth rate, a lower mortality rate, and the baby boom that followed World War II. However, the sizeable funded DB-component makes the Dutch situation different from that of many other Western economies. In those countries, the main concern is the sustainability of pay-as-you-go pension schemes. In the Netherlands, in contrast, policy makers must also be concerned about the effects of aging on returns on financial assets in international capital markets, the future purchasing power of current savings, and the macroeconomic effects of a wage-indexed, funded pension system. The aging of the population, together with the maturing of their membership, will narrow the premium base of occupational pension funds compared to their future obligations. The ratio between obligations and the annual premium base is currently about six but will rise substantially in the coming decades. This makes pension funds with DB benefits more vulnerable to unanticipated shocks in asset returns. Adverse shocks on financial markets require larger increases in premiums to guarantee defined benefits. These premium increases can in turn raise labor costs and harm employment.

At the same time, aging makes labor relatively scarcer than capital. This is bad news for maturing pension funds, which have their obligations linked to the wage rate but depend on the rate of return on capital for their income. Whereas lower returns harm assets, pension obligations rise as a result of wage increases. A compounding problem is that the increasing demand for nontraded goods and services (such as care for the elderly) caused by aging will tighten the labor market further, leading to additional wage inflation.

Finally, several European countries seem ill prepared for the aging problem. Aging will saddle these countries with considerable financial and budgetary problems. This can cause an inflationary spiral that harms the value of European firms, with adverse effects on the real return reaped by pension funds. All of these adverse shocks loom at a time when the pension funds are more vulnerable to risk because of their shrinking premium base. Thus, both pay-as-you-go pension systems and funded systems appear to be vulnerable to aging, especially if these funds are of a DB nature. This chapter quantifies this vulnerability.

We analyze the macroeconomic interdependencies among aging, risks, and pension funds in an applied general-equilibrium framework, explicitly taking into account various feedbacks between the economy and occupational pension funds. The two are linked in several ways. On the one hand, the value of the funds' assets and obligations depends on macroeconomic developments on the Dutch labor market and international financial markets. On the other hand, the level of pension premiums and benefits affects the Dutch economy in general and the labor market and commodity markets in particular. The two-way interaction between pension funds and the rest of the Dutch economy has important consequences for the distribution of income between active and retired generations.

We proceed as follows. After a short introduction to our model, we describe the benchmark scenario. We then explore different ways to address the financial burdens of aging. We discuss policy options for pension funds as well as the government, which is in charge of the pay-as-you-go (PAYG) system.

Both pension funds and the government start off in a state of disequilibrium. With currently expected financial returns and the current level of premiums, pension funds cannot finance future pension benefits that are fully indexed to gross wages. Raising premiums or reducing indexation are alternative ways to address this problem. We investigate the implications of these two alternative policy options for a number of macroeconomic variables (including wages, employment, and production) and for the standard of living for current and future generations.

The current levels of taxation are also insufficient to cover the future fiscal costs of aging. The rising net PAYG benefits, tied at present to net market wages, will force the government to pick up an increasing part of the PAYG bill through general taxation. This will cause either tax rates or the national debt to rise. We analyze the macroeconomic implications and intergenerational distribution issues and study a number of policy options: smoothing tax rates by cutting public debt and stimulating labor participation.

To explore the vulnerability of the Dutch pension funds and the national economy, we proceed by analyzing the effects of an adverse shock to the rate of return on capital. Lower rates of return may be caused by either worldwide aging or imported inflation from European countries suffering from fiscal imbalances.

Finally, we analyze how these results are affected if the tradability of goods and services declines. With the pension funds sustaining national consumption when the number of pensioners rises, prices of nontradables increase, causing wage inflation and therefore higher (defined-benefit) pension obligations for occupational pension funds.

The purpose of the chapter is twofold. It aims to identify through which different channels aging and pensions affect the economy, how these effects propagate, what the feedback effects are, and how the income distribution across and within generations is affected. As a second purpose, it intends to quantify these effects through numerical simulations, thereby allowing one to assess the relative importance of these different channels.

The IMAGE Model

The interactions among aging, pension funds, and the Dutch economy are studied using the IMAGE model. This dynamic overlapping-generations model is documented in Broer (1999). The analysis is conducted in the tradition of Auerbach and Kotlikoff (1987) and can be compared to Kotlikoff, Smetters, and Walliser (2001), Börsch-Supan, Ludwig, and Winter (2003), and Beetsma et al. (2003), among others. It differs from these approaches in a number of ways: we concentrate on aging in a small, open economy, which does not affect returns on

Table 8.1
Some key parameters.

Parameter	Value	Description
α	0.02	Labor-saving technical progress
β	0.02	Rate of time preference
r	0.04	Real rate of interest
γ	0.25	Intertemporal elasticity of substitution
η_H	0.25	Elasticity of productivity in the leisure preference of households
σ_u	0.56	Intratemporal elasticity of substitution between consumption of goods and the leisure-care composite
σ_v	0.65	Intratemporal elasticity of substitution between leisure and health care
σ_y	0.5	Elasticity of substitution between raw materials and value added in the tradable-goods sector
σ_H	0.5	Elasticity of substitution between labor and capital in the tradable-goods sector
δ	0.115	Technical depreciation of capital
ε	0.281	Net replacement rate of pay-as-you-go pension as a fraction of the average wage rate
ϕ_0	0.7	Total pensions as a fraction of the final wage at full pension build-up

international financial markets. Furthermore, we focus on the funded defined-benefit pension system and the ways in which policy choices in that system interact with the economy. Even though it is a part of our model, we do not analyze alternative policy choices in the pay-as-you-go pension system, as this has already been the subject of much analysis in the international literature. This section introduces the model without trying to be exhaustive: most mathematical detail is left out, for instance. Table 8.1 presents the key parameters. Two appendices give a short introduction to the structure of the model: appendix 8A provides some background on the optimization problem for households, and appendix 8B discusses the tradable-goods sector. For a complete overview of the model, we refer the reader to the documentation on our Web site (see ⟨http://www.netspar.nl/research/projects/image.html⟩).

In table 8.1, the constant relative risk aversion (CRRA) parameter γ is similar to that in Auerbach and Kotlikoff (1987), indicating a limited willingness to substitute intertemporally. The elasticity of the preference for leisure with respect to productivity, η_H, is positive to offset the income effect of higher cross-sectional productivity on the consumption of leisure. At the current value of η_H, cross-sectional labor supply increases slightly with productivity. The substitution elasticities in the utility function (σ_u, σ_v) determine the responsiveness of labor supply to endogenous changes in the wage rate. The current elasticities lead to a compensated wage elasticity of labor supply between 0.15 and 0.45, depending on the age of the worker. This is broadly in line with empirical findings. To illustrate, van Soest (1995) reports (uncompensated) elasticities of about 0.1 for males and 0.5 for females in the Dutch labor force. The survey of Theeuwes (1988) puts the uncompensated supply elasticity for the Dutch economy around 0.1. Production elasticities indicate moderate substitution possibilities between factors, which corresponds well with empirical results.[1]

In the IMAGE model, 560 types of households are active every period (the standard period is one year): there are eighty cohorts, and each cohort features seven types of workers, differing in exogenous productivity. These types thus represent different income groups in the economy. Each household consistently maximizes lifetime utility, using labor-leisure allocation and consumption as its instruments. All agents are endowed with perfect foresight. Appendix 8A contains the mathematical structure of the household problem. We calibrate the preference for leisure such that the age-specific participation rates roughly correspond to those found in the data, including a low rate of labor-force participation for those over fifty-five years of age.[2]

Firms maximize their value, defined as the present value of the stream of dividends. This yields optimal labor and investment demands. Firms face adjustment costs in investment (see appendix 8B). The associated barriers to international mobility of physical capital imply that gross wages are not fully determined by the world interest rate but also respond to domestic labor supply. While wages are thus determined in domestic labor markets, the return to capital is determined on international financial markets. We assume a constant real rate of return of 4 percent but also explore a case in which the rate of return declines.

The model is based on recent data and incorporates the institutions of the Dutch economy that are most affected by aging—the government, the health-care sector, and the pension funds. We assume a competitive labor market, so that wages are equated among the three production sectors—the government, the health-care sector, and the rest of the private sector. The size of these sectors can be read from table 8.2.

Table 8.2
Some key variables.

Employment volume per sector (1,000 work years)	
Government (with education)	728
Health care	661
Firms	4,963
Wealth (percentage of GDP 1999)	
Government debt	55.6%
Pension-fund assets	97.7%

The government levies (proportional) taxes on consumption and labor and capital income. That money is spent on government consumption, interest payments, subsidies, and lump-sum transfers. Public consumption is a fixed fraction of GDP; public transfers go to public health insurance, which is reimbursed a fixed fraction of its expenditures, and to the PAYG pensions, to the extent that the exogenously fixed premiums do not cover the costs. Age-specific transfers, which are subject to the income tax, are tied to the gross wage rate. The government aims to maintain a constant public debt-GDP ratio and uses the income tax rate to close its budget. Its initial debt rate is about 56 percent (see table 8.2).

The two mandatory pension systems are a pay-as-you-go scheme, which pays out a uniform basic minimum pension after age sixty-five that is tied to the wage rate, and a funded occupational pension scheme that provides benefits to top up the basic public pension. Dutch occupational pension funds are large: in 1999, their combined assets were almost equal to the nation's GDP. Pension funds are capital-based and receive premiums that are collected from working-age persons' wages.

The premium is levied on that part of the wage that exceeds the so-called franchise, and payment confers to the participant the right to a defined-benefit pension. Pensions are based on the last-earned wage and are subsequently tied to the level of gross wages in the economy. Their level depends on the accrued rights of the worker. The fund earns the international interest rate; discrepancies between its assets and the present value of its obligations are covered by adjusting the premium at a specified pace. Contributions to the pension fund are deductible from taxable income, while the benefits later in life are subject to income tax. In the PAYG scheme, the contribution rate is fixed, and deficits are covered by the state.

There are two types of health insurance, private and public, for agents on either side of a statutory income ceiling. Below the ceiling, agents have mandatory insurance through public health insurances. Public health insurance fixes its premiums, which are proportional to income, so that its budget is balanced each year. Privately insured households, in contrast, pay a lump-sum contribution. The private health-insurance sector transfers some of its premium income to the public insurance system to compensate that sector for the bad health risks of low-income households. Special medical treatments, which are difficult to insure on the private insurance market, are covered by a special insurance sector (AWBZ) to which all households contribute. Health expenditures, finally, require complementary time allocation from the consumers.

The model suffers from a number of limitations. We do not model differences between men and women. We abstract from bequests and assume perfect annuity markets along the lines of Yaari (1965). The absence of bequests may lead to an overestimation of the intergenerational effects of shocks, as bequests typically help smooth those effects across generations. Pension funds are homogeneous and represented by a single, representative fund. Markets, including the labor market, clear every period. Unemployment is thus ruled out. We abstract from business-cycle considerations to focus on the long-term effects of demographic trends.

The Benchmark Path

In the benchmark scenario, the starting point of our simulations, the assets of pension funds are not large enough to cover the obligations to current and future retirees (including an indexation of benefits to wages), while premiums are below their long-run level. This scenario is an attempt to approximate the current situation, even though much of the model is calibrated to 1999 data. The lack of funds in 1999, which was not actually observed in that year, can be explained as follows. First of all, we assume an average real return to capital of 4 percent, which is lower than the returns that were anticipated in 1999. Second, the stock markets had not yet reached their top in 1999.

On the base path, funds use their premiums, the percentage of income above the franchise that is paid to into the pension fund, as an instrument to cover the shortage in assets. The premium responds to the coverage rate (assets as a ratio of current pension obligations), which is

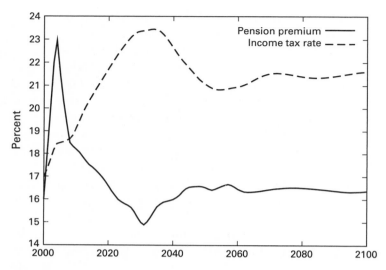

Figure 8.1
Income tax rate and pension premium rate on the base path, with premium instrument.

targeted at 1.05. The low premium rate in the base year, combined with the smaller-than-desired coverage rate, leads to a sharp increase in premiums in the base year. We have constrained the premiums to a maximum of 25 percent, with a maximum yearly increase of two percentage points.

The effects of aging for the cost level of pension funds and government can be seen from figure 8.1. The income tax rate increases when the dependency ratio goes up and reaches its highest level in 2040. Rising costs of the pay-as-you-go scheme play an important role in this increase. After an initial increase, occupational pension premiums stabilize at their long-run level around 16 percent.

Figure 8.2 contains gross wages (corrected for 2 percent technological growth). Wage costs peak around the time when the labor market is tight due to aging. Net wages[3] are contained in the same figure. These wages (also corrected for technological growth) are under pressure in the next decades due to rising tax rates and, initially, higher pension premiums. Higher tax rates also reduce the net occupational pension benefits contained in the same figure. However, as pensioners do not pay pension premiums, the decrease in net pensions is smaller compared to that in net wages.

Higher costs of labor reduce the demand for labor, while lower net wages depress labor supply. Together with demographic develop-

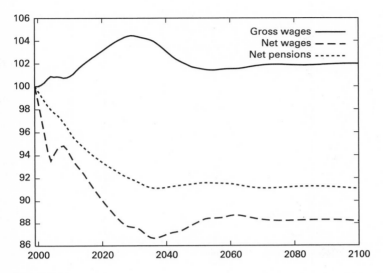

Figure 8.2
Gross wage, net wage, and net pensions in index numbers (corrected for technological growth) on the base path.

ments, this results in falling employment until 2030 (see figure 8.3). Gross domestic product (corrected for technological growth) reflects the downturn in employment.

Pension funds face two problems on the benchmark path—a low coverage ratio and a low initial premium. The tight labor market exacerbates these problems because the resulting inflationary pressure on gross wages increases pension fund obligations. Despite the tighter labor markets, net wages decline compared to net pensions due to higher occupational pension premiums.

Policy Instruments for Pension Funds

In the base case, the financial problems of occupational pension funds are shifted to active workers in terms of higher pension premiums. To protect the purchasing power of workers compared to that of the retired population, funds can opt for alternative instruments to address their financial problems. To complement the case with variable premiums, we discuss a number of alternative measures, which are also rather extreme but are intended to delineate the borders of the playing field for pension funds. In the end, pension funds probably will opt for a combination of measures.

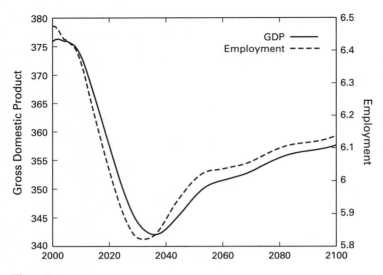

Figure 8.3
Employment in millions of FTEs (right) and GDP in billions of euros (left, corrected for technological growth) on the base path.

Fixed Premium, Variable Indexation

In our first alternative simulation, we let the pension premium increase to its long-run level of 16 percent straightaway. The fund's financial imbalances are thus no longer borne by the working population. Instead, current retirees carry the burden of the initial disequilibrium because their pensions are no longer indexed to gross wages as long as the fund's assets are too low to guarantee wage-indexed pensions with a long-run pension premium of 16 percent (figure 8.4).[4] Under this rule, additional indexation is possible if the coverage ratio exceeds 1.05. This way, pensioners share in both positive and negative shocks.

Pensions lag behind gross wages by an average of about 1 percent each year during the first decade. Figure 8.5 shows the effects of reducing indexation for net pensions. Reducing indexation leads to temporarily lower pensions, where net pensions lag behind net wages for two decades. The effect fades away after the generations whose pensions have been cut have passed away. Generations that start retirement in 2020 or later profit from increased indexation (see figure 8.4) and a relatively high gross final wage, caused by the tight labor market in 2020 (figure 8.2). This explains why net pensions grow faster than net wages between 2020 and 2040 (see figure 8.5). The use of the indexation instrument instead of the premium instrument moderates the

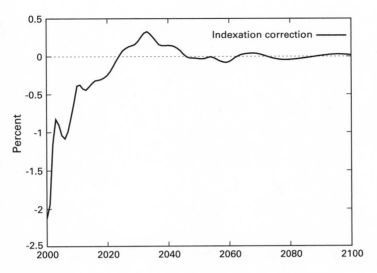

Figure 8.4
Indexation correction, expressed as missed yearly increase in pensions.

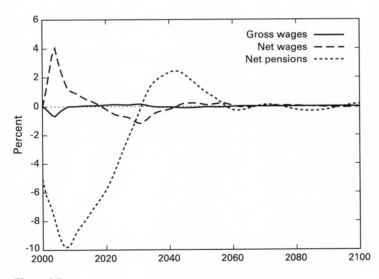

Figure 8.5
Changes in gross wage, net wage, and net pensions relative to the base path, with index-ation instrument.

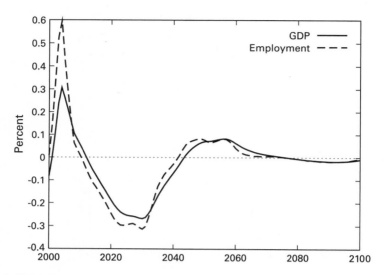

Figure 8.6
GDP and employment with indexation instrument relative to the base path.

costs on labor and protects net wages in the early years. This boosts employment (figure 8.6).

The welfare effects[5] on different generations are provided in figure 8.7. The year of birth of the different generations is on the horizontal axis. Generations that have just retired when indexation is reduced lose the most. Their benefits from funded pensions comprise the largest part of their income, as opposed to older generations, who rely more on the first (PAYG) pillar. Generations born between 1960 and 1990 do not retire until the period when indexation is no longer reduced. They gain relative to the base path because of lower pension premiums.

Career Average Pensions
Another policy option for pension funds is the use of average-wage pensions instead of final-wage pensions. Under the former system, pensions are based on the average wage earned over the worker's entire career, where the wages that are used to compute the career average are indexed to the sectorwide wage level. The switch takes place, unexpectedly, in the base year.

There is a transitory regime: for workers who had already entered into the final-wage system, the average wage until the base year is set

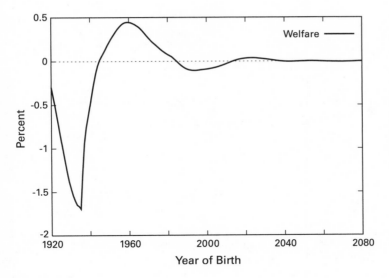

Figure 8.7
Welfare effects of the use by pension funds of the indexation instrument instead of the premium instrument.

to their wage at the time of the transition. The annual accumulation rate of pension rights is increased in this plan, so that the expected final pension is equal to that in the final-wage scheme. If premiums are adjusted to establish financial balance, pension benefits initially increase under the average-wage system because older employees benefit from this transition. Their current rights are protected, while they can increase their future rights using the new, higher, rate of contribution. The opposite holds for younger generations, who have not yet made their careers.[6] The higher rate of the accumulation of pension rights, which tends to improve benefits, is not enough to offset the loss as a result of the elimination of backservice when making a career.[7]

The welfare effects of a switch to career-average pensions show differences not only between generations but also between different income groups. Figure 8.8 shows the effects for three groups in current and future generations. The low incomes correspond to the 10 percent lowest incomes in a cohort; the high incomes are the top 5 percent of a generation. The latter lose from a switch to a career-average system because their individual wage profile goes up the most during their working lives, giving them a generous backservice under the final-wage

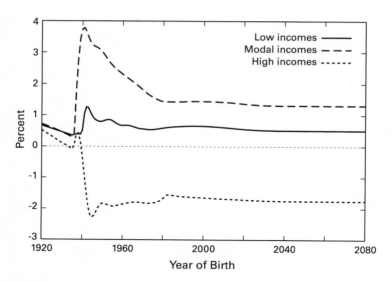

Figure 8.8
Welfare effects of a switch to an average-wage system, with premium instrument.

system. The lower and middle incomes profit from the new system since they have less steep careers. The gains for lower incomes are relatively modest, however, as most of their pension benefits originate in the PAYG system. Figure 8.8 further shows that the cohorts in the middle and lower incomes that profit the most are those that are just before retirement. As indicated above, these cohorts have little career (and hence, backservice) left but do profit from the higher accumulation rate.

Average-Wage Pensions with Conditional Indexation
A major advantage of the average-wage system over the final-wage system is the increased power of the indexation instrument to restore financial balance. Under this system, reducing the indexation of existing rights is possible not just for current retirees but also for those who are still active in the current labor force. The increased effectiveness of the indexation instrument is illustrated by the case in which the premium instrument is switched off by setting premiums at their long-run level immediately and only the degree of indexation of current (worker and pensioner) rights is employed to restore the coverage ratio to its desired value.

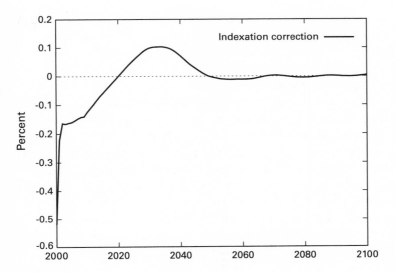

Figure 8.9
Indexation correction, expressed as missed yearly increase in pensions, under an average-wage system (with indexation instrument).

As the risk surrounding the funded pensions is borne by a much larger number of people, pensioners have to contribute less to pay off the funds' deficit; hence, their incomes remain relatively stable (compare figure 8.9 to figure 8.4, taking into account the different scale of the vertical axes). The broad use of the indexation instrument spreads the pain that is associated with the initial underfunding of the pension funds over a large number of agents. Indeed, if also the indexation of the rights of active workers is suspended under an average-wage system, the development of pensioners' incomes is more in line with that of workers, compared to the case in which the premium instrument is used or to the case of a final-pay scheme in which only the indexation of pensioners' rights is suspended.

Government Policy

The government has several policy options to address the fiscal problems associated with aging. The policy options have consequences for the national budget (including the costs associated with the first-pillar pay-as-you-go system) as well as for the occupational pension funds. This section analyzes the macroeconomic links among government policy, occupational pension funds, and intergenerational distribution. We discuss cutting public debt by raising taxes to their long-run levels immediately and the encouragement of labor participation.

Constant Taxes and Premiums

In the simulations so far, government debt was kept constant as a fraction of national income by adjusting the income tax rate on a yearly basis. Figure 8.1 shows that this policy implies that the generations that are in the labor market when the aging of society peaks in 2040 pay relatively high taxes. Several considerations—including the desire to spread the costs of aging more equally across generations and to avoid distortions due to fluctuating tax rates—call for smoothing tax rates over time. The level of a constant tax rate follows from the condition that the government has to stay solvent. In practice, this means raising rates at the present time to pay off a part of the national debt.

We simulate a scenario in which the government decides to enact this type of policy. Solvency restrictions put the (constant) income tax rate at approximately 21 percent, which is higher in the initial years of the simulation but lower in the later years (compare to figure 8.1). In this way, the costs of aging are in fact brought forward. Public debt (as a percentage of national income) decreases for two decades (figure 8.10) to stabilize at a level of 35 percent of GDP.[8]

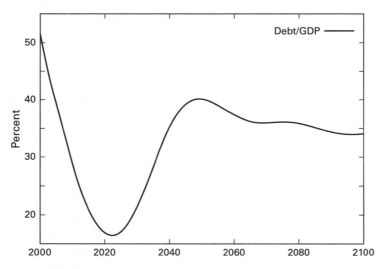

Figure 8.10
Government debt as a fraction of GDP, with tax smoothing.

Bringing the costs of aging forward influences labor supply. By keeping the income tax rate constant, the net wage will be lower in the base year but declines much less afterward. This stimulates labor supply at precisely the moment that the labor market is tight due to population aging. Constant rates of taxation thus help the price mechanism to allocate labor supply to those periods in which labor is most scarce. In this scenario, therefore, aging leads to a smaller fluctuation in the costs of labor, in production and in employment (combine figure 8.11 with figure 8.3). The welfare effects (figure 8.12) show that reducing the national debt in anticipation of an aging population burdens the current generations but benefits future generations.

Aging and Labor Participation

Population aging reduces the ratio between the number of working and retired members of society. This trend can be offset by increasing labor-force participation. Increases in participation are possible and have in fact occurred in the past. During the previous two decades, for instance, labor supplied by young women (between twenty and forty-five years) has increased markedly due to cultural changes and an increase in the educational level of that group. Also, increased opportunities to work part-time have made the labor market more accessible

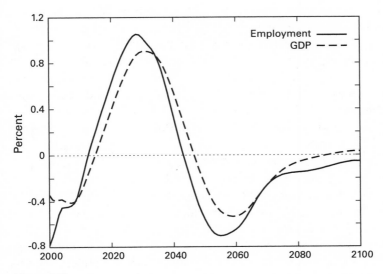

Figure 8.11
Change in GDP and employment relative to the base path after tax smoothing.

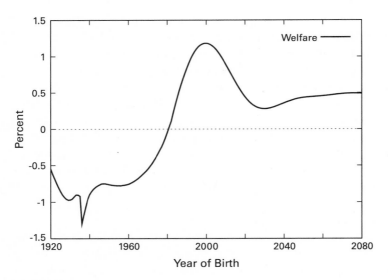

Figure 8.12
Welfare effects of tax smoothing.

for women with children. In the coming two decades, the women who have entered the labor market in recent years will be part of the older part of the labor force (between forty-five and sixty-five years). This part of the labor force, especially that older than fifty-five, has shown a decrease in participation over the last thirty years (although this trend appears to have reversed slightly during the last half of the 1990s). How labor-force participation of forty-five to sixty-five-year-olds will develop in the future is uncertain and will depend on cultural developments as well as government policy and employers aimed at stimulating participation of older workers.

CPB Netherlands Bureau for Economic Policy Analysis has developed several long-term scenarios for future labor participation. To explore the sensitivity of our simulations to changes in labor participation, we use an optimistic scenario for labor supply, the *European coordination* scenario (CBS/CPB, 1997). Table 8.3 compares labor participation on our base path to the development of participation in the CPB scenario. In our projection, participation declines over time, due to the increase in income tax rates over time (see figure 8.1). In the projection from CPB, in contrast, the participation rate rises; the recent increase in the participation of older employees is projected to continue into the next decade. This trend is explained by cultural changes that

Table 8.3
Participation in three age groups (percentage).

	Age 20–44	Age 45–49	Age 50–54	Age 55–59
Labor participation in 2000:				
IMAGE base path	73.9%	68.7%	61.5%	42.7%
CPB projection	73.4	70.5	63.5	42.2
Labor participation in 2010:				
IMAGE base path	70.5	66.8	58.6	38.6
CPB projection	75.2	76.6	69.3	49.5
Labor participation in 2020:				
IMAGE base path	71.5	65.9	57.3	35.7
CPB projection	76.3	78.5	74.3	53.9

stimulate participation among older women. Cutbacks in early retirement schemes also play a role. This allows us to interpret the CPB's scenario as a policy scenario in which labor participation is encouraged in a number of ways.

We exogenously introduce the increase in labor participation that is projected in the CPB scenario. The results of this simulation are in figures 8.13 and 8.14. Effective labor supply increases markedly for the next fifteen years, mainly due to the higher participation of older employees. The supply of labor does decrease when the baby-boom generation withdraws from the labor market, but the size of the decline is smaller than in previous simulations (compare figure 8.14 to figure 8.3). This mitigates the required increases in the pension premium and the income tax rate (see figure 8.13). The labor market goes through a cycle of relative abundance and relative scarcity.

Lower Rates of Return

The importance of funded pension schemes makes the Dutch economy vulnerable to adverse shocks in the rate of return on financial markets. This section explores the consequences of lower returns on capital for the Dutch economy.

Aging Reduces the Rate of Return to Capital

Aging countries in the Organization for Economic Cooperation and Development (OECD) supply the bulk of capital in world financial markets. The supply of capital will probably increase in the coming

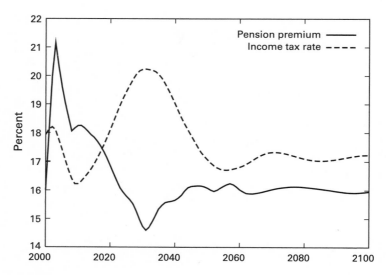

Figure 8.13
Income tax rate and pension premium with increasing participation.

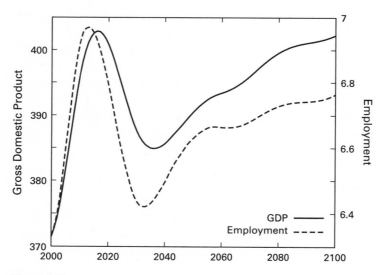

Figure 8.14
GDP (left, billions of euros) and employment (right, millions of FTEs) with increasing participation.

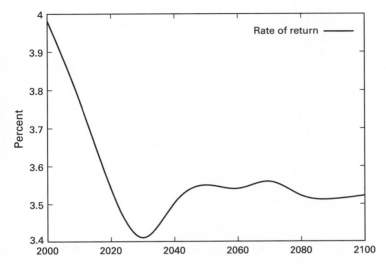

Figure 8.15
Projection of the rate of return to capital according to the INGENUE model.

years as the baby-boom generations save for their retirement years. The demand for capital, in contrast, will be low because fewer jobs need to be created for the shrinking labor force. It thus appears that the forces of supply and demand will put downward pressure on the rate of return on capital.

We employ the interest-rate projection of the INGENUE model, which is based on a worldwide demographic scenario (Aglietta et al., 2001). The projection in figure 8.15 confirms that the rate of return is under downward pressure. The model projects a declining rate of return for the next two centuries, after which a new equilibrium is found about fifty basis points below the real return of 4 percent that we employed in our base projection. The INGENUE projection accounts for the absorption of savings from the OECD countries by the developing world, where the population is relatively young.

A Lower Rate of Return Means a Lower Coverage Rate...
We analyze the effects of the INGENUE scenario for the world rate of return in our own model of the Dutch economy under the final-pay regime. The projected fall in the return to capital (together with the increase in wages caused by it) causes an immediate fall in the coverage ratio of pension funds. We study the effects of two possible responses

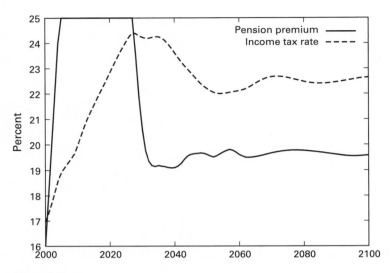

Figure 8.16
Income tax rate and pension premium after interest shock, with premium instrument.

of occupational pension funds to this problem—increasing premiums (figures 8.16 through 8.18) and cutting the indexation of current pension benefits (figures 8.19 and 8.20).

...with Higher Premiums...

When pension funds use the premium instrument to restore their coverage ratio, the premiums rise to the maximum level of 25 percent (see figure 8.16). Premiums are fixed at this level for the next twenty years, after which they return to their new steady-state level of just below 20 percent. This level exceeds the steady-state premium of 16.4 percent that was projected before, which is a consequence of the permanently lower rate of return (which is 3.5 percent instead of 4 percent).

...or Lower Benefits

An alternative course of action for the pension funds is to freeze premiums immediately at their new long-run level of 19.6 percent (corresponding to the new steady-state rate of return of 3.5 percent) and to cope with the shortages by limiting the indexation of pensioners' benefits. The growth of benefits will, in that case, lag about 4 percent behind the growth of wages for eight years. After this period, indexation of benefits to wages is gradually restored.

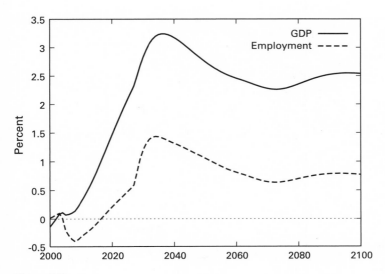

Figure 8.17
GDP and employment relative to the base path after interest shock, with premium instrument.

Lower Rates of Return Stimulate the Labor Supply

The lower rate of return required by financial markets serves to increase the level of investments. This is beneficial to labor productivity and leads to higher gross wages. In the long run, employment increases by 0.7 percent, while GDP grows by 2.5 percent (figure 8.17). Premiums are increased by a large amount if the premium instrument is used exclusively (figure 8.16), which causes labor supply and net wages to drop initially (figures 8.17 and 8.18). The use of the indexation instrument (figure 8.19) prevents sizable short-term effects on net wages and labor supply but severely decreases the value of net pensions in the initial years (compare figures 8.20 and 8.18).

Welfare Effects

Figure 8.21 shows the welfare effects of a negative shock in the rate of return for the different cohorts under two alternative pension-fund policies. In both cases, the fall in the rate of return harms the welfare of future generations: their lower income from capital dominates the (slightly) higher net wage. In the short run, the policy option chosen by pension funds is important. The cohorts that were born around 1980 pay most of the burden if the premium instrument is used.

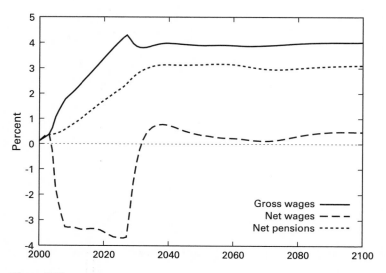

Figure 8.18
Gross wage, net wage, and net pensions relative to the base path after interest shock, with premium instrument.

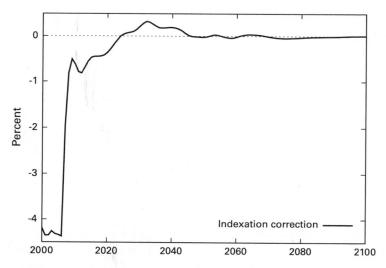

Figure 8.19
Indexation reduction, expressed in missed yearly increase in pensions, under a final-wage system after interest shock (with indexation instrument).

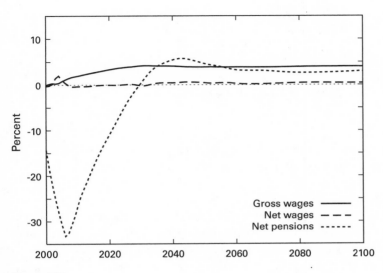

Figure 8.20
Gross wage, net wage, and net pensions relative to the base path after interest shock, with indexation instrument.

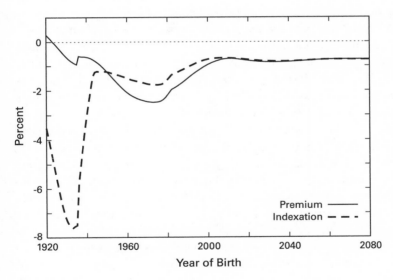

Figure 8.21
Welfare-effects interest shock with premium and indexation instrument.

Table 8.4
The size of the three sectors in 1999 (percentage).

	Sector		
	Tradables	Nontradables	Government and Health Care
Employment share	31%	44%	24%

Cutting the indexation of current pensions protects this generation but harms the welfare of those born around 1930.

Nontradables
When the baby-boom generation retires, the local supply of labor will decrease. This will limit Dutch production capacity, while at the same time the assets accumulated by pension funds provide the means to keep national consumption at a stable level. The money that was saved and turned into foreign investments can then be used to import consumption goods to finance domestic demand.

However, not all goods and services are internationally tradable and can be imported. A high demand for nontradables combined with a limited capacity to produce locally will cause the real exchange rate to appreciate; that is, nontradables will become more expensive relative to tradables. This change in relative prices will relocate production factors from the tradable to the nontradeable sector. With a limited pool of domestic labor, this is the only way in which the local production of nontradable goods and services can meet local demand.

The reallocation of scarce labor from the tradable to the nontradable sector is associated with a tight labor market. As sector-specific skills and capital need to be converted, wages rise. This process raises the price of nontradables and harms the competitiveness of the traded-goods sector and boosts the costs of (labor-intensive) government services. Pension funds, which have indexed their benefits to the wage level, see the value of their obligations rise.

We simulate a scenario in which the Dutch market sector is divided into two subsectors—tradable and nontradable. We use the definitions of *exposed* and *sheltered* sectors that have been used in the CPB's JADE model (CPB, 2003a). The government and the health-care sector constitute a third sector. The employment shares of these sectors are shown in table 8.4.

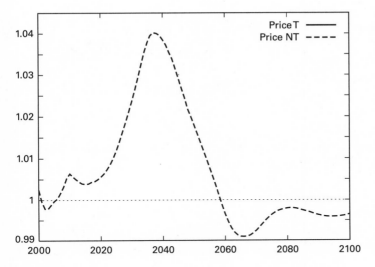

Figure 8.22
The price of tradable (T) and nontradable goods (NT).

Figure 8.22 shows the extent of the real appreciation due to the shift from tradables to nontradables production. After the transition has been completed, the price of nontradables returns to its initial value. The sectoral reallocation is quite large: in 2040, the employment share of the nontradables sector has risen by ten percentage points, from 44 percent to 54 percent.

The effects of the rising demand for nontradeables on the rest of the economy are shown in figure 8.23. Gross wages rise much faster than they did in the benchmark path (compare figure 8.23 to figure 8.2). Higher wage inflation due to a tight labor market raises the liabilities of pension funds, as pension benefits are tied to the level of wages. These higher liabilities cause an increase in pension premiums.

Conclusions

This chapter explores the interdependencies between an aging population and the costs of labor, net wages, (funded) pension premiums, and employment in a small, open economy. Aging leads to a tighter labor market, higher wages, and higher public spending on public pensions and health care. Developments on the international financial markets can, in addition to this, put pressure on the rates of return

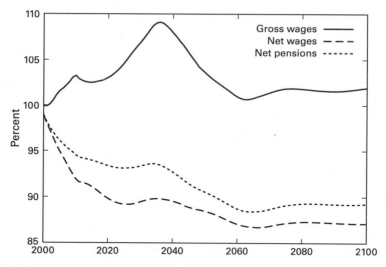

Figure 8.23
Gross wage, net wage, and net pensions in a scenario with nontradable goods.

that occupational pension funds can expect. The tight labor market at the peak of population aging exacerbates the funding problems that these pension funds experience because pension benefits are tied to the level of wages. The fact that part of the consumption bundle for consumers has to be produced locally adds to the pressure on local wages. An increase in the supply of labor, however, can reduce the impact of aging on the cost of labor. The same holds true for better tradability of goods and services. Especially an increase in older workers' labor-market participation can be a powerful tool to mitigate the effect of aging on labor costs, pension costs, and the costs of public spending.

The Dutch economy, with its mature defined-benefit pension funds, is vulnerable to the developments on international capital markets. Alternative rules for distributing capital-market risks across working and retired members of the funds have substantial effects on the distribution of welfare across generations. These risks are shared widely across the population if the pension rights of both workers *and* retirees can be decreased to repair a shortage in the coverage ratio. Moreover, compared to the premium instrument, the indexation instrument harms employment much less, thereby protecting the tax base. This makes the Dutch economy more robust to the risks of aging.

The changes to the funded pension system explored in this chapter leave intact the intergenerational risk sharing implicit in a defined-

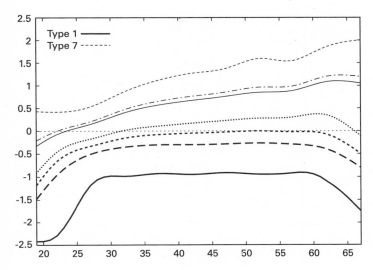

Figure 8.24
Wage profiles (logs) for different productivity types as a function of age.

benefit contract. One could envisage a more fundamental reform in which the pension contract is changed to an individual defined-contribution scheme.[9] Such a scheme would eliminate the intergenerational risk sharing that is implicit in DB schemes. We plan to extend the current model framework with risk so that we can study these fundamental reforms in our future research.

Appendix 8A Household Optimization

Households derive utility from the consumption of tradable goods, health care, and leisure over their remaining life. Households are distinguished by their year of birth (generation) t_0 and by their productivity type i. Productivity is exogenous to households but may vary with age. The relative productivity of a household of type i at age τ is $h(\tau, i)$, and its wage rate is given by $h(\tau, i)p_I(t)$ as a consequence of perfect substitution between types in the production of tradables.

We operationalize by specifying seven household types, whose wage profile can be found in figure 8.24. The share of these seven types in the population varies. We allow for a finer grid toward the higher earners to reflect the large variability in this segment. Shares can be read from table 8.5.

Table 8.5
Type shares and pension sizes (percentage).

	Type							
	1	2	3	4	5	6	7	Average
Share in population	12%	24%	24%	24%	12%	3%	2%	
Ratio funded occupational pension to public pension	0	0.14	0.31	0.65	2.14	2.48	5.33	0.694

Note: Of these seven productivity types, number 1 is the least productive, and number 7 the most productive. The second statistic, the ratio of supplementary pension income over public pension income, is an average over pension-age type members.

Denote the survival function of a household of generation t_0 at time t by $\Lambda(t, t_0) \leq 1$. Households maximize their expected utility, given by

$$E(U(t, t_0, i)|t)$$

$$= (1 - 1/\gamma)^{-1} \sum_{\tau=t}^{t_0+n_T-1} (1+\beta)^{t-\tau} \frac{\Lambda(\tau - t_0 + 1, t_0)}{\Lambda(t - t_0 + 1, t_0)} u(\tau, t_0, i)^{1-1/\gamma}, \quad (8.1)$$

where γ denotes the intertemporal substitution elasticity, and β the rate of time preference. Further, t_0 is the year of birth, and n_T is the maximum length of life (which we take to be 100). The flow of utility u is specified as

$$u(t, t_0, i) = [\theta_u^{1/\sigma_u} c(t, t_0, i)^{(\sigma_u-1)/\sigma_u}$$

$$+ (1 - \theta_u)^{1/\sigma_u} c_v(t, t_0, i)^{(\sigma_u-1)/\sigma_u}]^{\sigma_u/(\sigma_u-1)}, \quad \text{and} \quad (8.2)$$

$$c_v(t, t_0, i) = [\theta_{cv}^{1/\sigma_v} (\theta_v(t, t_0, i) v(t, t_0, i))^{(\sigma_v-1)/\sigma_v}$$

$$+ (1 - \theta_{cv})^{1/\sigma_v} (\theta_z(t, t_0, i) c_z(t, t_0, i))^{(\sigma_v-1)/\sigma_v}]^{\sigma_v/(\sigma_v-1)}, \quad (8.3)$$

where c denotes consumption of tradables, v denotes leisure, and c_z denotes consumption of health care (in units of output). The variable c_v denotes the consumption of the leisure–health-care aggregate. The weights θ_u and θ_{cv} are calibrated so that consumption of the different products matches actual consumption in the base year. Preference coefficients θ_v and θ_z depend on (1) the state of knowledge, reflected in the labor-productivity growth rate α, (2) the productivity type i, which represents the idea that human capital does not affect the labor-leisure choice (see Broer, 1999, p. 47), and (3) age $t - t_0 + 1$:

$$\theta_v(t, t_0, i) = \theta_0 h(t - t_0 + 1, i)^{\eta_h}(1 + \alpha)^{t_0}(1 + \theta)^{t_0 - t} \quad (\eta_h > 0), \tag{8.4a}$$

$$\theta_z(t, t_0, i) = \theta_1 h(t - t_0 + 1, i)^{\eta_h}(1 + \alpha)^{t_0}\theta_t(t - t_0 + 1, t_0), \quad \text{and} \tag{8.4b}$$

$$\theta_t(t - t_0 + 1, t_0) = \theta_t(t - t_0, t_0)\left((1 + \theta)^{\eta_1}\frac{\eta_2\lambda(\tau - t_0, t_0) + \eta_3}{\eta_2\lambda(\tau + 1 - t_0, t_0) + \eta_3}\right)^{1/(1 - \sigma_v)},$$
$$\tag{8.4c}$$

where h^{η_h} represents the effect of productivity, and θ and θ_t are the effects of age on leisure and health care, respectively. The effect of age on the demand for health care is linked to the mortality rate,

$$\lambda(\tau, t_0) = 1 - \Lambda(\tau + 1, t_0)/\Lambda(\tau, t_0).$$

Households can divide their time between leisure v, labor l, and health care c_z:

$$l = l_{max} - v - c_z \geq 0. \tag{8.5}$$

An important consequence of this formulation is that health care takes time that cannot be used for leisure or labor.

Appendix 8B   The Supply Side

Firms in the tradable-goods sector produce output using capital, labor, and raw materials. Production is subject to (internal) adjustment costs in capital formation. Technical change is purely labor augmenting at rate α. Labor and raw materials are variable inputs. As discussed above, labor is heterogeneous by age and skill type, but workers of all types are perfectly substitutable. With the productivity of a worker again equal to $h(\tau, i)$, the production function reads as

$$y(t) = F[M(t), H(t)] - \frac{1}{2}c_I\frac{I^2(t)}{K(t)} \tag{8.6}$$

$$F[M, H] = [\zeta_M M^{-\rho_y} + \zeta_H H^{-\rho_y}]^{-1/\rho_y}$$

$$H(t) = [\zeta_K K(t)^{-\rho_H} + \zeta_L(L_{eff}(t)(1 + \alpha)^t)^{-\rho_H}]^{-1/\rho_H}$$

$$L_{eff}(t) = \sum_{\tau = t - n_T + 1}^{t}\int_0^1 h(t - \tau, i)L(t, \tau, i)\,di.$$

Here, gross output F is a constant elasticity of substitution (CES) function of raw materials M and value added H. Value added H is produced by using beginning-of-period capital stock K and labor input in efficiency units L_{eff}. Internal-adjustment costs are subtracted in the definition of net output y, where I denotes composite investment.

The real market wage is defined as the marginal product of efficiency labor:

$$p_l(t) = F_L[M(t), K(t), L_{eff}(t)].$$

This means that the local stock of capital influences the wage rate. The adjustment costs of capital (equation (8.6)) and the associated barriers to international capital mobility imply that gross wages are not determined by the world interest rate through the factor price frontier.

Notes

A. Lans Bovenberg is a professor of economics and director of Netspar at Tilburg University. His e-mail address is ⟨a.l.bovenberg@uvt.nl⟩. Thijs Knaap is an assistant professor of economics at the Utrecht School of Economics and a fellow at Netspar. His e-mail address is ⟨t.knaap@econ.uu.nl⟩. This chapter is based on a research project commissioned by the Dutch Ministry of Social Affairs and Employment (SZW) and the Pension Research Foundation (SPW) and was conducted at Ocfeb, Erasmus University, Rotterdam. We thank Leon Bettendorf, Peter Broer, Juan Carlos Conesa, and seminar participants at CESIfo Munich for extensive comments. Any remaining errors are ours.

1. For example, CPB (2003a, p. 17) reports a substitution elasticity between capital and labor of 0.32.

2. The participation of older workers is more fully discussed below in the section on government policy.

3. *Net wages* refers to the payment that the worker receives after taxes, employer-paid premiums, and the pension-fund premiums.

4. We allow lower indexation up to 4 percent. This level of indexation corresponds to freezing of nominal pensions under 2 percent inflation and the assumed 2 percent technological growth.

5. Welfare effects are measured as a percentage of remaining lifetime utility, compared to the base path. The welfare effect reported in figure 8.7 is the average effect over the various income groups.

6. The intergenerational redistribution associated with the transition rule can be mitigated, for instance, by making the accumulation rate dependent on the age of the participant.

7. *Backservice* is the valuation of past contribution years at the current wage. Under a final-wage system, if there are relative wage increases over a career, this can be an important part of benefit buildup.

8. Recent computations by the CPB Netherlands Bureau for Economic Policy Analysis indicate that sustainable public finance (through constant rates of taxation) requires government debt to decline to 15 percent of GDP in 2030. See Centraal Planbureau (CPB) (2003b).

9. Such a change is discussed by, for instance, Westerhout et al. (2004).

References

Aglietta, M., R. Arezki, R. Breton, J. Fayolle, M. Juillard, C. Lacu, J. L. Cacheux, B. Rzepkowski, and V. Touzé. (2001). "INGENUE: A Multi-regional Computable General Equilibrium, Overlapping-Generations Model." Mimeo, CEPII, CEPREMAP, MINI-University of Paris X and OFCE. Retrieved from ⟨http://ideas.repec.org/p/sce/scecf0/178.html⟩.

Auerbach, A., and L. J. Kotlikoff. (1987). *Dynamic Fiscal Policy*. Cambridge: Cambridge University Press.

Beetsma, R., L. Bettendorf, and P. Broer. (2003). "The Budgetary and Economic Consequences of Aging in the Netherlands." *Economic Modelling*, 20, 987–1013.

Börsch-Supan, A., A. Ludwig, and J. Winter. (2003). "Aging, Pension Reform, and Capital Flows, a Multi-country Simulation Model." Mimeo, Institut für Volkswirtschaftslehre und Statistik, Universität Mannheim.

Broer, D. P. (1999). "Growth and Welfare Distribution in an Ageing Society: An Applied General-Equilibrium Analysis for the Netherlands." Ocfeb Research Memorandum 9908, Erasmus University Rotterdam. Retrieved from ⟨http://hdl.handle.net/1765/839⟩.

Central Bureau of Statistics/Centraal Planbureau (CBS/CPB). (1997). *Bevolking en arbeidsaanbod: drie scenarios tot 2020*. The Hague: Sdu Uitgevers.

CPB. (2003a). "JADE: A Model for the Joint Analysis of Dynamics and Equilibrium." CPB Document 30. Retrieved from ⟨http://www.cpb.nl/nl/pub/document/30⟩.

CPB. (2003b). "Vergrijzing en schuldreductie—een indicatieve update," CPB Notitie. Retrieved from ⟨http://www.cpb.nl/nl/pub/cpbreeksen/notitie/12feb2003/notitie.pdf⟩

Kotlikoff, L. J., K. Smetters, and J. Walliser. (2001). "Finding a Way out of America's Demographic Dilemma." NBER Working Paper 8258, Cambridge MA. Retrieved from ⟨http://www.nber.org/papers/w8258⟩.

Theeuwes, J. (1988). "Arbeid en belastingen." In *Preadviezen van de Vereniging voor Staathuishoudkunde*. Amsterdam: Kluwer.

van Soest, A. (1995). "Structural Models of Family Labor Supply: A Discrete Choice Approach." *Journal of Human Resources*, 30(1), 63–88.

Westerhout, E., M. van de Ven, C. van Ewijk, and N. Draper. (2004). "Naar een schokbestendig pensioenstelsel," CPB Document 67. Retrieved from ⟨http://www.cpb.nl/nl/pub/document/67/⟩.

Yaari, M. (1965). "Uncertain Lifetime, Life Insurance and the Theory of the Consumer." *Review of Economic Studies*, 32, 137–150.

9 Optimal Portfolio Management for Individual Pension Plans

Christian Gollier

Large numbers of European citizens who live in countries with a traditionally strong pay-as-you-go (PAYG) system now perceive that their social security benefits will not be sufficient to maintain their current lifestyles after retirement. As a consequence, there is a growing demand for individual long-term savings plans that would be designed for financing consumption after retirement. This phenomenon raises an interesting new decision problem for European consumers who used to save mostly for the short term. With these emerging markets, the typical time horizon for consumers' investments can now be as long as forty years. For such time horizons, the impact of the investment strategy on final wealth is enormous. Selecting this strategy is thus an important challenge for these consumers and their financial advisors.

During the twentieth century in the United States, the real return on bonds was 1 percent per year, whereas investing in stocks generated an expected return of 7 percent. Thus, a young worker investing 100 at age twenty-five would obtain a pension wealth at age sixty-five equaling 149 if she was 100 percent invested in bonds. This pension wealth would equal 1,497 on average if she invested everything in stocks. The equity premium puzzle is magnified by the exponential nature of compounded interests of long-term investors. Thus, the temptation is large for young households to take advantage of the large equity premium by investing a large fraction of their pension-plan wealth in the stock market. This is one of the arguments usually presented to advocate a move from a dominant pay-as-you-go system toward a more funded system. The problem, however, is that the expected benefit of this strategy and the associated risk for the final pension wealth are proportional to the time horizon of the investor. Investing in stocks for one year entails some risk, but investing in stocks for forty years is forty times riskier (if risk is measured by the variance of final wealth, assuming no serial correlation of stock returns). Thus, it is not clear a priori that younger investors should take more risk.

The problem implicit in dynamic portfolio choices is to determine how future investment opportunities affect instantaneous investment choices. Popular treatments suggest that short time horizons often lead to excessively conservative strategies. Samuelson (1989) and several others have asked: "As you grow older and your investment horizon shortens, should you cut down your exposure to lucrative but risky equities?" Conventional wisdom answers affirmatively, stating that long-horizon investors can tolerate more risk because they have more time to recoup transient losses. This dictum has not received the backing of scientific theory, however. As Samuelson (1963, 1989) points out, this "time-diversification" argument relies on a fallacious interpretation of the law of large numbers: repeating an investment pattern over many periods does not cause risk to wash out in the long run. This fallacy is illustrated by the following question raised by Samuelson (1963, 109): "I offered some lunch colleagues to bet each $200 to $100 that the side of a coin they specified would not appear at the first toss. One distinguished scholar ... gave the following answer: I won't bet because I would feel the $100 loss more than the $200 gain. But I'll take you on if you promise to let me make 100 such bets." This story suggests that independent risks are complementary. However, Samuelson went ahead and asked why it would be optimal to accept 100 separately undesirable bets. The scholar answered: "One toss is not enough to make it reasonably sure that the law of averages will turn out in my favor. But in a hundred tosses of a coin, the law of large numbers will make it a darn good bet."

This scholar misinterprets the law of large numbers. It is not by accepting a second independent lottery that one reduces the risk associated with the first one. If $\tilde{x}_1, \tilde{x}_2, \ldots, \tilde{x}_n$ are independent and identically distributed random wealth variables, $\tilde{x}_1 + \tilde{x}_2 + \cdots + \tilde{x}_n$ has a variance n times as large as the variance of each of these risks. What is stated by the law of large numbers is that $(1/n) \sum_{i=1}^{n} \tilde{x}_i$—not $\sum_{i=1}^{n} \tilde{x}_i$—tends to $E\tilde{x}_1$ almost surely as n tends to infinity. It is by subdividing—not adding—risks that they are washed away by diversification.

Table 9.1 provides some information about how U.S. consumers link their optimal pension portfolio to their age. It describes the actual portfolio compositions of individual TIAA-CREF plans as observed in June 2000. A simple pattern appears in this table: consumers tend to follow

Table 9.1
Portfolio composition as a function of age.

Allocation Pattern	Age			
	Under 35	35–44	45–54	Above 55
100% equity	34.9	32.6	30.1	28.1
75.1% to 99.9% equity	17.1	13.8	10.3	6.6
50.1% to 75% equity	19.5	20.4	19.5	17.2

Sources: TIAA-CREF Institute Research (2000); TIAA-CREF Actuarial Technical (1986).

the recommendation to rebalance their portfolio in favor of safer assets when growing older. Ameriks and Zeldes (2004), however, show that when taking care of the time effect, there is no clear evidence supporting a gradual reduction in portfolio shares with age among TIAA-CREF participants.

Following Jagannathan and Kocherlakota (1996), we show that there exist some convincing arguments sustaining the common wisdom that agents with a longer time horizon should take more risk. The next two sections present the benchmark model where an investor facing unpredictable financial markets invests at young age a specific amount to finance his consumption in n years from now. We explain why the optimal portfolio is independent of n in that case. We then show that the optimal portfolio risk is increasing in n if the agent can compensate early financial losses by saving more during her career and take into account the riskiness of human capital and the flexibility of labor supply. Finally, a short introduction to the effect of predictable returns (mean-reversion, stochastic volatility and Bayesian learning) on the dynamic portfolio strategy is presented.

The Initial Building Block: Optimal Static Portfolios

Let us start the analysis by assuming that the consumer is close to retiring and liquidating her portfolio. The consumer's current wealth in her individual pension account is w_0. The consumer's immediate problem is to determine the portfolio of financial assets that maximizes the expected utility of her accumulated pension wealth at the end of the period. Because of the short time remaining before the liquidation of the portfolio, this decision problem is essentially static. Assuming a complete set of Arrow-Debreu assets, this portfolio choice problem is written as

$$\max_{c_1,\dots,c_S} \sum_{s=1}^{S} p_s u(c_s) \quad s.t. \quad \sum_{s=1}^{S} \Pi_s c_s = w_0, \tag{9.1}$$

where $s = 1, \dots, S$ is an index for the S possible states of nature that could prevail at the retirement date, p_s is the objective probability of state s, Π_s is the price of the Arrow-Debreu security associated to that state, and c_s is the number of Arrow-Debreu securities s that are purchased. Because c_s is also the pension wealth of the agent at the end of the period, $u(c_s)$ is the utility that the retiree extracts from consuming this wealth over her remaining lifetime. We assume that u is increasing and concave. The degree of tolerance to risk on retirement wealth is measured by $T(c) = -u'(c)/u''(c)$. The budget constraint in (9.1) states that the accumulated pension wealth z at the beginning of the period is used to purchase a portfolio $(c_1, \dots, c_S)$ of Arrow-Debreu securities.

We do not restrict the investment opportunity set in any way. This means that households are allowed to invest in stocks, bonds, real estate, portfolio insurance, options, and other exotic assets. Our aim is to describe the unconstrained optimum. There are several reasons why regulators could want to restrict portfolio choices—for example, because of the implicit portfolio insurance that the state would provide if a financial crash would bring future (risk-loving) retirees into poverty. Constraining individual portfolio choices may be good to fight the moral-hazard problem associated with this implicit solidarity mechanism, but it introduces inefficiencies in the allocation of risk in the economy. The optimal portfolio management when upper limits to the portfolio risk are imposed is a difficult question that is not examined in this chapter.[1]

The first-order condition of program (9.1) can be written as $c_s = C(\Pi_s/p_s)$, where function C satisfies

$$u'(C(\pi)) = \xi\pi, \tag{9.2}$$

with ξ denoting the Lagrange multiplier associated to the budget constraint. The demand for the Arrow-Debreu security s is only a function of $\pi_s = \Pi_s/p_s$, the state price per unit of probability. C is nonincreasing in π: risk-averse investors accept having a smaller final wealth level in more expensive states. The riskiness of the optimal portfolio can be measured by how the riskiness of asset returns—which can be measured by the variability of $\pi_s = \Pi_s/p_s$—is transferred to riskiness of final wealth. The absolute value of the derivative of C with respect to π does exactly that. Fully differentiating the condition (9.2) yields

$$|C'(\pi)| = \frac{T(C(\pi))}{\pi}. \tag{9.3}$$

This means that more risk-tolerant agents purchase a riskier portfolio. In the remainder of the chapter, I examine how the riskiness of the optimal portfolio is affected by the age of the consumer.

Merton's Result: Age Is Irrelevant

In this section, the optimal dynamic portfolio strategy of a younger consumer is determined. This consumer with current pension wealth w_0 has n periods to go before liquidating her personal pension plan. Thus, contrary to what we assumed in the previous section, she does not consume the value of the portfolio at the end of the first period. Rather, she will reinvest the accumulated capital in an asset portfolio for another $n - 1$ periods. We are interested in determining how these future investment opportunities affect the attitude of the young consumer toward the current portfolio risk. To solve this problem, we use backward induction.

We assume that the investment opportunity set in each period t is not contingent to the past history. The investment opportunity set at each date is thus fully characterized by the vector of Arrow-Debreu prices $(\Pi_1, \ldots, \Pi_S)$. Assuming that this vector is independent of past events means that future asset prices are unpredictable: there are no mean-reversion, no learning, and no stochastic volatility in asset returns. Under this assumption, the only state variable of the dynamic problem is the accumulated wealth z at the decision date under scrutiny. Given z at date t, the consumer selects the portfolio to hold until the next date that maximizes the expected value of his pension wealth at date $t + 1$:

$$v_t(z) = \max_{c_1, \ldots, c_S} \sum_{s=1}^{S} p_s v_{t+1}(c_s) \quad s.t. \quad \sum_{s=1}^{S} \Pi_s c_s = z. \tag{9.4}$$

We first solve this problem for $t = n - 1$—when the agent has only one period to go before retirement. Because $v_n(c) = u(c)$ by definition, this portfolio problem is formally equivalent to the static portfolio problem that we examined in the previous section. We can thus interpret $v_{n-1}(z)$

as the optimal expected utility of final pension wealth conditional to accumulating pension wealth z one period before retirement age. Using this function, we can go one date backward to find value function v_{n-2} and so on.

To determine the impact of age on the optimal portfolio, we need to compare the solutions of program (9.4) for the various dates t from 1 to n. The only difference between these different programs comes from the transformation of the value function from v_t to v_τ. As explained in the previous section, an agent with age t should accept more portfolio risk than an agent with age $\tau > t$ if and only if the value function v_t exhibits more risk tolerance than the utility function v_τ or, equivalently, if $-v_t'/v_t'' \geq -v_\tau'/v_\tau''$.

Let us first compare v_{n-1} to $v_n \equiv u$. Fully differentiating the system of equations

$$\begin{cases} p_s u'(c_s) = \xi \Pi_s \\ v_{n-1}'(z) = \xi \\ \sum_{s=1}^{S} \Pi_s c_s = z \end{cases}$$

with respect to z yields

$$T_{v_{n-1}}(z) = -\frac{v_{n-1}'(z)}{v_{n-1}''(z)} = \sum_{s=1}^{S} \Pi_s T(c_s). \tag{9.5}$$

$T_{v_{n-1}}$ is the degree of tolerance to portfolio risk of the agent with two periods to go before retirement. Suppose that the agent has a power utility function $u(c) = c^{1-\gamma}/(1 - \gamma)$, which implies that absolute risk tolerance $T(c) = c/\gamma$ is proportional to retirement consumption c. Using the budget constraint, equation (9.5) is then rewritten as $T_{v_{n-1}}(z) = T(z)$. By backward induction, $T_{v_t}(z) = T(z)$ for all $t = 1, \ldots, n$: the degrees of risk tolerance of the value functions and of the utility function are identical. This means that the attitude toward portfolio risk is independent of age. Age, or the investment time horizon, is irrelevant for determining the optimal structure of the pension portfolio. Here, myopia is optimal in the sense that the best investment strategy is obtained by assuming in each period that this is the last period before retirement. This result has been independently discovered by Mossin (1968), Merton (1969), and Samuelson (1969).

Proposition 9.1 Consider the asset allocation problem with commited and defined contributions. Assume constant relative risk aversion and unpredictable asset returns. In such a situation, the optimal portfolio structure is independent of age.

Mossin (1968) observes that power utility functions are the only functions with such a nice property. This is easily seen from property (9.5) by using Jensen's inequality when T is either concave or convex or when $T(0) \neq 0$, as explained in Gollier and Zeckhauser (2002). However, calibrating the model shows that the nonproportionality of the absolute risk tolerance has only a marginal effect on the optimal portfolio of young investors.

This model relies on the assumption of frictionless financial markets. We assumed above the absence of any transaction cost and bid-ask spread. This is unrealistic. Taking into account these frictions implies that it may be optimal not to rebalance the portfolio in the case of limited capital gains or losses. But their effect on the optimal portfolio at a young age is ambiguous. Frictions in the housing market also have an ambiguous effect of the age structure of optimal portfolios.

Human Capital and Flexible Contributions to the Pension Plan

The previous dynamic portfolio problem isolates the problem of financing consumption after retirement from the other sources of needs, incomes, and risks faced by the consumer in her entire lifetime. In this section, we introduce intermediary consumption and labor incomes in the model. Suppose that the agent has n consumption dates $t = 1, \ldots, n$ to go before retirement. Her flow of labor incomes is denoted $(y_1, \ldots, y_n)$ and is assumed to be risk-free at this stage of the analysis. Let β denote the psychological discount factor of the agent, and let r be the risk-free rate.

Consider first a pension plan in which the agent must commit herself on the flow of her contributions $(q_1, q_2, \ldots, q_n)$ until retirement. This is equivalent to funding the plan with a single lump-sum contribution

$$w_0 = \sum_{t=1}^{n} \frac{q_t}{(1+r)^t}$$

at date $t = 1$. Given that initial pension wealth w_0, the problem of the optimal dynamic portfolio management is not different from the one that we examine in the previous section. In particular, if relative risk aversion is constant, myopia is optimal: if two agents have the same current pension wealth w_0, they should hold the same portfolio even if they don't have the same age. The optimal portfolio risk is proportional to $T(w_0)$.

Consider alternatively a pension plan with fully flexible contributions over time. At each date t before retirement, the agent decides how much to contribute to the plan and how to invest the pension wealth on financial markets. This dynamic consumption-portfolio problem is written as

$$h_t(z) = \max_{q, c_1, \ldots, c_S} u(y_t - q) + \beta \sum_{s=1}^{S} p_s h_{t+1}(c_s) \quad s.t. \quad \sum_{s=1}^{S} \Pi_s c_s = z + q.$$

(9.6)

From current labor income y_t at date t, the agent decides to save q and to consume the remaining $y_t - q$ at that date. Saving q is added to the past accumulated wealth z, and everything is optimally invested on financial markets. As before, we first solve this problem for $t = n - 1$, using the fact that $h_n \equiv u$. Solving this problem yields the optimal saving strategy s_0 and the optimal portfolio strategy $(c_1, \ldots, c_S)$ for that date. It also yields the maximum discounted expected utility h_{n-1} that is used to solve the consumption-portfolio problem for date $n - 2$.

Taking into account the equivalence of programs (9.4) and (9.6), we obtain that

$$T_{h_{n-1}}(z) = T(c_0) + \sum_{s=1}^{S} \Pi_s T(c_s),$$

(9.7)

where $c_0 = y_{n-1} - q$ is optimal consumption. Assuming again that relative risk aversion is constant and using the budget constraint, this implies that

$$T_{h_{n-1}}(z) = T(z + (1+r)^{-1} y_n),$$

where by definition $(1 + r)^{-1} = \sum \Pi_s$. By backward induction, we obtain that

$$T_{h_t}(z) = T(z + Y_t) \quad \text{where} \quad Y_t = \sum_{\tau=t+1}^{n} \frac{y_\tau}{(1+r)^{\tau-t}}$$

is the net present value (NPV) of future labor income—the human capital at date t. Because Y_t is decreasing in t, the degree of risk tolerance of the agent goes down when she grows older. Thus, agents with flexible contribution plans should rebalance their portfolio in favor of the risk-free asset when they are close to retirement. Notice also that because the agent starts initially with zero pension wealth $z = 0$, the optimal portfolio risk at young age with this fully flexible pension plan is proportional to $T_{h_0}(0) = T(Y_0)$. Thus, when we allow for flexible contributions, the portfolio risk is proportional to $T(Y_0)$, whereas it is proportional to $T(w_0) = (w_0/Y_0)T(Y_0)$ in the rigid case. Because the NPV w_0 of the flow of contributions in the rigid plan must be smaller than the NPV Y_0 of the flow of labor incomes, we proved the following proposition.

Proposition 9.2 Suppose constant relative risk aversion. When the contributions to the pension plan are predetermined, the optimal portfolio risk is independent of age, whereas it is decreasing with age when contributions are flexible. Moreover, the optimal portfolio riskiness at a young age is increased by a factor Y_0/w_0 if we allow for the contributions to the pension plan to be flexible compared to the rigid case, where w_0 is the net present value of the contributions in the rigid plan, and Y_0 is the human capital of the agent.

A crude estimate of Y_0/w_0 is around 10, which means that the flexible plan should invest ten times more in risky assets than if the plan has a preestablished and rigid flow of contributions. As explained in Gollier (2002), the intuition for such a powerful effect is the ability of the flexible plan to time-diversify shocks on pension wealth by splitting it into small shocks on consumption over the remaining lifetime. This effect goes down as the time horizon shortens, which yields a strong negative age effect on the optimal portfolio risk.

Uncertain Human Capital

Up to now, we assumed that the only source of uncertainty comes from the households' financial investments. For the sake of realism, we need to take into account the fact that the flow of labor incomes is also uncertain: young workers can face much uncertainty about the value of their human capital. In the same vein, future promotions and unemployment spells are uncertain. The uncertainty affecting human capital is expected to affect both the optimal wealth accumulation and the optimal structure of the pension portfolio. It has been well known since Leland (1968) and Drèze and Modigliani (1972) that prudent consumers will save more when their future incomes become riskier in the sense of Rothschild and Stiglitz (1970). Gollier and Pratt (1996) showed that risk-vulnerable consumers are more averse to portfolio risk when they bear an independent risk on their human capital. The concepts of prudence and risk vulnerability are related respectively to the third and fourth derivatives of the utility function. Consumers with constant relative risk aversion are both prudent and risk-vulnerable. Thus, under constant relative risk aversion (CRRA), the uncorrelated uncertainty affecting human capital raises the accumulation of financial wealth, and it reduces the share of this wealth invested in risky assets.

How does the uncertainty of human capital affect the relationship between age and the optimal portfolio structure? Because younger households face more uncertainty in their human capital, they should select a safer portfolio. This argument is particularly relevant when households are likely to face a liquidity constraint. The households' inability to borrow to finance consumption in periods of low labor incomes magnifies the riskiness of human capital. To sum up, age horizon has two contradictory effects on the optimal portfolio. As stated in proposition 9.2, younger households can better diversify their portfolio risk, which implies that they should take more portfolio risk. On the contrary, younger agents face more uncertainty on their human capital, which implies that they should select a safer portfolio. Which of these two effects dominates the other depends on the intensity of the risk for human capital.

Including an uninsurable background risk together with a liquidity constraint to the dynamic consumption-portfolio problem makes it unsolvable analytically. In the following calibration exercise, we consider an agent with constant relative risk aversion $\gamma = 10$. Both the risk-free rate and the rate of pure preference for the present are assumed to be zero. There is only one risky asset, which has an excess return of 7 percent per year and a standard deviation of 12 percent. We assume that the worker has fifteen years to live when he retires. At the exogenous retirement age, the pension wealth is invested in the risk-free asset to finance consumption over the remaining lifetime. Before retirement, the agent faces an unemployment risk that takes the following form: when he is employed, his yearly labor income is normalized to unity, whereas unemployment benefits equal only 50 percent of the labor income. When employed in year t, the agent faces the risk to become unemployed in year $t + 1$. This happens with probability 5 percent. On the contrary, if unemployed in year t, the agent finds a new

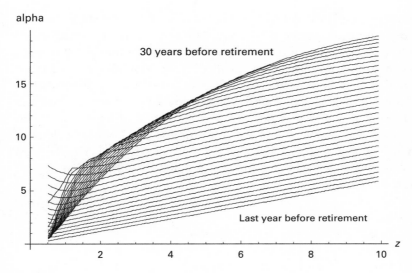

alpha

Figure 9.1
The optimal investment in stock (in the employment state) as a function of current
financial wealth, for different time horizons.

job in year $t + 1$ with probability 0.5. In figure 9.1, we draw the optimal
investment in the risky asset as a function of financial wealth z for different time horizons when the agent is employed.

When the agent has accumulated a large pension wealth, the riskiness of the optimal portfolio is decreasing with age, as stated in proposition 9.2. But when financial reserves are small, the riskiness of the
optimal portfolio is increasing with age. Because of the inability of
young households to time-diversify their unemployment risk, a safer
portfolio is optimal. When they grow older, this risk for human capital
becomes smaller, and they should rebalance their portfolio in favor
of the risky asset until the limited ability of old consumers to time-
diversify their portfolio risk becomes the dominant factor. In this
calibration, the effect of age on the demand for the risky asset is *ceteris
paribus* first increasing and then decreasing.

Flexible Labor Supply

Another unpleasant aspect of the benchmark dynamic model presented above comes from the assumption that households have no
control of their labor supply. Workers cannot compensate their financial losses in pension wealth by working more. Bodie, Merton, and

Samuelson (1992) examined the effect of a flexible labor supply on the optimal dynamic portfolio strategy. We can extend the benchmark model (9.6) to endogenize the labor decision. Suppose that the agent has one unit of time per period to allocate between leisure L and labor $1 - L$. For the sake of simplicity, we assume that the wage per unit of working time equals y, which is constant over time. Let $\hat{u}(c, L)$ denote the felicity of the agent who consumes a share L of leisure and who consumes $c = y(1 - L) - q$ of the consumption good, where q denotes savings. As usual, we assume that $\hat{u}$ is concave in (c, L). The decision problem of the household with accumulated wealth z at date t can then be written as

$$h_t(z) = \max_{L, q, c_1, \ldots, c_S} \hat{u}(y(1 - L) - q, L) + \beta \sum_{s=1}^{S} p_s h_{t+1}(c_s) \quad s.t.$$

$$\sum_{s=1}^{S} \Pi_s c_s = z + q. \tag{9.8}$$

We assume here that there is full flexibility in the sense that workers can increase or reduce their working time at any time and at their best convenience. In particular, the agent is here assumed to fully control his or her age of retirement. It is noteworthy that the above problem is strictly equivalent to problem (9.6), where function u would be defined as follows:

$$u(c) = \max_L \hat{u}(c - yL, L). \tag{9.9}$$

It is easy to check that the absolute risk aversion of the indirect utility function u equals

$$-\frac{u''(c)}{u'(c)} = -\frac{\hat{u}_{11}(c - yL^*, L^*)}{\hat{u}_1(c - yL^*, L^*)}$$

$$+ \frac{[y\hat{u}_{11}(c - yL^*, L^*) - \hat{u}_{12}(c - yL^*, L^*)]^2}{y^2 \hat{u}_{11}(c - yL^*, L^*) - 2y\hat{u}_{12}(c - yL^*, L^*) + \hat{u}_{22}(c - yL^*, L^*)}. \tag{9.10}$$

The second term of the right-hand side of the above equality is negative because of the concavity of $\hat{u}$. Also, $-\hat{u}_{11}(c - yL^*, L^*)/\hat{u}_1(c - yL^*, L^*)$ is the absolute of risk aversion of a worker who rigidly supplies labor L^*. These observations yield the following proposition.

Proposition 9.3 Consider two agents with the same utility function $\hat{u}$ on consumption and leisure. Let L^* denote the optimal leisure given wage y and consumption c. The agent who can adapt his labor supply to changes in income is locally less risk-averse than the agent who has a rigid labor supply L^*:

$$-\frac{u''(c)}{u'(c)} \leq -\frac{\hat{u}_{11}(c - yL^*, L^*)}{\hat{u}_1(c - yL^*, L^*)}.$$

The nature of the dynamic portfolio problem is not transformed by this form of labor flexibility. Labor flexibility just reduces the concavity of the utility function u in program (9.6). If the indirect utility function u exhibits constant relative risk aversion, the optimal portfolio structure is independent of age when contributions to the pension plan are preestablished. The only effect of the flexible labor market is to raise the share of the households' wealth invested in stocks at all ages.

The message will not be the same if we suppose alternatively that the flexibility of labor supply is limited to the decision on the age of (partial) retirement. In that case, only the risk aversion $(-u''/u')$ at old age is reduced, whereas risk aversion $(-\hat{u}_{11}/\hat{u}_1)$ when retirement is not allowed remains large. This implies that the degree of risk aversion of the value function is reduced for older households, yielding a riskier optimal portfolio.

Predictable Asset Returns

The absence of any predictability in asset returns has long been considered to be dogma in the theory of finance. Several empirical findings have reversed this idea over the last two decades. For example, Barberis (2000) estimates significant mean-reversion in U.S. stock returns: a high return of the risky portfolio in period t implies a lower expected portfolio return period $t + 1$. Because mean-reversion implies that stocks are safer in the long run, the intuition suggests that a long horizon agent should have a positive "hedging demand" for risk in the initial stage of the game. Kim and Omberg (1996) and Kogan and Uppal (2000) showed that this is indeed the case if constant relative risk aversion is larger than unity. Campbell and Viceira (1999) and Barberis (2000) have shown that the hedging demand for stocks is surprisingly large. For an agent with a relative risk aversion equaling 10 and a ten-year time horizon, the optimal investment in stocks is about 40 percent of current wealth without predictability. It goes up to 100 percent when mean-reversion is taken into account.

Predictability also arises from random time-varying volatility of stock returns. There is ample evidence that large negative returns tend to be associated with increases in volatility over long periods of time (see, for example, Ghysels, Harvey, and Renault, 1996). Chacko and Viceira (forthcoming) show that long-term investors with a constant relative risk aversion larger than unity should reduce their demand for stocks in that environment.

Predictability is an important element to take into account to discuss the age profile of optimal portfolios. For investors who are close to retirement, the existence of predictable future returns is irrelevant for their portfolio decision, since they will be out of the market when those changes will occur. On the contrary, households with a longer time horizon should take into account those future changes in their current choices. For example, we can infer from Barberis (2000) that the existence of mean-reversion in U.S. stocks returns multiplies the demand for stocks from investors with a ten-year time horizon by a factor larger than 2 when compared to the stock demand from investors with only one year to go before retirement.

The predictability of asset returns is linked to changes in the investment opportunity set over time. Asset returns are somewhat predictable if these stochastic changes are correlated with an observable variable. In the cases of mean reversion and stochastic volatility, this observable variable is the vector of past returns. More generally, when this observable variable is correlated to past returns, investors should insure against undesirable future changes in the investment opportunity set by investing more in assets that perform well when the opportunity set deteriorates. This is the hedging demand for stocks. For example, in the case of mean reversion of stock returns, the fact that stock returns are high when the investment opportunity set deteriorates induces a positive hedging demand for stocks. On the contrary, in the case of stochastic volatility, the investment opportunity set is improved (stocks become less risky) when returns are high. This implies a negative hedging demand for stocks. This effect is small compared to the effect of mean reversion, which implies that younger households should invest more in stocks.

In our benchmark model (9.4), the investment opportunity set at date t is characterized by the vector $(\Pi_1, \ldots, \Pi_S)$ of the prices of the Arrow-Debreu securities. Because we assume this vector to be stable over time, our model has no predictability in asset returns. Suppose alternatively that the vector of state prices at the beginning of the last period before retirement depends on the state of nature s_{n-1} that prevailed one period earlier. In the absence of intermediary consumption, the portfolio problem at that date can be written as

$$v_{n-1}(z; s_{n-1}) = \max_{c_1, \dots, c_S} \sum_{s=1}^{S} p_s u(c_s) \quad s.t. \quad \sum_{s=1}^{S} \Pi_s(s_{n-1}) c_s = z. \tag{9.11}$$

The value function v_{n-1} has now a second state variable, which is past history I. When u exhibits constant relative risk aversion γ, it is easy to check that

$$v_{n-1}(z; s_{n-1}) = K_{n-1}(s_{n-1}) \frac{z^{1-\gamma}}{1-\gamma} \quad \text{with}$$

$$K_{n-1}(s_{n-1}) = \left(\sum_{s=1}^{S} p_s \left(\frac{\Pi_s(s_{n-1})}{p_s} \right)^{(\gamma-1)/\gamma} \right)^{\gamma}. \tag{9.12}$$

Any change in history that yields a mean-preserving spread in the distribution of Π/p makes the agent better off—raises v_{n-1}. Observe that this means that such a change in the investment opportunity set reduces K_{n-1} if relative risk aversion is larger than unity. When γ is less than one, a MPS in Π/p raises K_{n-1}. Gollier (2004) shows that an increase in the equity premium or a reduction in the volatility of equity returns yield such a mean-preserving spread in state prices.

We are interested in determining the effect of predictability on the optimal portfolio two periods before retirement. The optimal demand for the Arrow-Debreu (AD) security associated with state s at date $t = n - 2$ is determined by the marginal value of wealth in that state, which is equal to

$$\frac{\partial v_{n-1}}{\partial z}(c_s; s) = K_{n-1}(s) c_s^{-\gamma} = \xi_{n-2} \frac{\Pi_s}{p_s}. \tag{9.13}$$

Suppose that the return of equity is low in state s, which means that Π_s/p_s is large. First-order condition (9.13) implies that the demand c_s for that AD security is negatively affected by this high price (negative substitution effect). But suppose that this expensive state in period $n - 2$ is associated to a mean-preserving spread in state prices in period n, as is the case with mean reversion. When γ is larger than unity, we know from (9.12) that it yields a reduction in K_{n-1}. This reduction yields a negative hedging demand for that AD security, thereby reinforcing the substitution effect. Symmetrically, the demand for AD securities associated to cheap states has a positive substitution effect and a positive reinforcing hedging effect. Ex-ante, the optimal portfolio in period $n-2$ is made riskier due to the presence of mean reversion.

Proposition 9.4 Consider the dynamic investment problem with constant relative risk aversion larger than unity and with mean reversion in equity returns. In such a situation, younger households should purchase riskier portfolios.

This recommendation is reversed for households with a constant relative risk aversion smaller than unity. This is because mean-preserving spreads in Π/p raise the marginal value of wealth in spite of the fact that these changes are desirable. Gollier (2004) generalizes this result to utility functions without constant relative risk aversion.

As observed by Chacko and Viceira (forthcoming), the fact that a drop in stock returns is generally followed by an increase in stock-return volatility (that is, a mean-preserving contraction in state prices Π/p) generates an effect on dynamic portfolio management that is exactly opposite to the one presented in proposition 9.4. Contrary to mean reversion where bad news on instantaneous returns is good news for the future investment opportunity set, stochastic volatility means that bad news on instantaneous returns is bad news for the future. Thus, stochastic volatility combined with a constant relative risk aversion larger than unity implies that younger investors should select safer portfolios.

In all these models, we assumed that investors know the distribution of stocks returns. Various authors since Detemple (1986) and Gennotte (1986) have argued that young investors may face considerable uncertainty about it. As investors grow older, they observe stock returns, and they update their beliefs by using Bayes's rule. How does this parameter uncertainty affect the optimal dynamic portfolio strategy? To answer this question, notice that good news on instantaneous returns are also good news for the future investment opportunity set, since Bayesian investors will update their beliefs in a more optimistic way after observing a large instantaneous return. Thus, as for stochastic volatility, we are in a situation opposite to the one presented in proposition 9.4. As shown in Gollier (2004), who provides a complete typology of predictability models, Bayesian learning on an uncertain equity premium implies that younger investors should select safer portfolios when absolute prudence $-u'''/u''$ is smaller than twice the absolute risk aversion. Under constant relative risk aversion, this is equivalent to γ being larger than unity.

Conclusion

Should younger households invest more in risky assets? To answer this question, we first considered a simple model where households who save exclusively for their retirement do not control their contribution to their pension plan. This benchmark model also assumed that assets returns are unpredictable and that households have no flexibility in their labor supply. Following the seminal contributions of Mossin (1968), Merton (1969), and Samuelson (1969), we showed that investors with a constant relative risk aversion should select a portfolio structure that is independent of their age.

This benchmark result led to two arguments in favor of a negative effect of age on the portfolio riskiness. The most convincing one relaxes the constraint that investors cannot adapt their contributions to their individual pension plan to shocks on their pension wealth. In reality, young households anticipate that they will save more during their careers if their pension plans do not perform well and that they will save less if their early portfolio return is large. This time diversification of the risk on pension wealth provides a strong incentive to invest more aggressively in the stock market at a young age. The second argument in favor of this recommendation comes from the observation that there is some mean reversion in stock returns. This implies that young investors face a long-term portfolio risk that is relatively smaller than in the unpredictable case. We showed that young investors with a relative risk aversion larger than unity should take into account this observation by investing more in stocks. These two effects are large. The first tends to multiply the demand for stocks from young investors by a factor 10, whereas mean reversion tends to multiply it by a factor 2.

However, there also exist various arguments going in the opposite direction. First, one should take into account of the fact that the return of human capital is highly uncertain for most young households. If they cannot time-diversify this risk because of liquidity constraints, for example, these young households should select a safer portfolio. The fact that younger investors face some uncertainty on the true distribution of the equity premium provides another argument in favor of their selection of a safer portfolio. Finally, the fact that the volatility of equity returns is increased after a crash also tends to reduce the optimal risk exposure of long-term investors.

The fact that households can react to shocks on their pension wealth by adapting their labor supply has no clear effect on the age profile of optimal portfolios. If the flexibility of labor supply is the same at all ages, the only effect of this flexibility is to raise the demand for stocks at all age. On the contrary, if the labor flexibility is limited to the decision on the retirement age, then this provides an incentive for older workers to invest more in risky assets.

The bottom line of the analysis is that there is no universal answer to the question of whether younger households should be less risk-averse. Its answer depends on individual characteristics such as, for example, the riskiness of the household's human capital, the intensity of potential liquidity constraints faced by it, the degree of flexibility of the household's labor supply, or the quality of the household's knowledge of the functioning of financial markets. Calibration exercises seem to favor a share of wealth invested in stocks that is decreasing with age.

Notes

This chapter benefited from comments by two anonymous referees and by Jacques Drèze, Thijs Knaap, Ali Lazrak, Pierre Pestieau, Eytan Sheshinski, and Richard Watt. It received the GSU-ARIA award for the best paper presented at the World Risk and Insurance Conference in Salt Lake City (August 2005).

1. For more details on this question, see, for example, Grossman and Vila (1992).

References

Ameriks, J., and S. P. Zeldes. (2004). "How Do Household Portfolio Shares Vary with Age?" Unpublished manuscript, Columbia University.

Barberis, N. (2000). "Investing for the Long Run When Returns Are Predictable." *Journal of Finance*, 55, 225–264.

Bodie, Z., R. C. Merton, and W. F. Samuelson. (1992). "Labor-Supply Flexibility and Portfolio Choice in a Life Cycle Model." *Journal of Economic Dynamics and Control*, 16, 427–449.

Campbell, J., and L. Viceira. (1999). "Consumption and Portfolio Decisions When Expected Returns Are Time Varying." *Quarterly Journal of Economics*, 114, 433–495.

Chacko, G., and L. M. Viceira. (forthcoming). "Dynamic Consumption and Portfolio Choice with Stochastic Volatility in Incomplete Markets." *Review of Financial Studies*.

Detemple, J. B. (1986). "Asset Pricing in an Economy with Incomplete Information." *Journal of Finance*, 61, 383–392.

Drèze, J. H., and F. Modigliani. (1972). "Consumption Decisions under Uncertainty." *Journal of Economic Theory*, 5, 308–335.

Gennotte, G. (1986). "Optimal Portfolio Choice under Incomplete Information." *Journal of Finance*, 41, 733–749.

Ghysels, E., A. C. Harvey, and E. Renault. (1996). "Stochastic Volatility." In G. S. Maddala and C. R. Rao, eds., *Handbook of Statistics* (vol. 14, chapter 14). Amsterdam: North-Holland.

Gollier, C. (2002). "Time Diversification, Liquidity Constraints, and Decreasing Aversion to Risk on Wealth." *Journal of Monetary Economics*, 49, 1439–1459.

Gollier, C. (2004). "Optimal Dynamic Portfolio Risk with First-Order and Second-Order Predictability." Mimeo, University of Toulouse.

Gollier, C., and J. W. Pratt. (1996). "Risk Vulnerability and the Tempering Effect of Background Risk." *Econometrica*, 64, 1109–1124.

Gollier, C., and R. J. Zeckhauser. (2002). "Horizon Length and Portfolio Risk." *Journal of Risk and Uncertainty*, 24(3), 195–212.

Grossman, S., and J.-L. Vila. (1992). "Optimal Investment Strategies with Leverage Constraints. Journal of Financial and Quantitative Analysis, 27(2), 151–168.

Jagannathan, R., and N. R. Kocherlakota. (1996). "Why Should Older People Invest Less in Risky Assets Than Younger People?" *Federal Reserve Bank of Minneapolis Quarterly Review*, 20, 11–23. Retrieved from ⟨http://minneapolisfed.org/research/qr/qr2032.pdf⟩.

Kim, T. S., and E. Omberg. (1996). "Dynamic Nonmyopic Portfolio Behavior." *Review of Financial Studies*, 9, 141–161.

Kogan, L., and R. Uppal. (2000). "Risk Aversion and Optimal Portfolio Policie in Partial and General Equilibrium Economies." Retrieved from ⟨http://finance.commerce.ubc.ca/~uppal/papers.html⟩.

Leland, H. E. (1968). "Savings and Uncertainty: The Precautionary Demand for Savings." *Quarterly Journal of Economics*, 45, 621–636.

Merton, R. C. (1969). "Lifetime Portfolio Selection under Uncertainty: The Continuous-Time Case." *Review of Economics and Statistics*, 51, 247–257.

Mossin, J. (1968). "Optimal Multiperiod Portfolio Policies." *Journal of Business*, 215–229.

Rothschild, M., and J. Stiglitz. (1970). "Increasing Risk: I. A Definition." *Journal of Economic Theory*, 2, 225–243.

Samuelson, P. A. (1963). "Risk and Uncertainty: The Fallacy of the Law of Large Numbers." *Scientia*, 98, 108–113.

Samuelson, P. A. (1969). "Lifetime Portfolio Selection by Dynamic Stochastic Programming." *Review of Economics and Statistics*, 51, 239–246.

Samuelson, P. A. (1989). "The Judgement of Economic Science on Rationale Portfolio Management: Indexing, Timing, and Long-Horizon Effects." *Journal of Portfolio Management*, Fall, 3–12.

Contributors

Theodore C. Bergstrom, University of California at Santa Barbara

A. Lans Bovenberg, Tilburg University and Netspar

Antoine Bozio, Institute for Fiscal Studies

Woojen Chung, Institute for Fiscal Studies

Juan C. Conesa, Universitat Autònoma de Barcelona

Gabrielle Demange, École des Hautes Études en Sciences Sociales (EHESS)

Richard Disney, Institute for Fiscal Studies and University of Nottingham

Carl Emmerson, Institute for Fiscal Studies

Robert Fenge, Ifo Institute for Economic Research

Luisa Fuster, University of Toronto

Carlos Garriga, Federal Reserve Bank of St. Louis

Christian Gollier, University of Toulouse, Groupe de Recherche en Economie Mathématique et Quantitative (GREMAQ), and Institut d'Economie Industrielle (IDEI)

John L. Hartman, University of California at Santa Barbara

Ayşe İmrohoroğlu, University of Southern California

Selahattin İmrohoroğlu, University of Southern California

Thijs Knaap, Utrecht School of Economics and Netspar

Georges de Ménil, École des Hautes Études en Sciences Sociales (EHESS)

Pierre Pestieau, University of Liège

Eytan Sheshinski, The Hebrew University of Jerusalem

Matthew Wakefield, Institute for Fiscal Studies

Index

Actuarial reduction factor (ARF), 27
Aging, 132, 211. *See also* Demographic
  shock
  and funded pensions, 239–240, 254–257,
    265–266
  and investment strategy, 274–275, 277–
    279, 282–283, 285, 288–290
  and labor market, 240, 255–257, 264–
    266
  and rate of return, 257–259
  and taxation, 254–255
Altruism, 214, 222
Annuitization, 12–13, 211–233
  and Approved Personal Pensions (APPs),
    176
  mandatory, 215, 219–221, 227–232
  and mortality rate, 220–221
  and Personal Savings Accounts (PSAs),
    218–221, 227–231
  and privatization, 213–215, 217
  welfare effects of, 227–231
Approved Personal Pension (APP), 176–
  186, 204

Balladur, Edouard, 37
Belgium, 4
Benchmark economy, 91–96
  funded pensions in, 245–247
  government in, 91–94, 96–106
  households in, 91, 93
  and life expectancy, 105
  market in, 92–93
  nontaxable pensions and, 99–101
  parameterization of, 93–96 ·
  Ramsey problem, 101–103
  social security in, 217–218
  taxation in, 92–94, 96–99, 106–108, 110
Beveridgean system, 141–143, 146, 155

Bismarckian system, 141–143, 146–148,
  151, 155
Bush (George W.) administration, 211

Caisse Nationale d'Assurance Viellesse
  (CNAV), 40, 44–45, 63, 73
Canada, 38
Capital, return on, 257–261
"Capital crowding-out" effect, 214
Capital integration, 159
Cohort effects
  and benefits age, 129
  of demographic shock, 88–90, 101, 109–
    110
  Dutch funded pensions, 251–252
  French pension reform of 1993, 42–43,
    53–54
Condorcet winner, 126
Constant relative risk aversion (CCRA),
  282

Defined-benefit (DB) pension plans, 172,
  174, 239
Defined-contribution (DC) pension plans,
  173–175, 189
Delayed retirement credit (DRC), 27–36
  labor disutility, 29–30
  and longevity, 34–35
  model, 28–29
  self-selection, 27–28, 30–33
Demographic shock
  cohort effects of, 88–90, 101, 109–110
  and dependency ratio, 2, 7–8, 87, 104–
    105, 119
  predictability of, 87–88
  strategies for absorbing, 89–90, 111–112
  and taxation, 90, 102–104
  transitory, 104–106

Dependency ratio, 2, 7–8, 87, 119
  and pivotal voting age, 121
  and transitory demographic shock, 104–
    105
Difference-in-difference methodology, 47–
    69, 194–195
  baseline estimates, 55–58
  common-trend assumption, 202
  disclosure effects, 59–60, 62–63, 78–80
  elasticity, 55
  quasi-difference-in-differences, 197–199
  response coefficients, 55, 58
  sources of bias, 58–60
Disability pensions, 60–62
Distortionary taxation, 90
Dynastic model, 214

Early retirement
  in Canada, 38
  in France, 67–74
  and PAYG systems, 6
Échantillon Interrégime de Retraités (EIR),
    43–44, 63–67, 73
Europe
  demographic shock in, 8
  mandatory contributions in, 141
  PAYG in, 1–2
  population aging in, 132
  sustainability of social security, 122–123,
    132, 136
European Union (EU), 141

Family Resource Survey (FRS), 191–192
Financial numeracy, 169–170
First pillar system, 141
France, 4. See also French pension reform
    of 1993
  complementary schemes in, 77–78
  PAYG reform in, 6–7
  pension system in, 40–41, 74–78
  population aging in, 132
  and U.K. system, 151–152, 155–156
Free choice model, 144–147
  intertemporal wealth, 145, 147
  liquidity constraints, 145
  proofs of propositions, 161–164
  rate of return, 147, 152
  stationary equilibrium, 149–150
Free choice systems, 141–164
  and capital integration, 159
  comparing, 148–152
  efficiency in, 155–156, 160–161

equilibrium under, 143, 149–160
  income and, 152–155
  myopic expectations, 159–160
  national, 147–148
  redistribution in, 142–143, 148, 151, 155
French pension reform of 1993, 37–80
  cohort effects, 42–43, 53–54
  contribution length, 41–42, 47, 49–59, 69–
    70
  disability pensions, 60–62
  labor-supply elasticity, 37, 70–71
  objections to, 37–38
  and pension rate, 75–76
  proportionality coefficient, 76
  reference wage, 42, 69, 77
  replacement rate, 43, 50, 69, 73
  retirement age, 45–47, 50–51, 67–74
  unemployment, 67–70, 74
  unpopularity of postponing retirement,
    71–73
Funded occupational pensions in
    Netherlands, 13–15, 239–270
  and aging, 239–240, 254–257, 265–266
  average-wage, 250–253
  and Dutch economy, 240, 264–266
  income groups, 251–252
  premiums, 245–247, 260–261
  and rates of return, 257–261
  variable indexation, 248–250, 252–253,
    260–261
  and wages, 246–247
Funded pension systems, 10–15

GDP, 95–96, 108
General-equilibrium model, 213, 215–
    217
  annuity payments, 220
  household types, 215, 222, 230–231
  parameters, 225–226
  preference structure, 221–224
Germany
  PAYG in, 4
  pension reform in, 16–18, 20–21
  population aging in, 132

Health insurance, 245
Hedging demand, 285–286, 288

Identification strategy, 47
IMAGE model, 241–245
  household optimization, 243, 267–269
  parameters, 242

rate of return, 243
tradable-goods sector, 269–270
Income
  and free choice systems, 152–155
  and funded pensions, 246–247
  and individual pension plans, 281–283
  and interest rates, 243
  and replacement rate, 218
  retirement pensions as, 97–99
Individual pension plans, 273–290
  and consumer age, 274–275, 277–279,
    282–283, 285, 288–290
  fixed/flexible contributions, 279–281
  and income, 281–283
  and investment risk, 274–275, 278–283,
    285, 288–289
  and labor flexibility, 283–285, 290
  optimal dynamic portfolios, 277–279
  optimal static portfolios, 275–277
  predictability of returns, 285–289
  and stock market investing, 273–274,
    285–286, 288–289
INGENUE model, 259
Initiative Fifty Plus, 18
Intergenerational redistribution, 1–2, 108,
  245, 266–267
Intertemporal wealth, 145, 147
Intragenerational redistribution, 9, 142
Investing. See also Individual pension
  plans
  and aging, 274–275, 277–279, 282–283,
    285, 288–290
  and labor supply, 283–285, 290
  in stocks, 273–274, 285–286, 288–289
Italy, 132

Labor disutility, 29–30
Labor-force participation, 38–39, 243, 246–
  247, 255–257, 266
Labor income. See Income
Labor supply
  and aging, 240, 255–257, 264–266
  and demographic shock, 89–90
  elasticity of, 37, 70–71, 123–124, 243
  and investment strategy, 283–285, 290
  and mobility, 141, 161, 176
  and rate of return, 261
  and taxation, 108
Life expectancy
  and benchmark economy, 105
  and early retirement, 73
Longevity, 34–35

Mandatory annuitization, 215, 219–221,
  227–232
Marginal labor tax, 36
Means-reversion, 286–287
Median voting age, 8–9, 120–121, 132
Merkel, Angela, 18
Microsimulations, 39
Migration, 141, 144
Minimum income guarantee (MIG), 202–
  203
Mitterand, François, 6
Mobility, workers', 141, 161, 176
Moral-hazard condition, 31–32

Netherlands. See also Funded occupational
  pensions in Netherlands
  aging in, 239–240
  labor-force participation in, 256–257
  market sectors, 264–265
  PAYG in, 4, 241
New Zealand, 39
Normal retirement age (NRA), 27

Occupational pension systems, 13–15. See
  also Funded occupational pensions in
  Netherlands
Optimal portfolio management, 275–279
Optimal taxation approach, 96–99
Overlapping-generations model, 216–
  217

Pareto improvement, 2, 90, 101
Partial-privatization plans, 12–13, 212,
  219–221, 232
Pay-as-you-go (PAYG) pension systems,
  1–8. See also Demographic shock; Free
  choice systems; French pension reform
  of 1993; Sustainability
  delayed retirement credit (DRC), 27–36
  in Europe, 1–2
  as insurance, 213, 232
  and migration, 141, 144
  and privatization, 213–214
  and retirement age, 5–8
Pension Credit Guarantee (PCG), 203
Pension-fund management, 15. See also
  Individual pension plans
Personal Pensions Scheme, 171, 173, 175–
  186, 204–205
  age-earnings profile, 179–180
  opting-out patterns, 181–182, 184–185
  rebate structure, 182–184

Personal Savings Account (PSA), 212, 218–221, 227–232
Pivotal voting age, 120–121, 126–128, 132
Population growth. *See also* Demographic shock
  and aging, 132, 211, 239
  and dependency ratio, 2, 7–8, 87
  and equilibrium benefit level, 131
  and social security, 130–131
Portfolio management. *See* Optimal portfolio management
Poverty condition, 30, 33
Private pensions. *See also* Retirement savings incentives in U.K.
  and annuitization, 213–215
  partial-privatization plans, 12–13, 212, 219–221, 232
  and PAYG systems, 213–214
  United Kingdom, 192–193, 201–202, 204
  United States, 211

Quasi-difference-in-differences model, 197–199

Rate of return on capital, 147, 152, 243, 257–261, 273, 286–287
Rational expectations hypothesis, 143
Redistribution, 141
  and efficiency, 155–156
  in free choice systems, 142–143, 148, 151, 155
  intergenerational, 1–2, 108, 245, 266–267
  intragenerational, 9, 142
Reference wage, 42, 69, 77
Replacement rate, 17, 43, 50, 73
  and contribution length, 49–50
  and earnings, 218
  and reference wage, 69
Retirement age. *See also* Delayed retirement credit (DRC)
  average, 45–47, 51
  and benefits age, 126–130
  and contribution length, 55–59, 69–70, 73–74
  early, 6, 38, 67–74
  and labor market, 38–40
  normal retirement age (NRA), 27
  and PAYG systems, 5–8
  self-selection, 27–28, 30–33
  statutory, 6–7, 17–19
  of women, 6, 19, 71–73

Retirement savings incentives in U.K., 169–206
  age-earnings profile, 179–180
  Approved Personal Pension (APP), 176–186, 204
  contracting out, 174–175, 177–179
  and financial numeracy, 169–170
  and household saving behavior, 170–172, 175–176
  opting-out patterns, 181–182, 184–185
  Personal Pensions Scheme, 171, 173, 175–186, 204–205
  rebate structure, 182–184
  reform of, 182–186, 202–203
  Stakeholders Pension Scheme, 10–11, 171–173, 186–193, 199–205
  State Earnings-Related Pension Scheme (SERPS), 172–173, 176–183
  tax relief, 173–174, 186–187, 190–191
Retirement savings model, 193–203
  and earnings groups, 196–199
  pension probabilities, 195–196
  and spouse's earnings, 193–202
"Riester" accounts, 16–17

Self-selection, 27–28, 30–33
Social security system, U.S., 87, 117–118
  and discount rates, 124
  and excess tax burden, 123–124
  political support for, 121–122, 125–126, 131, 134, 136
  and population growth, 130–131
  predicted benefits, 131
  present value of benefits, 119–120
  as social insurance, 135
Spain, 132
Stakeholders Pension Scheme, 10–11, 171–173, 186–193, 204–205
  contribution limits, 190–191
  and earnings groups, 187–190, 197–199, 201–203
  rationale for, 186–189
  response to, 191–193
  and spouse's earnings, 199
  and tax relief, 186–187, 190–191
State Earnings-Related Pension Scheme (SERPS), 172–173, 176–183
State Second Pension (S2P), 202
Statutory retirement age, 7
  in France, 6
  in Germany, 17–18
  in United Kingdom, 19

Steady-state equilibrium, 224–225
Stochastic volatility, 286, 288
Stock market investing, 273–274, 285–286, 288–289. *See also* Individual pension plans
Sustainability, 8–10. *See also* Free choice systems; Social security system, U.S.; Voter preferences
  and benefits age, 126–130, 136
  and concern for family, 134–135
  of European social security, 122–123, 132, 136
  median-voter model, 8–9, 130–131
  and pivotal voting age, 120–121, 126–128, 132
"Sustainability factor," 17

Taxation
  age-differential, 106–108
  and aging population, 254–255
  in benchmark economy, 92–94, 96–99, 106–108, 110
  and demographic shock, 90, 102–104
  distortionary, 90
  excess burden of, 123–124
  in Netherlands, 241
  optimal taxation approach, 96–99
  Personal Savings Accounts (PSAs), 219
  of retirement pensions, 97–99
  U.K. tax relief, 173–174, 186–187, 190–191
  variable, 7–8
Thatcher (Margaret) administration, 173
Thrift Savings Plan (TSP), 211
Transition probability matrix, 233

Unemployment, 67–70, 74
Unfitness pensions, 60–62
United Kingdom, 18, 20–21
  Approved Personal Pension (APP), 176–186
  defined-benefit (DB) pension plans, 172, 174
  defined-contribution (DC) pension plans, 173–174
  and French system, 151–152, 155–156
  National Insurance (NI) contributions, 178
  PAYG in, 3–4
  Personal Pensions Scheme, 171, 173, 175–186, 204–205
  private pensions in, 192–193, 201–202, 204

retirement age in, 19
Stakeholders Pension Scheme, 10–11, 171–173, 186–193, 199–205
State Earnings-Related Pension Scheme (SERPS), 172–173, 176–183
State Second Pension (S2P), 202
sustainability of social security, 132
tax relief in, 173–174, 186–187, 190–191
United States. *See also* Social security system, U.S.
  baby boomers, 89, 109, 117
  and Europe, 8
  investment returns in, 273, 286–287
  normal retirement age in, 27–28
  partial-privatization proposals in, 12–13, 211–212
  population aging in, 132
  replacement rate in, 218
  voter participation in, 120–121

Voter preferences, 135–136. *See also* Sustainability
  and access to information, 132–133
  benefits age, 126–130, 136
  median age, 8–9, 120–121, 132
  pivotal age, 120–121, 126–128, 132
  retirement age, 128
  and voter confidence, 125–126, 133–134

Wages. *See* Income
War pensions, 61–62
Women
  labor-force participation, 255–257
  retirement age of, 6, 19, 71–73
  and retirement incentives, 184